BLACK

WOMAN

REFORMER

BLACK

WOMAN

REFORMER

Ida B. Wells,

LYNCHING, &

TRANSATLANTIC

ACTIVISM

SARAH L. SILKEY

THE UNIVERSITY OF

GEORGIA PRESS

Athens & London

Designed by Kaelin Chappell Broaddus
Set in 11/13.5 Garamond Premier Pro by Kaelin Chappell Broaddus
Printed and bound by Sheridan Books, Inc.
The paper in this book meets the guidelines for
permanence and durability of the Committee on
Production Guidelines for Book Longevity of the
Council on Library Resources.

Printed in the United States of America
15 16 17 18 19 C 5 4 3 2 1

Library of Congress Cataloging-in-Publication Data
Silkey, Sarah L.
Black woman reformer : Ida B. Wells, lynching, and transatlantic activism /
Sarah L. Silkey.
pages cm
Includes bibliographical references and index.
ISBN 978-0-8203-4557-4 (hardcover : alk. paper) —
ISBN 978-0-8203-4692-2 (ebook)
1. Wells-Barnett, Ida B., 1862–1931—Travels.
2. African American women—Biography.
3. African American women civil rights workers—Biography.
4. African American women social reformers—Biography.
5. Lynching—United States—Foreign public opinion, British.
6. Civil rights workers—United States—Biography.
7. Social reformers—United States—Biography.
8. Public opinion—Great Britain—History—18th century.
I. Title. II. Title: Ida B. Wells, lynching, and transatlantic activism.
E185.97.W55S55 2015
323.092—dc23
[B]
2014024894

British Library Cataloging-in-Publication Data available

TO EVERY

phoenix

WHO EVER DARED

TO RISE FROM THE ASHES

Contents

Acknowledgments

A. A. Milne, author of *Winnie-the-Pooh*, wrote, "It's hard to be brave when you're only a Very Small Animal." He was referring to Piglet, one of my favorite literary characters. The world is a very big place. Sometimes the unanticipated challenges we face in life make us feel small. Piglet is Very Small not only in stature but also in confidence. He is timid. He worries, frets, and scares easily. Through the trials he faces, Piglet gives voice to our fears and insecurities. Even so, as Benjamin Hoff argues in *The Te of Piglet*, Piglet is the only character in the Hundred Acre Wood who rises to the challenges that confront him; he discovers that he can be brave. I have taken inspiration from Piglet's reluctant bravery whenever the challenges of this project seemed very large, even insurmountable. During his trials, Piglet "only blinched inside," according to Pooh, "and that's the bravest way for a Very Small Animal not to blinch that there is." In the process, Piglet is transformed. He becomes something greater than *only* a Very Small Animal; he embodied *te*—virtue in action.

Long before Piglet was conceived in Milne's imagination, Ida B. Wells embodied virtue in action. The challenges she faced must have felt insurmountable at times, yet she persevered. If she ever "blinched," she "only blinched inside." I love Wells not only for her *te* but also for her humanity. Her quick temper, pride, vanity, and stubbornness made her life more difficult at times than it could have been if she had "learned her place" or "acted more like a lady." But without these personality traits, she might never have believed that she belonged in the public sphere—that she could and should devote her life to reform. She accomplished great things not because she possessed some superhuman power but because she simply refused to settle or give up. I am proud to have had this opportunity to know her, even if only imperfectly through the distance of time.

Throughout this process, my friends and colleagues suffered good-naturedly through countless drafts and conversations about my ideas. But their contribution to this project went beyond refining outlines, copyediting, and challenging my ideas. Their support and encouragement carried me through the inevitable doubts and insecurities that arise along the way to achieving dreams. Gerald Gregersen, Mary Lebens, Colin Locascio, Andrew Mansfield, Nat and Alison Pitts, James Tejani, and Howard and Kitty Temperley offered their friendship, guidance, and enthusiasm for this journey. In addition to sharing their analytical and organizational skills, my aunts, Mariah Silkey and Bea Jones, kept me grounded on both sides of the Atlantic. Mariah also generously provided me with accommodation while I conducted research on a shoestring budget; Cita Cook, Bill and Jennifer Terry, and Jessica Wang did the same. Colleen Clayton, Aileen Davies, Lorraine Faith, Jacqueline Fear-Segal, Lyn Marsh, Octavia Phillips, Barb Stevens, Mari Ines Woodsome, and Joyce Wilson helped me navigate British and American bureaucratic mazes. During my years as a predoctoral fellow and visiting scholar at the University of Virginia, fellows and scholars at the Carter G. Woodson Institute, including Sandy Alexandre, Mieka Brand, Brian Brazeal, Vicki Brennan, Cheryl Hicks, Gordon Hylton, Kennetta Perry, and Lisa Shutt, together with Jaime Martinez, Brian Roberts, and Calvin Schermerhorn, challenged me to develop a more nuanced understanding of the transatlantic world in which Wells traveled. Wendy Perry helped me land the teaching position at Lycoming College I hold today. There I found a new family in my history department colleagues, Cullen Chandler, Robert Larson, Richard Morris, Christopher Pearl, and John Piper, who have supported me through the transition to becoming a teacher-scholar.

I was repeatedly blessed with the good fortune of finding great mentors. Christopher Waldrep offered valuable advice on creating a book manuscript, taking an interest in my research as well as my professional development. I miss his friendship dearly. Michael Fitzgerald has been involved with my project as long as I have. He introduced me to Ida B. Wells as an undergraduate and has supported me wholeheartedly ever since—even when I had this crazy idea to study the American South from the United Kingdom. Adam Fairclough supervised my work for five years and pushed me to take a broader, more comprehensive view of my project. He daily provided a practical demonstration of intellectual rigor, and my thinking and writing matured as a result. After Adam accepted his dream position at Leiden University, Richard Crock-

att graciously took on my supervision in addition to his many duties oversee-
ing the reorganization of the School of American Studies at the University of
East Anglia. Manfred Berg, Beverly Bond, William Carrigan, Kees van Minnen, Lindy Moore, Rob Riser, and Clive Webb encouraged my scholarship
and provided valuable feedback at different stages of my research. Catherine
Clinton opened many doors for me, perhaps most significantly by introducing me to Nancy Grayson, whose patient encouragement, enthusiasm, and
faith in the importance of this project helped me bring it to completion. Since
Nancy's retirement, many talented professionals at the University of Georgia
Press, including Sean Garrett, John Joerschke, and Beth Snead, have strengthened and guided this project through its final stages. Finally, Beatrice Burton
crafted an insightful index to complete this volume.

Many other scholars assisted in the development of this project. The anon-
ymous readers who commented on various aspects of my work made valuable suggestions and criticisms. Conversations with scholars at conferences
throughout the United States and Europe challenged me to better articulate
my ideas, led me to new sources, and broadened my perspective on the transatlantic world Wells inhabited.

I am also indebted to the numerous archivists and librarians at the British
Library and British Library Newspaper Reading Room, Colindale; the Rare
Book and Manuscript Library, Columbia University, New York; the Univer-
sity of Manchester Library; the Liverpool Record Office, Liverpool Libraries;
the National Library of Scotland; the Bodleian Library of Commonwealth
and African Studies, University of Oxford; the Modern Records Centre,
University of Warwick; the Library of Congress, Manuscripts Division; the
Special Collections Research Center, Joseph Regenstein Library, University
of Chicago; Special Collections at the Wilson Library, University of North
Carolina at Chapel Hill; the Alabama Department of Archives and History,
Montgomery; the Georgia Archives; the Library of Virginia, Richmond; the
Special Collections Library, Clemson University; and the South Carolina De-
partment of Archives and History, Columbia. I especially thank Lew Purifoy
and the Interlibrary Loan Services staff at the University of Virginia; Tom
Kanon and the Tennessee State Library and Archives (Nashville); Randall
Burkett and the entire staff of the Manuscript, Archives, and Rare Books Li-
brary, Emory University; the staff of Friends House and the Library of the Religious Society of Friends in Britain; and the entire staff of Snowden Library at
Lycoming College.

I could not have completed this project without generous financial support from several institutions. Lyndsey Stonebridge helped secure me the Humanities and Social Sciences Studentship that, along with the Overseas Research Students Award Scheme sponsored by Universities UK, enabled me to remain in England to pursue my PhD at the University of East Anglia. In the early stages of this project, the Arthur Miller Centre for American Studies provided crucial funding for travel to scholarly conferences and British archives, while grants from the Gilder Lehrman Institute of American History; the British Association for American Studies; and the Manuscript, Archives, and Rare Books Library at Emory University supported research travel to the United States. I am particularly grateful for the two years I spent as a fellow at the Carter G. Woodson Institute for African-American and African Studies at the University of Virginia. Finally, a Lycoming College Professional Development Grant allowed me to prepare the final manuscript.

I could not have finished this project, however, without the unwavering encouragement of my family. My mother, Shelley; brother, Keanan; and partner, Jesse Greenawalt, were enthusiastically and intimately involved with my project, even though it meant holding endless hours of conversation about lynching. They stood by me—even when I "blinched"—and in the process helped me reveal my *te*. They became my true north; I would have been truly lost without them.

BLACK

WOMAN

REFORMER

Introduction

On March 31, 2004, I sat in horrified disbelief watching the BBC evening news from my flat in Norwich, England. Had the newsreader really just declared that four American contractors had been "lynched" in the Iraqi city of Fallujah? As I watched the story unfold, the scenes recorded by reporters and by members of the attacking mob were eerily familiar: the four unidentified men had been shot and their bodies burned, mutilated, and dragged through the streets. Finally, two of the victims' charred remains were hanged from a bridge. Young boys participated in the event, learning from their elders to dehumanize the outsiders, whose presence was believed to threaten the Iraqis' way of life. A jubilant crowd of participants and spectators jostled around the bridge to have their pictures taken in front of the hanging corpses. There was no shame or fear of reprisal in the faces parading before the television cameras—the participants were proud of their actions and wished to record the event for the entire world to see.[1]

Turning back to my research for this book, I reviewed the many similar images that were recorded in communities throughout the United States less than a century ago. What happened to Wesley Batalona, Scott Helvenston, Michael Teague, and Jerry Zovko, the unfortunate victims of the Fallujah mob, had occurred countless times before. In 1909, Will James was hanged from the electric arch in Cairo, Illinois, in front of thousands of witnesses; then, his body was riddled with bullets, dragged through the streets, and set alight. When Laura Nelson and her teenage son were hanged from a bridge in Okemah, Oklahoma, in 1911, local townspeople dressed in their Sunday best and lined the bridge to pose with the bodies for a commemorative photograph.

A photographer captured the moment as friends lifted each other to obtain a better view as Jesse Washington was beaten, mutilated, and burned alive before thousands of spectators in Waco, Texas, in 1916. In Omaha, Nebraska, in 1919, William Brown was hanged and his body mutilated, riddled with bullets, and burned; afterward, a crowd of men and boys jostled for position within the photograph of his charred and smoldering remains. Likewise, the image on the front page of the *New York Times* the morning after the attack in Fallujah showed members of the mob angling for better positions in the photograph by scaling the beams next to the bodies. None of these acts were done in secret. The participants acted with impunity, using picture postcards and video cameras—the social media of their day—to share these lynchings with friends and family around the world.[2]

Among Americans today, the term *lynching* immediately invokes a brutal legacy of racially motivated attacks on African Americans.[3] However, such has not always been the case. The rhetoric of lynching is politically charged. Its meaning and significance evolved through a century-long transnational debate over the role of mob violence in American society. From its earliest usage, this label was employed for political purposes to distinguish particular acts of violence from murder or assault. Depending on the audience and on the commentator's intentions, the designation could as easily condone as condemn any particular incident of mob violence. The British newsreader's tone was clearly condemnatory when he declared the events in Fallujah a "lynching." Nevertheless, as numerous newspaper articles and lynching postcards attest, for more than one hundred years, American communities accepted and even celebrated such horrific acts of extralegal violence as important tools for preserving social order.[4] From their earliest applications of the term *lynching*, Americans and Britons debated the appropriateness of American mob violence through the transatlantic press. As Americans argued that "lynch law" was necessary to maintain order in their developing society, journalists refined reports of mob violence to strengthen the case for lynching's international acceptance. For a significant portion of the nineteenth century, British commentators accepted these arguments and sustained Americans' "right" to lynch.

British acceptance faltered in the 1890s, however, when a series of high-profile lynching cases brought American justifications for mob violence under renewed scrutiny. Ida B. Wells capitalized on this moment of uncertainty to introduce an alternative interpretation into the transatlantic discourse. An African American civil rights activist from Memphis, Tennessee, Wells traveled to Great Britain in 1893 and again in 1894 to gather support for a transatlantic campaign against lynching in the United States. More than a century later, Wells's campaign remains a compelling story of individual courage and resourcefulness.[5] An outspoken journalist, Wells was thrust into the national and international spotlight after her protests against mob violence prompted an infuriated mob to destroy her press and drive her into permanent exile from the South. Wells turned this misfortune into an opportunity to continue her campaign against lynching on a broader scale. Her public speeches captured the attention of a British woman, Catherine Impey, who invited Wells to become the spokesperson for a nascent British anti-imperialist organization. Wells eagerly seized the opportunity to travel to Britain to speak out against the injustices faced by African Americans in the United States. Inspired by Wells's activism, the remnants of the old abolitionist and freedmen's aid society networks joined a new generation of British social reformers to fight against American lynching.

Through her transatlantic antilynching campaign, Wells enticed the American and British public into a vibrant debate on the causes and consequences of American lynching and, through that debate, redefined mob violence as a tool for maintaining white supremacy. Late nineteenth-century American leaders remained deeply invested in preserving the illusion that lynching was in some way honorable and distinct from murder. For a nation striving to attract foreign investment and prove itself worthy of becoming an imperial power on par with European nations, the rampant lawlessness of lynching threatened to embarrass the United States and stunt its development during a period of great economic upheaval. Although African Americans did not necessarily account for the majority of nineteenth-century victims of mob violence, Wells promoted an interpretation of lynching as a racist act of violent oppression directed specifically against African Americans.[6] Through this critique, Wells sought to undermine the narratives employed by local communities to make their actions appear heroic. These narratives formed the foundation of lynching culture; without them, "lynching" amounted to little more than an archaic form of riotous murder.

Because scholars have traditionally undervalued the rhetorical power of lynching and the transnational context in which the term was applied, they have underestimated the impact of Wells's activism and British influence on American society. Wells's outspoken attacks against southern lynching culture received substantial press coverage in both the United States and Great Britain. Historians generally agree that Wells's transatlantic campaign brought lynching to the attention of white Americans but have struggled to assess the value of that contribution. Too often, scholars have used equivocal lynching statistics to evaluate her success or failure, concluding that because lynching persisted after 1894, Wells's campaigns had little lasting impact.[7] Since the term *lynching* was a political label, its application depended on the attitudes and motivations of reporters located close to the scene of events. Therefore, the evolving rhetorical power of the word remains particularly significant, not just the specific number of times it was applied.[8]

Similarly, although scholars have noted the transatlantic connections among the reformers Wells rallied to her cause, they have neither explored the impact of these networks on Wells's ability to influence British public debates nor questioned why cultivating British public interest in American lynching may have been important for reasons beyond simple publicity.[9] Despite the nom de plume Wells adopted while abroad, she was not simply an "Exile" in Britain. She exploited lingering race and gender roles established by African American abolitionists in Britain to legitimate her activism as a "black lady reformer"—an identity unavailable to her in the United States—to claim the right to act as a spokesperson for African Americans. Through her personal testimony and her supporters' sometimes subtle efforts to inject her arguments into broader public debate, Wells's campaign redefined the way in which the British public understood the nature of mob violence and American race relations. British tolerance for American lynching quickly dropped. Outraged by the attention garnered by a "troublemaker," southern politicians and newspaper editors launched vitriolic attacks to discredit Wells's campaign, but they had little success. Mounting British criticism of lynching pressured prominent Americans, especially southern political leaders desperate to maintain positive relations with potential foreign investors, to choose whether to defend or decry lynching.

The rhetoric of isolationism and the mythology of American exceptionalism have largely hidden from our collective memory the transnational connections that have always been a vital part of the development of American society. The exportation of cotton and wheat to Europe dictated the fortunes of farmers throughout the South and Midwest, while Euro-Americans maintained close intellectual, cultural, and familial ties with their native lands. Industrialization, agricultural expansion, and urbanization increased the demand for new immigrants, who could provide cheap labor and settle the frontiers of the West and South, encouraging states and territories to compete with one another to attract quality workers and investment capital from Europe. Europeans, in turn, eagerly watched American development as a testing ground for democratic evolution. British leaders repeatedly invoked American successes and failures in domestic debates about British democratic reform. Long before Wells first traveled to Britain in 1893, therefore, American lynching had become an important symbol in these political debates.

The nineteenth century saw the rise of many successful transatlantic reform movements, including antislavery, temperance, and women's suffrage. Although largely excluded from political participation, women played an essential role in the creation and expansion of these reform networks. Technological innovations and the extension of women's roles into the public sphere during the mid- to late nineteenth century provided women with unprecedented opportunities to travel and exchange ideas with men and women on both sides of the Atlantic. Whether transmitted through telegraph wire, print journalism, personal travel, or correspondence, this movement of ideas back and forth across the Atlantic is vital to understanding the world in which Wells operated.[10]

This book ultimately explores not individual cases of lynching but the exchange of ideas. It traces the nineteenth-century evolution of American and British discourse about lynching and reveals how Ida B. Wells exploited this discourse to initiate a new transatlantic debate. Wells's activism called into question the basic assumptions about the role of mob violence in American society and permanently altered the way in which Britons and Americans understood lynching and American race relations. This volume explores the dissemination of Wells's ideas through British social, political, and religious networks into the transatlantic debate, enabling her ideas to penetrate mainstream American debates from which she had been excluded. Although white Americans could easily ignore an outspoken black woman, many felt compelled to respond to British criticism and struggled to find plausible arguments to defend their tolerance of mob violence. Their responses in turn strengthened and perpetuated the transatlantic debate on lynching. Long after the memory of her campaign faded, the British public continued to embrace Wells's assertion that lynching was motivated by racism and to press Americans to develop more plausible explanations for their continued indulgence in mob violence. Wells's campaign, the transatlantic debate she initiated, and her interpretation of lynching as a racist act of violent oppression ultimately helped to decrease transatlantic social tolerance of lynching.

Chapter 1

BRITISH RESPONSES TO

AMERICAN LYNCHING

When Ida B. Wells launched her transatlantic antilynching campaign in 1893, the British public was already well aware of the problem of American mob violence. From the first appearance of the phrase *lynch law* in the transatlantic press during the 1830s, British social commentators and newspaper editors enthusiastically joined Americans in debating the appropriateness of extralegal violence in American society. In her campaign, Wells played off of these pre-existing British concerns about American lawlessness. Therefore, in order to appreciate the impact of Wells's activism on British public discourse, we must examine the evolution of British perceptions of American mob violence.

Lynching and *lynch law* were politically charged labels. American reporters applied these terms to distinguish particular incidents of violence from common criminal assault, murder, and rioting. What constituted lynching, however, was never clearly defined; instead, this rhetorical construct was constantly negotiated and renegotiated through a transnational public discourse. As a powerful rhetorical tool, the term *lynching* was employed by American and British commentators both to condone and to condemn acts of mob violence. Acting through the guise of "Judge Lynch," the mythical personification of community-sanctioned justice, some Americans claimed the right to employ lynching as a form of extralegal punishment for perceived violations of the community peace. At the same time, some British commentators denounced lynching as evidence of public disregard for modern conventions of social behavior, minority rights, and the principle of due process. Throughout the nineteenth century, Americans remained sensitive to such British disapproval and strove to develop increasingly effective rhetoric to justify lynching as an honorable form of extralegal violence. In effect, lynching became the subject of a century-long public relations campaign waged by both opponents and apologists.

THE TRANSATLANTIC DEBUT
OF JUDGE LYNCH

During the summer of 1835, news of two Mississippi lynchings spread throughout the United States and Great Britain and launched the first significant transatlantic debate about the acceptability of this novel form of extralegal violence. Vicksburg residents hanged five gamblers in an attempt to cleanse the town of their immoral influence, while seventy miles away in Madison County, a "lynch court" condemned and executed several white men and enslaved African Americans accused of fomenting insurrection.[1] These two cases created a sensation in the United States and attracted the attention of the British press. Although the terms *Judge Lynch* and *lynch law* had previously been used, at least informally, in the United States, British commentators appeared unfamiliar with the concept.[2] While violence had always been a part of American society, the Vicksburg and Madison County incidents established *lynching* as a part of American culture in British eyes.

From these early days, Americans defended their right to employ summary execution outside the system of judicial due process. Vicksburg residents were "proud of the public spirit and indignation against offenders displayed by the citizens" when they rallied together to banish professional gamblers from their community. Although regrettable, drastic measures were necessary to protect and purify their community from "a class of individuals, whose shameless vices and daring outrages have long poisoned the springs of morality, and interrupted the relations of society." In the view of Vicksburg's leading citizens, gamblers were outsiders "unconnected with society by any of its ordinary ties" and therefore lacked "all sense of moral obligations" to the community. They violated the community peace by encouraging young men to engage in dissipation: to drink alcohol, employ the services of prostitutes, and go into debt rather than becoming productive members of society. Finding the legal system "wholly ineffectual" in prosecuting these offenses, Vicksburg residents resolved to find another way to banish professional gamblers from their community. Facing armed resistance, residents concluded that simply expelling the gamblers would not be enough to maintain the community peace. Hanging five gamblers not only rid the community of the immediate menace but also sent a clear message that Vicksburg residents would not tolerate unsavory characters in the future. Most important, the residents of Vicksburg established lynching as an expression of community will. As one witness to the incident observed, "we have never known the public so unanimous on any subject."[3]

Fears of an impending slave insurrection prompted Madison County's white residents to take similar decisive action to protect their community peace. Participants in that lynching attempted to distinguish their actions from those of common mobs by conducting an investigation into the alleged insurrection plot, examining witnesses, and holding "something like a *trial*" in a hastily formed lynch court for the white men accused of masterminding the plan. The plantations' relative isolation and the rapidly increasing number of slaves in the area—more than 40 percent of the county's total population in 1830 and nearly 75 percent a decade later—created a tremendous sense of vulnerability among the county's white citizens. Only four years after Nat Turner's bloody rebellion claimed dozens of lives in Southampton County, Virginia, the threat of an alliance between poor white men and slaves against the slaveholding elite would have made the situation appear particularly menacing. Distrustful of lawyers and legal procedure, slave owners demanded the certainty of summary justice to put down what they feared was a massive plot. In the final tally, six enslaved African Americans and six white men were publicly hanged over three weeks.[4]

From the earliest applications of the term *lynching*, Americans sought to justify their resort to mob violence. In 1836, Thomas Shackelford, a local attorney, published a pamphlet arguing that the Madison County lynching had been an act of community self-defense. After two days of interrogations, the enslaved suspects had made full confessions that implicated several white men in the alleged plot. Although the confessions were probably obtained through physical violence, they were used as prima facie proof that the community's actions were justified. Residents resolved to make examples of the enslaved "ringleaders" through summary execution to "strike terror among the rest, and by that means crush all hope of their freedom." Because the evidence against the alleged white conspirators included hearsay and the inadmissible testimony of slaves, the regular courts would not have convicted the whites involved. Therefore, Shackelford insisted, bypassing the judicial system was justified "under the law of self-preservation, which *is paramount to all law*." Shackelford praised the community for acting with "manly energy" to preserve "all which we hold most dear in this world."[5]

Although Shackelford assumed that his reasoned and carefully documented account would receive public approval, his attempt to present lynching as a necessary and honorable method of community defense met with disdain in Britain. Just two years after the 1833 Emancipation Act abolished slavery throughout the British Empire, few British commentators had sympathy for American slaveholders who claimed the right to set aside the rule of law to protect their interests in human bondage. To a British audience, Shackelford's "evidence" of an imminent slave insurrection seemed ludicrous, almost hysterical. Although any discontent openly expressed by a slave would have immediately alarmed southern slaveholders, *The Times* was not surprised that a slave might "utter the treason" that she was "tired of waiting upon the 'white folks'" and "wanted to be her own mistress." Charges against the alleged white conspirators appeared equally flimsy. While perhaps indicating regrettable personal preferences, "being out all night" without "satisfactory explanation," "being deficient in feeling and affection for his second wife," or "trading with the negroes ... and enjoying himself in their society" hardly seemed to warrant death by extrajudicial hanging.[6] Shackelford's pamphlet clearly indicated that the participants in the Madison County lynchings acted with impunity, believing their actions to be both necessary and just. Yet in British eyes, if residents had the time, organization, and forethought to hold "trials," record confessions, and conduct public executions, then they could have convened proper legal proceedings. If American lynching apologists wished to receive broad public approval, they needed to better substantiate the necessity of mob violence in American society.

In the 1830s, Britons were intrigued by all aspects of American society; the addition of lynching to the list of peculiar American folkways only piqued that interest. Europeans viewed the United States as a bold experiment in republican government and democratic equality. Curiosity about this new social and political experiment created a tourism industry that brought thousands of upper- and middle-class travelers to the United States. Intellectuals and social critics such as Alexis de Tocqueville and Charles Dickens toured the United States and then returned home to report their experiences. British travelers produced copious volumes on American society during the 1830s and early 1840s, discussing wide-ranging cultural issues in what have been described by some historians as the earliest sociological studies of the United States.[7] The genre quickly became popular reading among the upper and middle classes in both Great Britain and the United States. As one contemporary commentator observed, "There is scarcely a theme with which English readers are more familiar than that of American manners."[8]

Sociologist Harriet Martineau, former naval captain Frederick Marryat, novelist Frances Trollope, and other British visitors to the United States during this era witnessed one of the most violent periods in American history. Riots and other forms of mob violence increased suddenly and dramatically between 1835 and 1837. This apparent explosion in extralegal violence demanded attention, and American newspaper reports chronicling these outbursts made the violence appear epidemic, as though the hangings in Mississippi had unleashed a torrent of lynchings.[9] Although British newspapers and travel narratives did not begin to describe extralegal violence in the United States as lynching until after the 1835 Vicksburg hanging, by the end of the decade, British authors who dissected American society for British readers routinely commented on lynch law. Trollope, for example, added a footnote to the 1839 edition of her popular travel narrative, *Domestic Manners of the Americans*, remarking, "It was not till after I had left the United States [in 1831] that the frightful details of Lynch law reached me. These details are now well known throughout Europe, and must surely be received as a confirmation of the . . . insufficiency of the laws, or at least of the manner in which they are enforced, for preventing and punishing crime."[10] In just a handful of years, British commentators had come to perceive lynching as an inextricable if regrettable component of American society.

Although Trollope's commentary reveals a strong association between lynching and the punishment of crime, the contentious politics surrounding American slavery complicated the emerging debates about lynching. American abolitionists coming under attack by northern mobs appropriated the word *lynching* to label their persecution, conflating the violence in Vicksburg and Madison County with antiabolitionist riots in the North. Abolitionists constituted a small and intensely unpopular movement in antebellum America, important more for the social reactions they generated than for their influence on American political and social institutions. The strain of abolitionist ideology advocated by William Lloyd Garrison and his supporters, which included an immediate end to slavery with no compensation for slaveholders, was not widely supported in Great Britain, and such ideological cleavages led to serious ruptures in the transatlantic antislavery movement.[11] To slaveholders and those who profited from the fruits of slave labor in the North and Britain, abolitionists advocated "theft" of valuable property by aiding escaped slaves, threatening to incite widespread slave insurrections, and undermining the South's economic welfare. Such a strategy, one American commentator concluded, "forced the good people" of the South to lynch the abolitionists.

Confronted with growing hostility, abolitionists embraced the term *lynching* as a propaganda tool and identified the practice as a symptom of the moral and social disruption slavery caused in American society; if left unchecked, they argued, the spreading infection of southern immorality threatened to corrupt the body politic and create national anarchy. The abolitionist critique of lynching as evidence of slavery's immoral influence would have resonated with many Britons during this period of intense reform activism, when similar concerns about the capacity of corrupt institutions to spread moral decay throughout society had prompted the restructuring of the British legal and penal systems and the elimination of British colonial slavery.[12]

Indeed, the concurrence of antiabolitionist attacks with the development of "lynching" raised British concerns about the general stability and morality of American society. In her 1837 travel narrative, *Society in America*, Martineau described a mob attack on Garrison and the ladies' meeting of the Boston Anti-Slavery Society. Handbills had been posted at the City Hall threatening to kill "as sure as fate" any women who dared attend the meeting and offering a reward for tarring and feathering the guest speaker. Refused protection by local law enforcement, the meeting came under attack "by a howling, shrieking mob of gentlemen." Although Martineau expected the mob to be composed of "a rabble of ragged, desperate workmen," she was shocked to learn that the attackers were members of Boston's elite. This revelation turned Martineau's understanding of American mob violence on its head. While European riots typically involved members of the lower classes protesting their oppression by the aristocracy, American mobs seemed to be composed of, instigated by, and led by "gentlemen"—those who most clearly benefited from the existing social order. Garrison, who had escorted his pregnant wife to the meeting, was caught by the mob, pelted with brickbats, and dragged through the streets. Indeed, only the intervention of a working-class man saved Garrison's life. In Martineau's view, American society was seriously diseased if the upper classes were driven to riot and only the working classes could show compassion for human life. If American gentlemen could openly target defenseless (even pregnant) ladies for no crime other than exercising their constitutionally protected right to free speech, then the constraints of civil society had ruptured, and those entrusted to set the standards for American society might be capable of even greater horrors.[13]

From the American perspective, however, claims that the attack in Boston had been conducted by gentlemen rather than the lower classes gave credibility to the mob's actions and calmed fears about the outbreak of social anarchy. Some Americans insisted that the disturbance in Boston could not by definition qualify as a "mob" attack. In the early 1830s, the term *mob* held two distinct connotations—either "rioters or destructive crowds" or "the lower orders in general." Not until the end of Andrew Jackson's turbulent presidency in 1837 did *mob* became specifically associated with violence and dissociated from the poorer masses. As one "eminent lawyer" from Boston explained to Martineau, "O, there was no mob . . . I was there myself, and saw they were all gentlemen. They were all in fine broad-cloth." From this viewpoint, the rioters' respectability excused their lawless actions. Indeed, antiabolitionist mobs generally consisted of "gentlemen of property and standing" who attacked organized antislavery to protect their elite status. Although prompted largely by self-interest, antiabolitionists often portrayed themselves as America's best citizens, stalwart patriots who were defending society from those bent on its destruction.[14] Martineau's elite American informants felt sufficiently reassured by the equally elevated social status of the Boston mob's members; after all, when well-heeled citizens took matters into their own hands, they did so to preserve rather than wreck the social order.

Because Martineau was a popular reformer and respected social commentator, her criticism received widespread attention that helped to popularize the connection between lynching and antiabolitionist riots and made lynching appear ungentlemanly; her influence can be measured in part by examining how Marryat countered her position in his narrative, *A Diary in America*.[15] Marryat viewed Martineau with contempt for cultivating sympathy for disruptive abolitionists. Writing to his mother from the United States, he concluded that the United States was "a wonderful country" that had been unfairly criticized by "all the prejudices of little minds," and he resolved to "do [the Americans] justice, without praising them more than they deserve." "All that I have yet read about America written by English travellers is absurd," he complained, "especially Miss M[artineau]'s work." He went on to mock her widely known hearing loss (she often traveled with an ear trumpet) in describing the thirty-five-year-old as an "old woman [who] was blind as well as deaf."[16] As socially conservative as Martineau was radical, Marryat assailed her presuppositions as well as her powers of observation in arguing that mob violence was simply an organic part of American society that Britons had not yet sufficiently attempted to understand.

Marryat offered a great deal more sympathy to the lynchers than to the victims of their attacks. Largely ignoring the issue of antiabolitionist violence, Marryat focused on the alleged criminal activity that purportedly sparked incidents of mob violence in Vicksburg and elsewhere. He made a sharp distinction between "primitive" lynching as an organic form of natural law and mob violence exercised in opposition to the established legal system. Marryat reported that however distasteful, lynching "has occasionally been beneficial, in the peculiar state of the communities in which it has been practiced." Marryat described situations where "lynch law was called in to *assist* justice on the bench," with mobs waiting outside courtrooms to ensure punishment where legal technicalities, reluctant jurors, or clever lawyers might otherwise have prevented conviction. Improperly worded indictments, inadmissible evidence, and cunning legal arguments vexed impatient communities whose concept of jurisprudence required that those who perceived a wrong felt satisfied that justice had been done. Lynching became a panacea for the supposed failings of the judicial system or in cases where "from excitement the majority will not wait for the law to act."[17]

Furthermore, attempts to prosecute members of the mob faltered when sympathetic judges and juries refused to indict or convict lynchers. In 1836, Francis McIntosh, an African American man accused of murdering two law enforcement officials, had been burned alive by a St. Louis mob numbering in the thousands. When a grand jury convened to investigate the lynching, Missouri judge Luke Edward Lawless presented the jurors with a legal rationale for lynching. He instructed the grand jury to answer a "preliminary question, namely, whether the destruction of McIntosh was the act of the 'few' or the act of the 'many,'" before deciding whether to indict any of the participants in the lynching. If it could be determined that only "a *small* number of individuals, separate from the mass," burned McIntosh alive, then the grand jury "ought to indict them all without a single exception." If, however, McIntosh's "destruction" was the act of "the multitude . . . seized upon and impelled by that mysterious, metaphysical, almost electric phrenzy, which . . . has hurried on the infuriated multitude to deeds of death and destruction," then the case lies "beyond the reach of human law."[18] Lawless in effect proposed a legal justification for extralegal violence, arguing that the scale of the mob and the spirit of its actions could mitigate individual culpability. Coupled with the concept of "primitive" lynching as a form of common law, the "electric" and "metaphysical" character of lynching became the standard excuse for more than a century of extralegal violence and judicial inaction. If prosecutors refused to indict, juries refused to convict, and witnesses refused to identify participants in mob violence, lynchings could proceed unchecked. According to the St. Louis grand jury, even though more than two thousand people witnessed Mc-

Intosh's death, the spirit of mob violence, not those individuals who applied the torch or stood by watching, was to blame. Throughout the nineteenth century, countless newspaper reports and coroner's inquests echoed the sentiment behind Judge Lawless's charge to the grand jury, reaching the standard conclusion that lynching victims met their deaths "at the hands of persons unknown."

Arguments in defense of lynching largely rested on the assertion that American society was at its core wholly different from European society. Despite the dangers mob violence posed, the unprecedented history of the United States—a former British colony with seemingly limitless natural resources, a steadily growing population, and increasing political and economic power—required the adoption of new moral and social standards. For example, in *The Americans in Their Moral, Social, and Political Relations*, Francis Grund attempted to defend lynching as "a species of *common law*," deeply rooted in American colonial history and perfected during the Revolutionary War. In Grund's estimation, lynching was used not in "opposition to the established laws of the country . . . but rather as a supplement to them." By providing a time-honored commonsense counterbalance to the imperfections and shortcomings of the legal system, lynching had "been productive of some of the happiest results."[19] Americans "seriously defended" lynch law as "the only law of which some portions of the Union are capable," and their confidence in the "necessity" of lynching ultimately "bar[red] all discussion" of the suitability of mob violence for maintaining law and order.[20]

British commentators who accepted the premise of American exceptionalism found it difficult to question assertions that lynch law was required to maintain order in the former colonies. Lynching "in its primitive state," Marryat observed, was a tool invented by necessity, "acted upon in support of morality and virtue, and . . . regulated by strict justice." Without an established legal system, frontier communities required a form of popular justice to maintain order. Without lynch law, he concluded, "all security, all social happiness would have been in a state of abeyance" in early American communities. "We have often in England made a great mistake," London's *Penny Illustrated Paper* agreed, "in supposing that Lynch law was necessarily either cruel, unjust, or unnecessary," for without it "there would be no law at all." The implementation of a rude "mode of organization in the outskirts of a spreading empire," *The Times* concurred, was simply a condition of territorial expansion; Americans could not otherwise defend their property or safeguard their families.[21] Still in its infancy, the United States could not be fairly compared to European nations. As American society became more organized, the need for this rough form of justice would presumably diminish.

Nevertheless, Americans' willingness to forgo fair trials in exchange for swift vengeance appeared symptomatic of the moral deficiencies of American society and did not sit well with British social leaders. In response to Grund's argument that American colonists had resorted to lynch law only when they deemed English common law too lax and to his assurances that lynching was "not a child of democracy" but was inspired by the Bible, an incredulous reviewer in *The Times* exclaimed, "Mr. Grund, not content with offering an excuse for the atrocious barbarities practised under the name of 'Lynch law,' actually becomes the advocate for its adoption, and justifies its infliction by a reference to the Bible!" The reviewer similarly choked on Grund's seemingly hypocritical declaration that slavery reinforced the democratic principles of slaveholders by making them "cherish doubly those rights and privileges, without which they would sink to a level with their slaves." Rather than work to improve American society, Grund merely diminished the plight of American slaves and sullied Britain's reputation by excusing American inadequacies with the claim that American qualities had been derived from England. The reviewer despaired "that republicans are more addicted to pull down their superiors to their own level than to exalt those beneath them to their own equality."[22]

Accordingly, tolerance of mob violence became a mark of distinction between the two societies. To British observers, the United States was populated by "the canting zealots of liberty and lashes" whose "religious revivals" and "love-feasts" merged with "slave auctions" and "Lynch-law."[23] British commentators scoffed at the notion that a "country of lynch-law and negro slavery" thought itself "the home of justice and of equal right," when "the high principles maintained in England on the equal rights of all mankind, whether white or coloured," had been established firmly by the 1833 Emancipation Act.[24] American society did not meet British moral standards, and the continued tolerance of slavery and mob violence diminished U.S. moral authority. Consequently, Britons placed little stock in the opinions of "slave-driving, Lynch-law, tar and feathering Yankee[s]!"[25]

Evaluating the success of the American experiment in democracy became increasingly important to British social and political leaders in the 1830s. Growing political instability in Europe and the death of King George IV in 1830 raised debates regarding the value of constitutional reform in Britain. The success of the second French Revolution inspired a wave of rebellions across Europe between 1830 and 1832; fearing that civil unrest might spread across the English Channel, British politicians passed a limited series of reforms in 1832. Although these reforms redistributed parliamentary representation to better reflect the growth of major industrial centers in the North and Midlands and extended the franchise to members of the middle classes, the 1832 Reform Act fell far short of radical aspirations to implement the secret ballot and grant universal manhood suffrage.[26] Therefore, as debates over democratic reform continued, Britons looked to the United States to anticipate the results of democratic reform at home.

American tolerance for mob violence prompted some Britons to question whether democracy was in fact an intermediary step along the path to anarchy. British fears that American democracy equated with mob rule were reinforced by the seemingly endless stream of lynching reports coming from the United States. Abolitionists' claims that lynching was used to suppress dissenting opinion resonated with British aristocrats fearful of sharing power with the masses. If democratic reforms placed Britain's future in the hands of the uneducated, unguided masses, the country's elite might find themselves facing similar forms of persecution for advocating unpopular policies. Consequently, the narrative of lynching as antiabolitionist violence, developed by American abolitionists and promoted by Martineau and other British sympathizers, allowed conservative British critics to conflate democracy with mob rule.

Conservative politicians in particular denounced lynching as evidence of the inferiority of American society. The Tory Party suffered a striking defeat after the 1832 reforms. Under the leadership of Robert Peel, the Tories reinvented themselves as the Conservative Party and cultivated middle-class anxieties about the spread of American lawlessness to England as a means of averting further democratic reforms. The Conservative Party positioned itself as "the consistent supporter of the constitution," endeavoring "to avert the wicked designs of those Whigs, Papists, and Unitarians" who called for universal suffrage, religious freedom, and the separation of church and state. To Conservatives, lynching was a symptom of the excesses of Jacksonian democracy. British political leaders denounced the "mob constituencies" and "mob flatterers" that drove American politics. If Britons were to embrace universal suffrage, they, too, might become subject to an American-style "mobocracy." Therefore, Conservatives had a duty to defend England from the anarchy that threatened to engulf the United States. Declared Conservative member of Parliament Wilson Jones, "Let us thank God for the blessings we enjoy, and buckle on our armour, with a determination to preserve them."[27]

Lord Sandon's 1836 speech before the Liverpool Tradesmen's Conservative Association captured the character of Conservative Party attacks on American democracy and parliamentary reform. Although other nations struggled for liberty, according to Lord Sandon, none had "attained the stable liberty that England has so long enjoyed." True liberty grew out of a respect for law, tradition, and Protestant religion. Even the United States, "that greatest of free states, that noble descendent of ourselves," had found not true liberty but only the false liberty of absolute personal freedom. How, he asked, could Britons "covet that perfection of personal freedom which subjects any one uttering a sentiment displeasing to the ruling party to be taken up and tried by what they call Lynch law?" When citizens did not receive the due process of the courts but were "summarily tried, and hanged at the first lamp-post" or "tarred and feathered and banished for life," democracy became distasteful. Although Americans may "have done what, perhaps, suits best the peculiar situation in which they found themselves," Britons "have nothing for which to envy them."[28] If, as Lord Sandon argued, lynching inevitably followed the spread of democracy, Britain's present leaders might find themselves the targets of unruly mobs, facing the same potentially deadly fate as American abolitionists or French aristocrats. Such a catastrophic restructuring of British society could be prevented only by stopping the democratic reform movement.

As conservative British rhetoric linking democracy and extralegal violence became more widely accepted, British politicians and social commentators adopted the term *lynch law* as shorthand for the failings of American society. The editor of *The Times* ridiculed a radical British political reform group for claiming the motto "Democracy or Despotism." To the editor, "'Democracy or Despotism' is about as foolish a motto as 'Lynch-law or no-law' . . . for what despotism of an individual has the world produced which was half so arbitrary and cruel as the despotism of mobs?"[29] The editor equated democracy with anarchy and mob rule and dreaded them as much as any dictatorship. Even those British liberals who desired radical democratic reform, another editorial insisted, looked "with loathing" on the example of the United States, "a polity corrupted with the foulest venality. The more sober, but not less bold admirer of practical liberty shrinks with disgust from the contemplation of a republic which belies its high pretensions by the vindication of slavery and the toleration of Lynch law." A letter to the editor of *The Times* signed "Anti-Lynch" scolded the actions of a British mob in Guildhall, declaring that they "would have been a disgrace to the most recent settlement in the back woods of Amer-

18

ica."[30] Lynch law became the symbol of American hypocrisy, and toleration of lynching diminished British respect for American society. For Britons, to become more like the United States was to regress as a civilization.

Even though it did not reflect the reality of American democracy, tying democratic reforms to the rule of Judge Lynch was an effective Conservative Party political strategy. Conservative attacks on American mob violence were successful enough that by the late 1830s, anyone wishing to defend American democracy or democratic reforms to a British audience needed to defuse the issue of American lynching. British and American writers sympathetic to the United States tried to place the blame for lynching anywhere but on democracy. While Martineau cited the moral corruption of slavery as the root of American lawlessness, others sought to defend lynching as a form of common-law justice deeply rooted in the formation of American society. Americans were aware that the prevalence and severity of lynching threatened to tarnish their international reputation. Consequently, some newspapers called for Americans to denounce lynching and advocated the adoption of antilynching legislation.[31] Mobs based on local fears and formed for local reasons could be used as examples of national failings and symptoms of national disorder. Therefore, the relationship between the rhetoric of lynching and the reality of mob violence was not as important as the effectiveness with which the concept of lynching was employed in social and political discourse.

BUILDING TRANSATLANTIC TOLERANCE FOR LYNCHING

Throughout much of the nineteenth century, lynching apologists struggled to develop a narrative that would deflect criticism and justify lynching. American newspapers tested the boundaries of public tolerance for mob violence through frequent reports of lynchings, with positive and negative reactions establishing consensus constraints on mob actions. When British commentators complained about the excesses of American lynching, American journalists refined news reports to make *lynch law* seem honorable and justified. In the process, reporters helped to develop ground rules for what separated lynching from lawlessness. Over time, these constraints evolved into an unwritten code of conduct for the proper exercise of extralegal punishment.

The British press responded favorably to reports of lynchings that conformed to the code but offered harsh condemnations of violence that exceeded those limits. Future mobs then courted public approval by modeling their behavior to follow established patterns. Appropriate applications of extralegal violence tended to observe specific customs: the lynch court was made up of the area's "best citizens," and prominent participants were openly identified; the proceedings were conducted in a calm, sober manner during daylight hours; and the participants observed the ceremony of the lynch court, including some form of impromptu trial, confession of guilt, expressions of repentance (or lack thereof), prayers for the soul of the condemned, and a clean hanging with only a short public display of the body. In contrast, common or illegitimate mobs conducted midnight raids and tribunals, assumed the guilt of suspects and forced them to prove their innocence, used torture to extract confessions, and burned their victims alive or inflicted other forms of brutal punishment.[32] As lynching protocols became more formulaic, Britons evaluated the conduct of communities to determine the appropriateness of individual lynching cases. What emerged in the 1830s as a series of unrelated instances of extralegal violence had become by the following decade a series of civic rituals that foreigners could easily identify and evaluate.

British authors repeatedly celebrated the restraint demonstrated by "lynch courts." The press often reported trials by "people's courts," made up of local citizens of good community standing, held shortly after the alleged crimes. Just as in debates over antiabolitionist violence, reports of lynching employed as a form of summary justice emphasized the respectability of mob participants. Representatives for the defense and prosecution might appear, and testimony could be given under oath. Judgment might be passed by the consensus of a designated committee or by a general vote.[33] In keeping with the theory that attempts to hold prisoners wasted scarce resources and manpower and invited rescue or retribution by people who sympathized with the accused, the entire process was often accomplished in a matter of hours.[34]

In 1846, *The Times* reported the lynch court trial of Yeoman, a white man accused of stealing slaves in Florida. Having confessed to membership in "an organized gang" that "had stolen negroes in Thomas and Lowndes counties, Georgia, and Jefferson County, Florida, to the value of over 10,000 dollars," Yeoman was transported to Florida for punishment. He must have profited greatly from his criminal activity because he offered his captors a thousand dollars if they released him. Refusing the bribe, Yeoman's honorable captors delivered him to the citizens of Jefferson County for punishment. Ninety residents assembled, heard evidence, and in true democratic fashion "took a formal vote, which resulted 67 in favour of hanging, and 23 against it. Yeoman was accordingly executed at 12 o'clock." The article claimed that "The principal reason for this summary execution of the law was the insecurity of the [gaols], and the fact of his having a band of accomplices in the community, who would, in all probability, have effected a release."[35] The attention given to the details of the case against Yeoman and his trial by lynch court demonstrated the lynchers' desire to win outside approval for his summary execution. The community had a lot at stake in its quest for vengeance. Slaves were valuable property— often as expensive as real estate—and the execution of even one member of this gang of thieves would have sent a clear message that his partners should stay away from the slaves of Jefferson County. At the same time, the residents wanted to appear civilized and restrained in contrast to the criminal element they wished to eliminate.

To justify the circumvention of judicial due process, newspaper reports provided extensive accounts of the shocking, deliberate crimes that allegedly precipitated lynchings. Murder became a common justification for lynching, particularly in cases where the victims were given no chance to defend themselves. In 1857, Eli Grifford was reported to have "approached his victim from behind to within 15 feet and shot him in the head" with a rifle.[36] Similarly, after a personal dispute, Jefferson Gray confronted his unarmed opponent with a gun later the same year. The other man "acknowledged himself in Gray's power" and "turned his back to him to walk off" when Gray "shot him in the back."[37] While such dishonorable attacks offended public sensibilities, the mutilation of bodies was even more disturbing. In 1873, while under arrest on robbery charges, James Cullen secured an axe and "deliberately chopped off the heads of Sheriff Hayden and Hubbard, his assistant," as they camped overnight on their return to town. Cullen reportedly burned down the tent containing his victims' bodies so that nothing was left "but some heaps of ashes, a few fragments of charred bones, and a bunch of keys." The crime was so shocking that it "naturally caused wild excitement."[38] This account leaves many unanswered questions, such as how a man on the run could have created a fire so intense that it utterly destroyed two corpses, while evidence of their decapitations survived the flames. Nevertheless, descriptions of such barbaric and cowardly crimes tempered outside criticism of extralegal violence by placing the alleged perpetrators beyond the pale of civilized society.

Lynching reports customarily included confessions establishing the victims' guilt and demonstrating that the correct people had been punished. When their impending fate at the hands of the mob became clear, lynch victims such as Martin H. Gilliam and Eli Grifford chose to unburden their souls. "Seeing no hope of escape," Gilliam "confessed his guilt, manifested contrition for his past deeds, sought forgiveness at the Throne of Mercy in a feeling prayer, and earnestly called upon those present to be admonished by the example before them."[39] Although he had originally protested his innocence, "when Grifford found that the citizens were determined upon hanging him, and there was no probability of escape, he made a clean breast of it, confessing that he shot Ingalls" in the head from behind. He went on to reveal that his uncle had paid him to kill John Ingalls to end an escalating personal conflict. For good measure, Grifford also confessed to the attempted murder of a local man and woman. Regardless of their veracity, reports of such detailed confessions would have convinced many readers that men such as Gilliam and Grifford had earned their fates at the hands of the mob and that the formality of a legal trial would inevitably have led to the same result.[40]

Confessions of guilt legitimated mob actions by removing public doubt that innocent men might have been unjustly punished on unproven charges. Yet confessions of guilt could also benefit mob victims by tempering punishment, delaying execution, or increasing the chances that a final request would be granted. In one case, two Texas robbers confessed to membership in a secret gang of thieves and identified other members in exchange for clemency from the mob. Although both men were severely whipped before and after their confessions, neither was hanged.[41] Gray reportedly swore his innocence until a member of the mob "cried out, 'Hang him up; he is determined to die with a lie in his mouth.'" The mob moved to hang Gray without proper preparation, essentially condemning him to a slow, agonizing death by strangulation. Gray then changed his strategy, begging for time to confess his crime so that proper preparations might be made for his execution. Gray admitted shooting Robert Abernathy in the back following an altercation. He then proclaimed "that his wife was a good woman, and he hoped she would be taken care of; that Abernathy was a good man, and he believed was gone to Heaven; as for himself he could see the flames of hell blazing under his feet like dry broom sage." Through his declarations, Gray humbled himself in the hope of receiving mercy from the mob. He began to pray and begged members of the mob to pray for him. The mob then nominated Major Steele to pray "for the spiritual welfare of the prisoner, and for the sanction of Heaven upon their proceedings." As Gray apologized to each of Abernathy's brothers, the mob took up a collection for Gray's wife and child. If Gray had not confessed, it was unlikely the community would have demonstrated compassion for his family, given him an opportunity to come to terms with his impending execution, or granted him a humane, quick death.[42] The lynchers' acts of mercy also reinforced their claims to legitimacy. Rather than a howling, bloodthirsty mob set on revenge, the lynch court had performed its solemn duties in a sober and compassionate manner that achieved justice.

Confessions were often accompanied either by evidence of remorse, signaling to American and British readers that the actions of the lynchers were just, or by a total lack of remorse, demonstrating that the accused was entirely irredeemable. Like Gray, Grifford "acknowledged the justice of his punishment," and in return, a local preacher offered a prayer for Grifford's soul.[43] In contrast, the Reverend George Andrews remained wholly unrepentant for his crimes. Presented with a summons to appear in court in 1861 on charges of seducing and severely whipping a young female relative in his care, Andrews chose to shoot his way out of his predicament, killing two men and badly wounding two others before finally being subdued. The following morning, members of the local community gathered at the home of one of the victims to decide Andrews's fate. The deliberate nature of his crimes prompted seventy citizens to sign his death warrant, and he was hanged the same day. Defiant to the end, "the last words of this hardened wretch were, 'I am only sorry that I did not kill three or four more.'"[44] The unanimity of local residents in the production of a death warrant demonstrated community sanction for the lynching, but Andrews's status as a Methodist minister and lack of repentance made his crimes all the more shocking and his extralegal execution appear particularly well justified.

Concerns that lynching eroded legal authority or promoted anarchy were tempered by the disruptive nature of the crimes committed and the scale of the lynching event. British newspapers did not object to isolated, small-scale lynchings of individuals accused of theft, counterfeiting, or gambling. Lynching was understood as a direct community response against transgressions that threatened the fabric of American society. Thefts, especially of slaves, eroded the security of the local political economy. Likewise, counterfeiters threatened the stability of an economy dependent on faith in bank notes. Gamblers, often associated with criminal gangs and various forms of vice, were accused of corrupting youth and destabilizing community relations.[45] While lynching was regrettable and might erode established legal authority, the serious nature of these crimes against society tempered British disdain for lynching.

Despite its repeated criticism of American lawlessness, *The Times* delighted in reprinting what it viewed as humorous or creative lynching incidents. In 1836, Nicholas County Circuit Court Judge Brown was "lynched" in Carlisle, Kentucky, by the disgruntled populace for granting a new trial in a murder case. The crowd gathered outside the courthouse with a fire engine "and gave him a handsome ducking, as he passed out after the court adjourned." The crowd hanged and burned the judge in effigy the next morning and then "hoisted a black flag and tolled the bells" as he scurried out of town. The American author of the report gave the people "great credit ... for this modification of Judge Lynch's code. It evinces much humanity, and its tendency is as likely to produce the end designed as the more severe inflictions of 'Lynch law.'" The report concluded with the commonwealth's attorney, who had been soaked while leaving the courthouse with the judge, joking "that his misfortune resulted alone from keeping bad company."[46] Another report detailed how residents of a boardinghouse conducted the "moral lynching" of a man in Bloomington, Indiana, who had left a young woman pregnant, alone, and in ill health. When he returned to visit the boardinghouse in 1852 where his child had been born, the landlady locked the man in a room while her boarders fetched a minister, the clerk of court, and a marriage certificate. Everything was "made ready for tying the noose in the tightest manner" and he was "told in emphatic terms the part he had to play in the proceedings." Despite his objections, "the couple were united," with the groom looking miserable and "wishing himself a thousand miles away."[47] Reports of such amusing cases helped to make lynching seem more publicly acceptable; if Britons could laugh at these humorous incidents, they were more likely to tolerate more brutal cases of extralegal violence. But these cases also demonstrated the fluidity of the definition of lynching. If the term could be applied equally to the hanging of gamblers and murderers, a shotgun wedding, and the burning in effigy of a circuit court judge, then mid-nineteenth-century Britons defined *lynching* according to the spirit of extralegal "justice," not the actions of the mob or the alleged crimes committed.

The link between lynching and justice was reinforced in the 1840s as lynching opponents and apologists sought to establish effective lynching narratives—rhetorical frameworks designed to explain the motivation for lynching and the role extralegal violence played in American society. As transatlantic debates over mob violence evolved, several lynching narratives competed for dominance during this period. Although lynching opponents during the 1830s had experienced some success in defining lynching as antiabolitionist violence, vigilance committees in California rehabilitated lynching in the late 1840s by defining it as a form of "frontier justice." Based on the principle of popular sovereignty, they argued, local citizens had the right to employ mob violence to establish order when unscrupulous gold seekers brought rampant lawlessness into frontier communities.[48] This interpretation put the honor back in lynching by combining a romanticized image of "primitive" justice and common law. According to this narrative, communities without ready access to effective legal systems required popular justice to maintain order. Remote communities required the labor of every citizen, and delegating precious manpower to guard prisoners for six months or more while awaiting the arrival of a circuit court judge threatened survival. Long delays and poor security provided ample opportunity for friends or family members to assist the accused in escaping.[49] Therefore, upstanding citizens had a duty to take on the roles of judge, jury, and executioner to protect the more vulnerable members of their community. Rather than being considered shameful, extralegal violence was framed as an essential obligation, and shirking it would have brought dishonor.

By the 1850s, lynching had won a grudging respectability, at least as long as it was confined to frontier communities. Overwhelmed by the migration of large numbers of single men seeking to attain quick wealth, Californians relied on "a corps of volunteers . . . formed of respectable persons to preserve some degree of security against the outrages of the mobs of suspicious gentry who are flocking to this country from all quarters."[50] "In this aggregate of homeless, reckless, and lawless adventurers," Californians claimed, "an extemporized code of honour or honesty" supplied "the function of civil government."[51] After all, Americans insisted, lynching was the act not of wild mobs of drunken and disorderly men but of "men of Anglo-Saxon blood, decent education, and respectable political training" who transformed what had previously been viewed as "a barbarous process of vengeance or violence . . . into a recognized operation of popular justice." The administration of lynch law had become "so far naturalized" in some parts of the country by 1851, *The Times* remarked, that "American journals look with approval on these proceedings" even when lynching superseded "the ordinary administration of the law."[52]

British commentators who had witnessed American frontier conditions, particularly those in the gold fields of California, defended the use of lynching as a form of frontier justice and in the process justified their personal participation in or tolerance of mob violence. In a letter to the editor of *The Times* recounting his experiences during the California gold rush, William Kelly lauded the important role "the famous judge Lynch" played in deterring crime. According to Kelly, the knowledge that any wrongdoing would result in summary violence had "stricken terror into the evildoers"; as a result, "our rude society" in the mining camps had assumed "a placable and honest air." Security of property was especially important in such remote tent communities, and sudden, dramatic consequences for attempted theft deterred future transgressions. The knowledge that attempts to steal another man's treasure might result in death or physical mutilation would make any would-be thief take pause. Consequently, "honesty, even though it may be constrained, pervades this region," and the fruits of a man's labor were "as safe in your canvas tenement as if deposited in a metal safe" with a pick-proof lock. Other correspondents similarly applauded the San Francisco Vigilance Committee for transforming the community into "a habitable condition" and accomplishing "more good in the detection of crime than could have been accomplished by the police in a lifetime." "Popular feeling" quickly grew "in favour of Lynch law in preference to the uncertainties and delays of constitutional enactments," and frontier residents who found state laws "inadequate" began to consider lynching "more operative than legal justice."[53]

This "remarkable movement of opinion" was not lost on British commentators, particularly those with interests in the Australian gold fields that opened in 1851.[54] Arguing that the police force was both inadequate and corrupt, Australian settlers patterned their justifications for resorting to lynch law after those of Californians. The social disruption accompanying massive migration to remote regions, they argued, led to increasing crime rates. Unable to rely on an ineffectual police force for protection, the people of Australia were "crying out for Lynch law."[55] As in San Francisco, Australians in the mining districts reported the salutary effect lynch law had on local crime rates and argued that "the sooner it gets general" adoption, "the better," for it would "get rid of the hordes of ruffians who are prowling about." Fears about potential mob excesses did not appear to concern these commentators, since, they asserted, "lynch-law has no terrors for an honest man."[56] Some observers even claimed that British settlers could improve the practice. In Melbourne, for example, local citizens displeased with the poor performance of the police planned to form "a private rifle corps for the apprehension of thieves." Rather than inflicting summary punishment in the manner of California's vigilance committees, however, these citizens planned to deliver suspected thieves "to the constituted authorities" for trial: "That," a reporter proudly concluded, "is how Englishmen realize the idea of Lynch law." Lynch mobs in the rest of Australia apparently were less high-minded, as evidenced by the many reports of lethal applications of lynch law that surfaced from the gold mining regions.[57] Nevertheless, these attempts to make lynching appear safe and honorable reveal continued British discomfort with the practice.

Despite the British public's tacit approval of extralegal punishment, American lynch mobs could and often did exceed the limits of British tolerance. In September 1841, *The Times* denounced the mass lynching of a gang of gamblers and counterfeiters in Mississippi. Local citizens captured between fifty and seventy-five gang members, brought them by boat to a deserted stretch of river, and then "shot and drowned them all." The mob then turned the men's families out of their homes and burned their property to the ground. Although British audiences might find it difficult to understand how "the mere vice of gambling" could warrant death, authors such as Marryat and Grund defended the "purification" of fledgling American communities of the threat of "unprincipled characters" and "the pernicious influence of example."[58] Nevertheless, *The Times's* editors felt that such an excessive demonstration of mob violence exceeded the bounds of justice: "The laws and the good order of society have received a more dangerous blow" from this mass killing "than could possibly have resulted from a long life of crime." Although the mob's victims "were no doubt rascals of the deepest die" and might have "violated every law," their "numberless crimes can offer no excuse for the cold-blooded murder of so many men." "This cruel and damnable act of the mob" made "the crimes of the sufferers sink into insignificance."[59] If American communities wanted to maintain British public support for extralegal violence, they would have to be careful not to create such sensational news stories.

As Britons embraced the argument that the special circumstances of American frontier life necessitated lynching, criticism of the practice gradually waned in the latter half of the nineteenth century. The intense debate over parliamentary reform that had prompted Conservative politicians to denounce lynching and democracy in the 1830s and 1840s had substantially diminished by 1860. Although the question of slavery and the American Civil War helped inspire a second wave of constitutional reform debate in Britain, the country's 1867 Reform Act approximately doubled the British electorate, defusing the crisis.[60] British politicians no longer needed to use the United States as a negative example of a democratic society. While the American Civil War resolved the question of American slavery and erased tensions regarding American abolitionists' strategies, the outcome of the war still strained relations between the United States and Britain. Economically dependent on cotton exports from the South, Britain had hesitated to offer its full support to either side during the war. It had, however, allowed the Confederacy to purchase war supplies, including munitions and the *Alabama*, a fast cruiser designed to disrupt Union supply lines by destroying merchant vessels. Lingering diplomatic friction over British assistance to the South made Britons reticent to criticize or insult the

United States. Although both sides agreed to use arbitration to resolve the *Alabama* claims, the threat of war with the United States hung over the lengthy proceedings. Seeking normalized diplomatic, social, and economic relations with the United States, British leaders tried not to unduly anger Americans during the Reconstruction era.[61]

Britons not only lodged less criticism of American lynching following the Civil War but also became fascinated by lynching stories. Although the graphic details of mob violence printed in the daily newspapers offered some voyeuristic pleasure for British readers, voyeurism alone cannot account for this shift in sentiment. The concept of lynching as frontier justice became entwined with a larger cultural mythology that flourished in the 1870s and 1880s. Dime novels relating "true" stories of the Wild West became popular reading in both the United States and Britain, depicting brave lawmen and vicious outlaws as powerful icons of the American frontier. One of the principal ambassadors for American frontier mythology during this period was Buffalo Bill Cody, whose traveling Wild West show repeatedly toured England and Europe from 1887 to 1904. His first British tour coincided with Queen Victoria's Golden Jubilee celebrations, and his May 11, 1887, command performance before the monarch received widespread attention in the British and American press and made the show an instant success. More than 2.5 million people attended the Wild West show in London, including many of the European dignitaries and royalty who traveled to England to honor the queen during the summer of 1887. With the growth of frontier mythology, Britons began to admire the rugged individualism settlers needed to protect their families and build civilized communities in a harsh and hostile environment filled with dangerous outlaws and wild "Red Indians."[62] Lynching as frontier justice began to appear honorable, even admirable, and Britons came to perceive lynching as part of the authentic American experience. By the time of his 1892 "Farewell Visit to Europe," Cody had incorporated "TWO NEW PICTURES of historical interest," "Lynching a Horse Thief" and "Burning at the Stake," into his spectacular presentation of Sioux Indians, American cowboys, bucking horses, and wild buffalo. The show received favorable reviews, and audiences were "entranced by these vivid representations of lynch law . . . in the Far West."[63]

The frontier justice narrative was so successful that the British public began to view lynching as an organic force, much like fires, floods, tornadoes, and other hazards of the American landscape, accounts of which appeared alongside those of lynchings. An October 1868 *Times* report of "American . . . disasters for the last three days," listed seven fires that destroyed more than

$650,000 worth of property and killed five people, four fatal railway accidents, a political riot, an assassination, the collapse of a mine shaft that killed four men, and the lynching of a criminal who had murdered an Arkansas sheriff and wounded three deputies while trying to escape capture. "By this series of disasters," the American correspondent concluded, "26 persons were killed, 49 injured, and a large amount of property burnt up or otherwise destroyed."[64] Another report filed days later recounted a lynching and an attempted lynching alongside two fires, three railway accidents, three shipwrecks, the collapse of a wall, and the abduction of a Kansas family by Indians.[65] By the second half of the nineteenth century, lynching had become just another peril lurking in the American wilderness.

As audiences became more comfortable with the practice of lynching and more willing to assume the guilt of victims of mob violence, journalists shifted their focus away from establishing the justification for an individual act of lynching in favor of detailed reports of the lynching itself, with some British authors even relaying their encounters with lynch mobs as colorful adventure stories about rural American folkways. A. H. Paterson told British readers of an 1887 edition of *Macmillan's Magazine* about his participation in a lynch party when the area's most respected citizens had joined forces to protect their small western community from the threat of murderous anarchy. Confident in the morality of his actions and writing for a literary audience, Paterson described at length the deliberate process involved in the lynching. After an allegedly corrupt jury acquitted two accused murderers, the settlement's leaders met in secret to deliberate the fate of the two men. Holding a second "trial," the secret court convicted the two men by authority of "Judge Lynch," swearing they had "given judgment without malice toward any one." R. B. Townshend's 1892 account of frontier lynching in the *Nineteenth Century*, a journal intended for an educated audience, was set in a community with no law-enforcement facilities. The community organized a "people's court" and conducted an impromptu trial for an accused murderer within hours of the crime. The accused was quickly found guilty and hanged, prompting "many of the worst characters in town" to leave the same night. Townshend claimed that the lynching he witnessed purified "the moral atmosphere of Morgan City" and prevented further murders.[66]

Although British commentators had been appalled by the use of a lynch court in Madison County in 1835, half a century later lynching had become an integral part of transatlantic popular culture. The British public craved thrilling tales of life on the American frontier and eagerly received such accounts.

Depictions of lynching as an honorable form of American frontier justice affirmed the delight with which British audiences consumed these tales. Even as the frontier began to close, lynching no longer offered any moral ambiguity to British audiences; the "best citizens" of fledgling American settlements required popular justice to impose law and order. Lynching thus revealed not the lawlessness of American society or the weakness of American character but the moral strength of brave pioneers.

THE CLOSING OF THE
FRONTIER JUSTICE NARRATIVE

While lynching as frontier justice remained celebrated in transatlantic popular culture, the vast majority of American lynching reports that reached Great Britain during the early 1890s did not fit this description. Lynchings in settled areas were becoming ever more frequent, and fears that lynching might undermine the judicial system increasingly began to trouble British observers. Such fears appeared justified after the March 14, 1891, lynching of Italian nationals in a New Orleans prison. More than two thousand local citizens, displeased with the verdict in a murder trial, "broke into" the city jail and shot and hanged eleven Italian immigrants. The incident sparked an international diplomatic crisis and shocked Great Britain. New Orleans was not a remote frontier community with limited access to the court system but a thriving port city with a population of more than 240,000. Several of the victims had been formally tried and acquitted of the murder charges they faced but remained in jail awaiting trial on lesser charges. Furthermore, legal authorities admitted that they had known the lynchers' intentions but made no attempt to intervene. Baffled British journalists scrambled to explain lynching's apparent new role in American society.[67]

The lynched prisoners had been accused of ambushing and murdering police chief David C. Hennessy, who had won popularity in New Orleans and international renown for his tough stance against the Mafia. In 1881, Hennessy had played an instrumental role in tracking down, identifying, and arresting Giuseppe Esposito, a Sicilian bandit who had fled Italy after kidnapping a British merchant and holding him for ransom in 1876. When a shootout between rival stevedore gangs battling for control of New Orleans's lucrative South American fruit trade docks led to the arrest and prosecution of local Mafia leaders in 1890, Hennessy was once again the arresting officer. The prosecution's case rested heavily on Hennessy's extensive knowledge of Mafia activities, and his testimony threatened to unmask the central leadership of this secretive criminal organization. Hennessy was shot six times outside his home on October 15, 1890, the night before his scheduled testimony, and died of his wounds several hours later, insisting to the end that he had been shot by "Dagos."[68]

Hennessy's murder shocked and outraged the citizens of New Orleans because it represented the first open Mafia murder of a high-ranking white city official. City authorities declared war on the Mafia, nominating a "Committee of Fifty" distinguished citizens to investigate and disrupt these secret gangs. Chaired by Edgar H. Farrar, a prominent lawyer and white supremacist leader of the Louisiana disfranchisement movement, the committee collected evidence to prosecute Hennessy's assailants. More than one hundred Italian immigrants were questioned—some held in custody for weeks—before nineteen suspects were indicted on charges related to the murder.[69] Despite popular excitement and the mounting evidence against them, none of the first nine defendants tried were convicted. Amid allegations of jury tampering, intimidation, and bribery, the nine defendants were returned to the parish prison on March 13, 1891.[70]

Outraged by the verdict, Farrar published a notice in the morning newspapers calling for "all good citizens" to attend a mass meeting at the statue of Henry Clay "to remedy the failure of justice in the Hennessy case." The brief notice, signed by sixty-two of New Orleans's most prominent citizens, ended with the ominous instruction, "Come prepared for action." The following morning, William S. Parkerson, a local lawyer and politician, "harangued" the crowd that gathered at the statue "until they were in a state of frenzy for the blood of the men in the hands of the officers of the law." "Armed with weapons seized from some gun stores that had been pillaged," the members of the mob marched to the prison. Along the way, "the mass grew larger at every corner," until it contained as many as ten thousand participants.[71]

When the guards refused to hand over the prisoners, the mob broke down the prison door and stormed inside. Facing certain death if they remained locked in their cells, the prisoners begged for release or arms with which to defend themselves. Unwilling to concede to either request, the guards unlocked the cell doors and allowed the prisoners to hide inside the prison. According to one news service report, the leaders of the mob selected fifty men to enter the prison and "execute the sentence of Judge Lynch." "Only these" men, assured the reporter, "were allowed to enter" the prison and carry out the gruesome task of hunting and killing the trapped and frightened prisoners. The executioners proceeded calmly and efficiently. "Not a word was spoken" while nine prisoners, "caught like rats in a trap," were pulled from their hiding places and their bodies riddled with bullets.[72]

Disappointed at their inability to witness the carnage, the mob outside grew impatient and "demanded that the victims should be brought out and hanged in sight of all." Two prisoners were dragged outside to appease the crowd, which contained "many women and children." The multitudes in the streets "had heard the shots within the gaol but had not seen the slaughter. Now was their opportunity." One of the prisoners, already mortally wounded, was hanged from a tree as "men and women watched the scene with opera glasses" from neighboring balconies. Finally, a reporter noted, "a fusillade from a score of weapons ended his sufferings." The final victim of the mob was inexpertly hanged from a lamppost on the other side of the prison, shot repeatedly, and left dangling.[73]

Political calculations affected responses to the crisis on both sides of the Atlantic. To maintain his control of a fragile coalition government, Italian premier and foreign minister Marquis Antonio di Rudini needed to resolve the crisis quickly in Italy's favor. Under pressure from political rivals, di Rudini severed bilateral diplomatic relations with the United States, recalling ambassador Baron Francesco S. Fava on April 1, 1891. Fava's recall sparked a war scare that was exploited by the press and politicians in both countries. American military advocates used the crisis to lobby for the creation of a modern, standing navy—the establishment of which enabled American expansion into Central and South America and the Philippines at the turn of the century—while advocates of immigration control exploited American fears about the growing Italian immigrant community to open debates on immigration and franchise restrictions.[74] The situation soon stagnated. As the *Economist* explained, the Italian government "cannot sit still, they cannot fight, and they cannot obtain the redress they want without fighting."[75] Neither President Benjamin Harrison nor the diplomatic service had the constitutional authority to levy funds to pay an indemnity to the families of the mob's victims. Since murder was a state rather than federal crime, Louisiana was responsible for prosecuting the lynchers. But local sympathies meant that even if indictments could be obtained, the mob's leaders—some of the "most prominent citizens of New Orleans"— were unlikely ever to be convicted. Moreover, federal demands that the state compensate the victims' families would only have been "ridiculed by the local authorities." Unwilling to alienate southern voters, the Harrison administration refused to acknowledge American negligence or obligation to pay reparations along standard international law principles. Moreover, confusion about the citizenship of the Italian prisoners at the time of their deaths brought into question the extent of American government responsibility. If the prisoners were in fact naturalized American citizens, then international treaty obligations would not apply.[76] With no clear solution, the conflict between Italy and the United States dragged on for more than a year, bringing unprecedented, sustained transatlantic media attention to the issue of American lynching.

Excessive, deliberate, and cruel, the New Orleans lynching shocked the British public. Accustomed to contemplating lynching as a by-product of frontier settlement, newspaper-reading Britons could not fit the New Orleans case into one of their existing categories of perception. It was clearly not "frontier justice." Formal local authorities were in firm control and could have chosen to prevent the lynching but did not; instead, Mayor Joseph Shakespeare "bluntly declared that Mr. Parkerson and his associates did quite right" when they took the law into their own hands and that he "did not regret" his decision not to take "measures to prevent the tragedy" because the Italian prisoners "deserved hanging."[77] Britons, however, saw that the Italian prisoners had been tried and acquitted in a court of law. The price of civilization was that the legal process—and not particular outcomes—was sacrosanct. Claims made by lynching apologists that extralegal violence maintained social order appeared ludicrous when that violence nullified the authority of a working judicial system.[78]

American lynching apologists offered an alternative narrative to excuse the actions of the mob: in this case, lynching was an exercise of "popular sovereignty"—an excess, perhaps, but not a defect of republican government. Parkerson, one of the celebrated leaders of the mob, articulated the rationale behind this lynching narrative: "Under our Constitution," he claimed, "the people are the sovereign authority, and when the Courts and their agents fail to carry out the law the authority is relegated back to the people." While "the citizen hands over the right of government to law-makers and custodians of the law," John R. Fellows, a member of the U.S. Congress and former Confederate Army officer, explained in an interview with *Lippincott's Magazine*, "the right of government still belongs to the citizen" and "can be withdrawn" at any time in the name of self-defense. This ex post facto constitutional apology had a seductive if ersatz logic. Americans claimed that Mafia interference with the trial had led to a miscarriage of justice that left the court system corrupted and ineffective. New Orleans's leading citizens merely exercised their right and duty to reassert the authority of the people at large and restore order to an outraged citizenry by providing substantive justice—that is, justice that accorded with prevailing opinion in the local community rather than legal due process.[79]

Like the logic that underpinned it, the popular sovereignty narrative was flexible, covering a wide variety of situations. It could be used to excuse most acts of mob violence provoked by a variety of perceived miscarriages of justice, whatever their causes.[80] The popular sovereignty narrative emphasized active, voluntary, civic-minded democratic participation to right "imbalances" in the justice system. This strategy retained the aesthetics of the frontier justice idea but removed the restrictive geographic component.

The New Orleans lynching prompted the British press to issue a flurry of articles on lynch law and its legal and international implications. Citing interference by the Mafia in the original trial, some British authors accepted the logic of the popular sovereignty narrative and concluded that the citizens of New Orleans had been justified in bypassing the corrupt legal system to reassert their authority. Membership in the Mafia alone would have been enough to convince many Britons and Americans that the accused men were criminals even if they were not directly responsible for the Hennessy murder. Although the *Spectator* disapproved of the lynching on principle, the editor acknowledged that the citizens of New Orleans had been seriously provoked by the Mafia. While "the natural impulse of all law-abiding citizens" would be to denounce "the usurpation by an excited mob of the functions of Courts of law," in this case, the editor of *The Times* came down on the side of the lynchers. "All law rests ultimately upon force, and when the Courts are dominated by the criminals they exist to punish," the editor concluded, "nothing remains but to go back to first principles to effect their deliverance."[81]

In a surprising twist, a small, outspoken group of British commentators chastised the mob for lynching the wrong people, arguing that the corrupt judge and jury should have been targeted. "It is a bad feature of the American remedy for the defects of juries that its justice is not even-handed," complained the *Saturday Review*. The real criminals were not those who had availed themselves of the legal process to get away with their criminal activity but the citizens who had failed to defend their community by returning the proper verdict. The logic of the popular sovereignty narrative was so flexible that there was no limit to how it might be applied. If the mob could be excused for murdering criminals who escaped conviction through the shortcomings of due process, then the mob could just as easily be excused for killing anyone who participated in the corrupt legal system and thus contributed to the acquittal. "On the strict principles of wild justice," the author argued, "a better exam-

ple" might be made by "at least tarring and feathering or cow-hiding the jury."
The *Spectator* agreed that "those who incidentally benefit" from the faults of
a corrupt judicial system were not the problem. "No one at heart would have
blamed the citizens of New Orleans" if they had hanged the jury members
who "had returned false verdicts, either from terror of the Mafia, or because
they had accepted bribes at its hands." Although killing the Italian prisoners
was inexcusable, the *Spectator* concluded, vengeance against corrupt jurymen
"would not have been essentially unjust."[82]

Nevertheless, the legal proceedings against the mob's victims contradicted
claims made by members of the New Orleans mob that their actions served
"justice." If one of the central justifications for the toleration of lynch law was
the assertion that only criminals were lynched, how could anyone argue that
victims of mob violence who had been legally acquitted of the charges against
them were unquestionably guilty? Although the citizens of New Orleans
might have felt confident in their position, the *Washington Post* warned that
"Italy will surely not be inclined to think the massacre justifiable when, despite the prejudice and excitement arising from Mr. Hennessy's murder, a New
Orleans jury failed to convict the alleged authors of the crime." Furthermore,
the possibility that any foreign national might be subjected to extralegal execution *after* being legally acquitted raised concerns for all European citizens
who traveled to the United States under the assumption that the international
customs and treaties designed to protect their safety would be upheld. The
New Orleans lynching cast serious doubts on the American "disposition to
afford adequate protection to foreigners, whether by shielding them from in-
jury or by providing those who are accused with just and dispassionate trials,"
and raised concerns that Americans might hesitate to travel abroad for fear of
retribution.[83]

Despite threats and appeals from the Italian government for legal redress
against the lynchers, the U.S. government washed its hands of the affair, maintaining that it had no constitutional mandate to interfere in what was essentially a state matter. While politically convenient, the Harrison administration's position did not conform to contemporary international law principles.
Both the 1871 U.S.-Italian Treaty and international customs held the United
States and Italy "liable directly for violations of international law in whatever
department, judicial or executive, they may have occurred." Notwithstanding
the decentralized organization of the U.S. government, federal officials retained the duty to uphold American treaty obligations to extend equal protections to foreign nationals on American soil.[84]

British commentators were intrigued by U.S. government claims that it could not force states to abide by the terms of international treaties. Supporters of Irish Home Rule, the Irish right to self-governance, had advocated the adoption of a similar federal system to oversee Britain's semiautonomous colonies. But after the failure of American federalism in the New Orleans case, conservative politicians questioned whether Britain could ensure that its self-governing colonies would abide by British foreign policies and international legal obligations. Although the United States might be able to ignore its international obligations because of its physical isolation, Britain could not. In London, commentators questioned whether a federal system could work for Great Britain and other nations with "wide external interests." The federal system "worked with success in the United States," the Tory *Globe* insisted, only "because until recently that country had no foreign policy." "If this country were to adopt the federal institutions dreamed of by our Separatists," the editor of *The Times* warned, "it needs little imagination to conceive of similar complications, involving far greater perils" than the suspension of diplomatic relations.[85] If a semiautonomous Irish government violated British treaty obligations with a powerful European nation, Britain might find itself drawn into a costly and dangerous European war.

U.S. secretary of state James G. Blaine provoked angry responses from the international community when he argued that the United States had not violated its treaty obligations because the murdered Italians had been afforded the same rights and privileges as any American citizen. "The United States," Blaine insisted, "did not by their treaty with Italy become the insurer of the lives and property of Italian subjects." Although the government should take reasonable steps to ensure public safety, no government could protect "against violence promoted by individual malice or sudden popular tumult." Foreign residents, he contended, were only "entitled to such protection as is afforded to our own citizens."[86] Since American citizens could and did lose their lives at the hands of the mob, those foreign subjects who chose to live within the United States could not expect to be immune from the same risks. If, as American lynching apologists maintained, only criminals were subject to lynch law, one might avoid being lynched by simply refraining from engaging in criminal activity. Blaine's position troubled British government officials enough that they began investigating how this policy would affect British subjects in the United States.[87] British journalists derided the secretary's position, ironically asking whether "liability to lynch law" should be considered "a right and privilege" "enjoyed" by all foreign visitors.[88]

The Harrison administration ultimately agreed to pay a twenty-five-thousand-dollar indemnity from the civil service operating budget to the families of three of the victims identified as Italian nationals if Italy agreed to drop demands for punishment of the lynchers. Italian officials welcomed this face-saving maneuver, accepting the payment and immediately reopening bilateral diplomatic relations with the United States.[89] While the diplomatic crisis may have been resolved, the same could not be said for British public debates about American lynching.

For more than a year, American lynching and its repercussions had been a persistent theme in the transatlantic press. As public interest grew, international wire services increased their coverage of American lynchings to satisfy and sustain British curiosity about American mob violence. Sensationalism in the American press gradually created a cultural divide between the United States and Britain over the issue, as British and American audiences developed differing interpretations of those stories. Newspaper reports had shifted from trying to justify lynching to presuming that lynching was indeed justified. Therefore, American reports detailed the actions of the lynch mob, not the crime that had precipitated the violence. And because Britons had so completely embraced the frontier justice narrative, British editors had seen little need to contemplate other aspects of or explanations for mob violence and reprinted reports of American lynchings without questioning the details presented by American reporters. In the mid-1890s, however, a series of dramatic incidents called into question the reliability of American newspaper reports and British assumptions about lynching.

On January 5, 1893, *The Times* reported that the local sheriff and his officers had heroically resisted a mob attack on the Bakersville, North Carolina, jail. Although this display of valor ultimately ended their lives, the sheriff's men reportedly killed more than twenty of their attackers.[90] Subsequent reports placed the total number of dead at forty-two, with more than forty others wounded. A second attack reportedly resulted in twenty-five more deaths.[91] The scale of the incident seemed unfathomable, but Britons recalled earlier incidents in which Americans had killed as many as seventy-five men in a single lynching. Located in the Blue Ridge Mountains along the border with Tennessee, the remote region around Bakersville remained fraught with lingering Civil War tensions that had split many families. Since Americans also were known for feuding, the story seemed to fall within the realm of possibility, and the story gained credibility from the detail with which it was reported in the American press.[92]

The Times printed a lengthy editorial denouncing this "astounding tale of lawless outrage." The Bakersville incident did not fit American explanations for lynching. Despite the town's remote location, it was clearly not a case of frontier justice. Although lynchings in "the unsettled regions of the Far West" might be expected, this "outburst of savagery" had occurred "in the heart of the older States." Nor was this a case that could be justified by the popular sovereignty narrative, since there was no such "qualified justification for the conduct of the lynchers as existed in New Orleans," where "the course of justice had been defeated by the terrorism of the Mafia." The editor insisted that any law officers who "so gallantly braved death in defending" the suspected murderers from a lawless execution would surely "have held them securely until they were brought" to trial. He denounced the community's "impulsive resort to violence" and cautioned "Americans that they cannot afford to play fast and loose with lawlessness." Although *The Times* had initially embraced the popular sovereignty narrative as justification for the New Orleans lynching, broader applications made this narrative a dangerous doctrine. By circumventing the legal process to attain personal visions of justice, American lynchers had undermined the authority of a working judicial system and spawned chaos "rising almost to the level of civil war."[93] If Americans were not careful, they might soon descend into anarchy.

Although the editor of *The Times* had initially been skeptical about the sensational reports, he concluded that the story came "with so much circumstantiality of detail that it is impossible to dismiss it as a mere freak of a Transatlantic journalist's imagination." American newspapers had printed the case in excruciating detail, including a lengthy backstory and lists of the deceased. Nevertheless, as international indignation over the Bakersville lynching mounted, subsequent telegraphs repudiated the entire incident. Claiming that the town had been isolated for days by a severe snowstorm and could not respond sooner, Bakersville officials denied the "desperate affray" and insisted "that there has been no disturbance whatever, and that none is expected."[94] American newspapers reported that the named parties in the case were alive and well and had read about their supposed lynching with great amusement.[95]

The British public lacked the context for interpreting sensationalized reports of lynching transmitted by international wire services that American reporters expected. American newspapers prepared their readers to accept and interpret violence in specific ways, and American readers grew to expect certain patterns of violence and rationalization.[96] Because British editors selectively reprinted stories to share with readers, Britons had only limited exposure to the interpretation of American society suggested by American newspaper coverage. Shielded from repeated exposure to American sensationalism, Britons were left to draw their own assessments. Consequently, British readers received a perplexingly brutal picture of American society.

British newspaper editors were "extremely crestfallen" after the Bakersville lynching battle was revealed to be "an absurd invention." "The London papers," one American correspondent complained, "leaped upon the long, ghastly tales of seventy men slain in cold blood" to condemn the failings of "American institutions and . . . attempts to appear civilized." Even if the retractions had proven that Americans "were not a nation of bloodthirsty lynchers," that revelation came at a cost, for they had been demonstrated to be "at least rather unusual liars." Yet whether or not the details of the Bakersville case were accurate, the American press had consistently presented evidence of American enthusiasm for lynch law and lawlessness. Whoever was responsible "for the cabled Reuter reports during the last six months from America" had done the United States a great disservice by providing a "long, exasperating chronicle of prize fights, giant conspiracies . . . swindles, murders, and crimes of one sort or another, with never a lightening gleam of any respectable event."[97] The United States could not sustain a respectable reputation abroad when reports of such unseemly events were consistently transmitted from its own shores. Americans who wished to be regarded by the British elite as peers needed to abide by the accoutrements of civilization, including adherence to and respect for the law.

Less than a month after the Bakersville hoax, reports of an even more shocking case of lynching reached Britain. The transatlantic telegraph cable enabled reports of a lynching in Paris, Texas, to appear in British papers within hours of the incident. As with many incidents in which a mob targeted an African American victim, initial reports were brief, stating simply that a "negro" accused of assault had been lynched by an infuriated mob.[98] But accounts released over the next several days revealed that this lynching had been anything but a spontaneous act of grief and vengeance.

On February 2, 1893, more than ten thousand spectators had flooded into the streets to witness the torture and burning alive of Henry Smith, a black man accused of raping and murdering Myrtle Vance, a four-year-old white girl, tearing her "asunder in the mad wantonness of gorilla ferocity."[99] Unlike the New Orleans incident, the Texans did not wait for a trial but took only enough time to ensure widespread attendance at Smith's slaughter. Schools and businesses were closed, special excursion trains brought residents of neighboring cities and counties, and a scaffold displaying the word *Justice* was erected to ensure that all those in attendance could witness the proceedings. Smith was paraded through the streets of Paris on a float before being led to the scaffold, bound to a stake, and stripped to the waist. Male relatives of the dead child were given the honor of searing Smith's flesh with red-hot irons for fifty minutes, leaving his entire body covered with burns. They then thrust the irons into his eyes and down his throat. Finally, Smith was soaked in kerosene, covered in cottonseed hulls, and set on fire. When the ropes securing him to the scaffolding burned through, Smith rolled himself—blind, deaf, and in excruciating pain but still alive—out of the fire. Unsatisfied, spectators kicked and dragged him back into the flames. When at last the fire burned itself out, the mob dug through the remains to collect souvenirs of Smith's bones, teeth, and charred flesh. Picture postcards of the lynching soon circulated across the country.[100] The premeditation and elaborate planning of the incident horrified the British public and called into question the validity of all that Britons had previously understood about American lynching.

British newspaper editors did not know how to react to the detailed reports from Paris, Texas. Just a month after the Bakersville hoax, the story seemed too sensational, too horrific, to be believed. British editors were not alone in their incredulity; the *New York Herald* reportedly "refused to believe its correspondent," demanding "further proof and particulars" before printing the story.[101] Despite such skepticism, within a week newspapers from every corner of the British Isles carried detailed reports of the lynching. Even *The Times*, which rarely reported on lynchings of African American men, ran stories on the incident.[102]

The British public generally accepted the necessity of extralegal violence but found the execution of Henry Smith's lynching deeply disturbing. There seemed to be nothing heroic in torturing and burning a man alive, and in this case, the courts had not failed since they had not been used. Through the development of the frontier justice narrative, Britons had grown to accept American assertions that criminal activity precipitated acts of lynching and that only criminals were lynched. Therefore, British observers found it difficult to denounce lynching on principle, even when the behavior of the mob appeared excessive. The editor of London's *Daily Chronicle* struggled to make sense of the "tragedy" in Texas. Although it was "not wonderful" that the white community had engaged in "the most terrible revenge," he reminded his readers that the rape and mutilation of little Myrtle Vance provided the community with "strong provocation." The *Bristol Mercury and Daily Post* ridiculed "the Texan Paris" for attempting to emulate the "elegance of manners" exhibited

by its European namesake. While "in other places lynching is a vulgar unpre-
meditated affair," the editor sneered, in this case "the entertainment is provided with a programme" advertised in advance. Back in London, the *Daily
News* marveled at the depravity of the Texas mob, which tried to repay Smith's
violence "with interest" by burning him alive. "Men, or even devils might have
paused here from sheer lack of invention," yet Smith was tortured as well. The
paper's editor felt "very little pity" for Smith but cautioned that "concern may
be felt for the communities to which his executioners belong," for "they are
forming a taste in cruelty which they will find it hard to correct." Rather than
accomplishing their purported goal of deterring future crimes, white southerners merely set an instructive example in brutality, "which certainly will not
be lost upon the [black] savages on the other side."[103] Britons accepted that
Smith's alleged criminal behavior had placed him beyond the pale of due process and into the hands of the mob, yet the mob's brutality remained difficult
to countenance.

Furthermore, Smith's elaborate and premeditated torture called into question the validity of claims that lynching was a spontaneous act of vengeance
and brought a backlash not only in Britain but also in the United States. A
cartoon published in the *New York Press* recalled not only the Paris lynching
but a February 1892 incident in Texarkana, on the Texas-Arkansas border, in
which Edward Coy had been burned alive in front of as many as fifteen thousand onlookers after being accused of raping a woman. The cartoon showed
"Texas trampling on law and order and justice with her hands outstretched in
holy horror, but helpless, while a woman applies the torch to a negro rapist in
Texarkana and Paris," and asked, "Has civilization gone mad?" The *Fort Worth
Gazette* responded with a "picture of Henry Smith with his foot on the naked
body of little Myrtle Vance, a blasted home in the background, while he holds
in his right hand a dagger dripping with the blood of this little innocent he so
cruelly mangled." The *Gazette*'s caption emphatically asserted that civilization
had indeed gone mad if it could produce monsters such as Smith, but many
commentators nevertheless noted that white men controlled the South's judicial system and that any African American rapist, particularly one who had
also murdered his child victim, would be unlikely to go unpunished.[104] The
Michigan House of Representatives passed a resolution condemning the mob
for refusing due process to "colored people accused of crime and calling upon
the authorities at Washington to exercise the power of the Nation to prevent
the wholesale lynching of these defenseless people."[105] A dispute broke out
at a meeting of the Chicago Pastoral Alliance when one member proposed

a resolution condemning the Paris lynching on the grounds that Smith had been "burned at the stake . . . because he was a negro." Although a series of ministers denounced the "inhuman" or "devilish barbarity" of the lynching, a Methodist Rev. Leach objected to the vilification of the Paris community, arguing "that Smith was executed not because of his color but on account of his crime, and that he was treated just right." The cries of "Shame!" that hissed around the church in the wake of Leach's protest were no less than John G. Rankin, editor of Texas's *Brenham Daily Banner,* expected. "Many people remote from the 'theater of action,'" he complained, "especially up 'up North,' will raise their eyes in holy horror" at the brutality of the lynching. "Let us keep silent and permit them to enjoy their" righteous indignation, he advised. Apparently comfortable in the conviction that Paris, only 250 miles away, was like any other American community, Rankin argued that a universal, passionate sympathy for the Vance family led the incensed mob to wreak such terrible vengeance. Anyone faced with a similar tragedy, he insisted, would have been "ready to say: 'Let me, too, get hold of the hot irons.'"[106]

Under harsh criticism for failing to take measures to prevent the lynching, Texas governor James Hogg denounced the Paris mob scene as "the most revolting execution of the age, in which large numbers of citizens openly, in broad day, purposely became murderers by methods shameful to humanity." The lynching was "a disgrace to the State. Its atrocity, inhumanity, and sickening effect upon the people at large cannot be obscured by reference to the savage act of the culprit himself in brutally taking the life of an innocent child." Hogg called on the state legislature to pass an antilynching law and to empower him to prosecute the leaders of the Paris mob. Dismissed as "political claptrap" designed to "catch negro votes," Hogg's propositions received little support from either the public or officials in Texas, and no one was ever prosecuted for Smith's murder. Rankin reminded readers of the *Brenham Daily Banner* that the international attention generated by the Paris lynching had placed Hogg in a difficult position: the public "can not reasonably expect Governors and other officers to perjure themselves by official endorsement" of extralegal violence.[107]

Searching for a narrative through which to understand the actions of the Paris mob, British newspapers fell back on the rhetoric of antislavery activism. The various levels of filtering that occurred as American reporters decided what to write, international wire services chose what to transmit, and British editors selected what to print meant that few detailed accounts of the lynching of African Americans had been reported in the British press. When these lynchings were reported, British newspapers often provided only sketchy accounts or lumped reports into summaries of general events. Consequently, British editors sought context for the Paris lynching in the only American racial discourse many Britons knew: the struggle against slavery. One *London newspaper, the Star,* printed the story of Smith's lynching under an ironic headline, "A Man and a Brudder," invoking the memory of a popular antislavery slogan and supplicant image of a naked slave in bondage pleading for mercy. "The awful story, if accurate," the editor of the *Daily Chronicle* asserted, "shows how well-nigh insoluble is the problem which negro slavery has entailed on the United States." Slavery kept African Americans in a degraded and barbarous state and corrupted white southerners. Although the institution of slavery had ended, its demoralizing influences had created both the black rapist and the depraved white mob. If Smith were a monster, then white southerners had created the social structures that produced him, and the children of Paris were reaping the evil that previous generations of southern whites had sown. As the editor sadly concluded, "The evil that we do lives after us."[108]

With the Paris incident, the Americans had presented the British with an unfamiliar narrative—that lynching was prompted by community outrage over the rape of white women by black men, a crime so horrific that the legal system could never deliver adequate punishment. The purpose of justice, the *Brenham Daily Banner* maintained, was to strike fear into the hearts of would-be criminals. Yet "no law exists that can, with sufficient force, strike terror to men so full of hell as to be capable" of outraging "womanly virtue" or "mangling and murdering an innocent child." In the editor's eyes, only a true monster would have destroyed both the life and innocence of a four-year-old girl. A simple death by legal hanging was too good—too easy an end for black rapists. White southerners thus had a moral obligation to punish sexually based offenses through inventive applications of lynch law. "As no law fierce enough exists" to punish the sexual violation of white women and girls, the *Banner* insisted, "let the demons of lust understand that in every case one will be made by the people."[109]

The "lynching for rape" narrative was truly a foreign concept for Britons. Without indoctrination into the culture that supported lynching narratives in the United States, the British public had not embraced the core fear of the "black beast rapist," whose uncontrollable animal lust for white women allegedly posed an ever-present menace in American society.[110] Although typically characterized as a pervasive feature of southern society, the "southern rape complex"—an unwarranted preoccupation with the threat of black rapists—did not manifest in the United States until the late 1880s and early 1890s.[111]

It is therefore not surprising that the British press remained largely unaware of these anxieties. Lynching had not previously been discussed as a racially motivated act of violence; British authors assumed that victims of mob violence were chosen for their criminal behavior, not their color. Writing in the *Juridical Review,* N. J. D. Kennedy explained for Britons the various degrees of punishment employed by lynch mobs: *a*lthough the favorite punishment for "venial delinquencies" remained public flogging, more serious offenses were "sufficiently expiated by the accused being shot or hanged." However, "burning alive is usually reserved for negroes or Indians in cases where popular feeling is strongly excited" and at times would be "ingeniously combined" with the other punishments. While Kennedy's analysis calmly described the torture and burning of African Americans, it did not suggest that these acts, collectively referred to as lynchings, were motivated by the racist categories in which the mob interpreted the supposed crimes and criminality of African Americans in Paris, Texas. Although black men might receive harsher treatment at the hands of the mob, British authors maintained that criminal behavior, not race, triggered lynchings. Even then, British authors acknowledged only that lynching was used to resolve cases of black-on-white rape; they did not embrace the assertion that African American men posed an imminent threat to all unprotected white women. For example, the *Spectator* questioned the value of lynching black men accused of assaults on white women, insightfully arguing that "the only effect is that fear of [rape] has become the governing terror of the South."[112]

Britons were not, however, unfamiliar with the existence of the problem of black-on-white rape in America. As far back as the end of the eighteenth century, British travel narratives and newspaper reports recounted cases in which black men accused of raping white women were burned alive. In his 1807 travel narrative, *The Stranger in America, 1793–1806,* Charles William Janson described a slave accused of raping his master's daughter in Chowan, North Carolina: after capturing the man, his "enraged pursuers tied him to tree, collected wood around him, and immediately consumed his body to ashes." Martineau described an 1837 case in which two Alabama slaves accused of assaulting two white women and raping and murdering two small white children were seized by "the gentlemen of Mobile," who "heaped up faggots on the margin of the brook, and slowly burned them to death." In 1862, *The Times* reported the case of an African American man accused of attempted rape and murder who was hanged, shot, and then dragged through the streets of Denton, Maryland, to the riverbank, where his corpse was "cut into small pieces" and thrown into a fire. In another incident related in *The Times* just over two decades later, a black man was "roasted to death" in Austin, Texas, after he confessed to the murder of a local white woman.[113] These stories indicate that at least in some communities, burning alive was considered a standard punishment for African American slaves accused of raping elite white southern women, and the practice persisted following emancipation.[114] What changed, however, was the definition of such acts as *lynching*.

Prior to the Paris lynching, Americans had not pushed Britons to accept the "lynching for rape" narrative. The growing British horror at the brutality of lynch mobs and consequent increases in British resistance to earlier justifications for lynching caused American apologists for the practice to shift their tactics again, now claiming that without the paternalistic guidance and control of slavery, African American men had become savage rapists. But this explanation never satisfied British audiences. The lynching for rape narrative did not match British colonial experiences with black men, leading Britons to begin to fear that white southerners' violent responses undermined American moral integrity and civilization.

In the two years between the New Orleans lynching and the lynching of Henry Smith, the British public had been introduced to three distinct lynching narratives. For different reasons, each of these narratives appealed to the British public yet failed adequately to excuse mob violence, and the inadequacies became greater with each successive explanation. The frontier justice narrative resonated with Britons' images of American settlement and colonial experiences but remained limited in scope and could not explain urban lynching. The popular sovereignty narrative employed a seductive, flexible logic that could be applied to a wide array of alleged miscarriages of justice in the American legal system. Although that approach proved effective in the case of the New Orleans lynching, Britons remained reluctant to accept its regular application to the increasingly frequent and outrageous acts of extralegal violence reported by the transatlantic press in the early 1890s. The lynching for rape narrative proved least satisfactory of all, given its foundational idea that some crimes were so heinous that they could only be handled extrajudicially—the precise definition of anarchy.

Britons refused to accept this argument and turned to questioning Americans' moral integrity and the truthfulness of their excuses for these lawless excesses. This uncertainty created an opportunity for renewed debate about the nature and prevalence of American mob violence, and this debate offered a space in which potentially more satisfying alternative interpretations of lynching might be considered. Ida B. Wells stepped into this debate.

Chapter 2

THE EMERGENCE

OF A TRANSATLANTIC

REFORMER

Into this realm of confused British perceptions of American lawlessness strode Ida B. Wells, civil rights firebrand, promoting an alternative narrative about events in the South. Wells had come of age during a tumultuous period in American race, class, and gender relations, and in her, history and circumstances had fashioned an unusually effective advocate.

Ida Bell Wells was born into slavery amid the upheaval of the Civil War on July 16, 1862, in Holly Springs, Mississippi. Her father, James, was the son of a slave named Peggy and her master, Morgan Wells, a white plantation owner from Hickory Flats. Morgan Wells and his wife had no children of their own, and Morgan favored Jim and apprenticed him as a carpenter with Spires Bolling, a white architect and builder from Holly Springs, a growing town located approximately twenty miles to the west of Hickory Flats. In Holly Springs, Jim met his future wife, Elizabeth Warrenton, a young cook in Bolling's household. Born to enslaved parents in Virginia, Lizzie and two of her sisters had been sold south to Mississippi as children. Unable to reunite with her family following the end of the Civil War, Lizzie's loss underscored for her children the importance of maintaining family connections.[1]

Her parents' efforts to embrace their newfound opportunities as American citizens following emancipation provided Ida Wells with strong examples of political, religious, and educational community involvement. After the war ended, Jim's valuable carpentry skills provided him with greater opportunities than were available to most freedmen. Despite the dangers inherent in black political participation during Reconstruction, Jim insisted on exercising his right to vote. When Bolling locked Jim out of his carpentry shop for refusing to vote for Democratic Party candidates, Jim quickly found a new house, purchased tools on credit, and obtained a new employer. The need for skilled carpenters to repair the destruction of the Civil War and Jim's willingness to help his neighbors, both black and white, during times of crisis made him a valued member of the Holly Springs community. Jim had enough financial security to adopt middle-class gender roles, allowing Lizzie and their children to attend a local school established by the Freedman's Aid Society of the Methodist Episcopal Church in 1866. A devout woman, Lizzie learned how to read the Bible and oversaw her children's academic and religious education. As Ida Wells later recalled in her autobiography, "Our job was to go to school and learn all we could."[2] When the 1878 yellow fever epidemic devastated the Mississippi Valley, spreading to more than two hundred communities across eleven states, the courage and selflessness Jim Wells demonstrated tending to the afflicted taught Ida to take action when serious problems arose. Both her parents and infant brother died during the epidemic, leaving sixteen-year-old Ida to provide for her five surviving brothers and sisters by working as a schoolteacher.[3]

Seeking better employment, Wells relocated to Memphis, Tennessee, in 1881. Starting in the country schools and working her way up to a position in the city, Wells quickly joined the growing ranks of Memphis's black middle class. This thriving urban community offered access to stimulating social and intellectual opportunities, and Wells participated in literary societies, took elocution lessons, and eventually became a journalist. Nevertheless, life for a young, independent black woman in a budding New South city in the 1880s presented serious social challenges as southern state legislatures attempted to codify racial segregation.

NAVIGATING A GENDERED WORLD

The new generation of educated young black men and women who came of age at the end of the nineteenth century asserted the right to pursue professional opportunities and enjoy the benefits of middle-class status. Born and raised outside the rigid social structure of slavery, these African Americans expected access to the rights and privileges associated with social and economic success in American society, including the right to be considered ladies and gentlemen. In the nineteenth century, the combination of class status and respectability signified by these labels conferred certain social privileges and legal protections not available to the broader public. These protections were especially important for women. As long as they conformed to expected behavior codes and dressed respectably, middle class "ladies" were assumed to be innocent, delicate, and honorable and thus had the right not to be subjected to the abuses or offenses to which their lower-class counterparts were vulnerable.

On September 15, 1883, Wells boarded a train traveling from Memphis north to Covington, Kentucky, intending to disembark at Woodstock, Tennessee, ten miles north of Memphis in Shelby County. She had been visiting her aunt and sisters in Memphis and was returning to her position as a teacher in the Woodstock public school system. As a young, single lady traveling alone, Wells entered the first-class car designated for ladies and their gentlemen companions. Late-nineteenth-century social mores dictated the segregation of public accommodations along the lines of sex and class. First-class passenger coaches afforded middle-class ladies protection from men who smoked, drank alcohol, or used coarse language in public. Only well-mannered gentlemen, particularly those escorting ladies, were allowed to ride in first-class carriages, commonly referred to as ladies' cars. Unaccompanied men might travel in ladies' cars at the discretion of train conductors; however, as seats filled, gentlemen were expected to give up their seats to ladies and stand or move to the smoking car. In addition, ladies' cars were located at the rear of the train, affording the quietest, most comfortable ride and the safest position in case of a train collision or derailment—an all too frequent occurrence. These rules established a protected gendered and class-defined space that extended the "domestic sphere" into public transportation, allowing ladies to maintain their respectability and travel safely. The act of riding in the ladies' car also visibly confirmed a woman's status as a lady.[4] Therefore, when Wells chose a seat in the first-class carriage, she was publicly asserting her right to be considered a lady.

Although racial segregation or exclusion was commonly practiced nationally in rail travel throughout the second half of the nineteenth century, the division of first- and second-class carriages into ladies' and smoking cars left African American women in a particularly difficult position when Tennessee and other southern states began passing segregation ordinances in the 1880s.[5] Rather than investing in additional first-class cars, many rail companies adapted less well-appointed smoking cars to serve as "first-class" coaches for black passengers. Located closer to the engine, smoking cars were hot, loud, and airless, filled with engine exhaust and cigar smoke. Men were permitted to indulge in gambling, drinking, and raucous behavior. Unlike the plush couches in the ladies' car, smoking cars typically provided serviceable wooden benches designed to endure the abuse of cigar ash and tobacco juice. Additional amenities and services commonly found in first-class accommodations, such as plush carpets, separate bathrooms for men and women (no small consideration on swaying carriages), and supplies of ice water, were not provided.[6] Conversely, even where enforced, racial segregation was not complete. Black women traveling as nurses for white passengers or accompanying white children were routinely admitted to first-class cars designated for white passengers. As racial segregation laws became more rigidly enforced, domestic servants continued to be admitted to first-class carriages, but black middle-class women were increasingly forced to forgo the protections of the ladies' car.[7]

Where tickets were sold with specific service designations, passengers who could not afford higher first-class fares, men traveling alone on lines where the only first-class car was designated for ladies and their companions, and black passengers seeking to avoid the humiliation of being refused admittance to the first-class car designated for white passengers might choose to pay second-class fares. However, on rail lines that sold only common fares, individual train conductors had discretion to determine who would be allowed to ride in the ladies' car and who would be directed to the smoking car. This system left unprotected those women who, based on behavior or appearance, did not outwardly qualify as ladies. Unless they were accompanying white employers, black women of low social status were expected to ride in second-class coaches or smoking cars, where they were more likely to be subjected to sexual and other harassment.[8] Moreover, the act of consenting to ride in a second-class carriage demonstrated that a woman lacked sufficient respectability to be deemed a lady, thus justifying any ungentlemanly behavior directed toward her. As white frustrations over the advancement of African Americans grew, black women, regardless of their education, wealth, or social status, were increasingly denied the right to be considered ladies. Many southern whites believed that African Americans diminished white power and social status by claiming access to these privileges. The easiest way to reassert white dominance was to restrict the progress of middle-class African Americans. Although conductors might theoretically refuse admittance to anyone deemed "obnoxious" regardless of race, in practice, middle-class African Americans were much more likely to be excluded than even the poorest whites.[9]

Wells was a frequent rail traveler, visiting family and friends as well as attending educational conferences and social events in various states. She routinely sought passage in the ladies' car and, like many middle-class black women in the early years of segregation, was typically successful. If Wells claimed a seat in the ladies' car without objection before the conductor took her ticket, she could expect to proceed unmolested on her journey.[10]

On September 15, 1883, Wells purchased a ticket on the Chesapeake, Ohio, and Southwestern (CO&S) Railroad's accommodation train, which provided daily service for the small communities between Memphis and Covington. Since there was no distinction between fares on the CO&S line and the train had only two passenger cars, Wells took a seat in the first-class ladies' carriage at the rear of the train, as she had on previous occasions.[11] When the conductor, William Murry, came to collect tickets, however, he refused to accept Wells's ticket in the ladies' car, insisting that CO&S regulations required that all "colored people must ride in the forward coach." Wells had noted the presence of smokers and at least "one drunken white man" in the forward car and consequently refused to relinquish her seat in the ladies' car despite the conductor's repeated requests. When the train reached the first station, Frayser, the conductor and two white passengers attempted to drag Wells from her seat. Wells wedged her feet under the seat in front of her and fought her attackers—quite literally tooth and nail. Encouraged by the white onlookers, the conductor eventually wrested Wells from her seat, dragged her from the carriage, and dropped her on the train platform, tearing her dress.[12]

Although Wells's resistance may have appeared undignified, it demonstrated the high stakes involved in the situation. Throughout her life, Wells struggled to protect her reputation and control her temper to conform to public expectations for middle-class ladies. Nevertheless, she was willing to engage in unladylike behavior to defend her right to be acknowledged as a lady by remaining in the first-class carriage.[13] Other respectable black women similarly fought for recognition as ladies. African American activist Mary Church Terrell, for example, used a parasol to fight off a brakeman who tried to force her into a second-class car. When her father sought to intervene on her behalf, the brakeman fled, leaving Terrell to enter the first-class car with her father and shattered parasol. On another occasion when she was forced to travel alone at night, Terrell persuaded a conductor to allow her to ride in the ladies' car by threatening to leave the train at the next stop and have her father, prominent businessman and wealthy real estate investor Robert Church, "sue the railroad for compelling his daughter who has a first class ticket to ride in a second class car." Fearing harassment or sexual assault, she concluded "that anything would be preferable" to being subjected to the immoral atmosphere of the smoking car, "even death itself."[14]

Unlike Terrell, Wells had no male protector to champion her cause either in person or in absentia. If she wanted to maintain her public status as a respectable middle-class black woman, she simply could not move to the second-class car. So, disheveled and incensed, Wells left the train at Frayser and sought legal redress against the CO&S Railroad for her violent ejection from the ladies' carriage.[15]

Steamboats, streetcars, and passenger rail companies were licensed as common carriers, a status that granted them distinct legal powers. Common carriers were required by common law to provide passage to any traveler who paid the standard fare and complied with all company regulations established "to protect the comfort and safety" of all travelers. As long as those regulations were made known to passengers and consistently enforced, company regulations on common carriers might encompass any reasonable restriction, including the prohibition of dangerous or antisocial behaviors and the segregation of passengers based on sex and class. Carriers were permitted by law to eject any passenger who violated company regulations as long as those regulations were deemed reasonable and the carrier's agents used no undue force in enforcing company policy.[16]

Therefore, the CO&S Railroad could legally segregate passengers by race if the company evenly enforced the regulations for all passengers. In addition, the CO&S needed to comply with Tennessee's 1881 and 1882 statutes requiring equal accommodations where segregation was based on race. Although the actual carriages provided by the CO&S Railroad were used interchangeably for white and black passengers, Judge James O. Pierce found that the rules governing passenger conduct in the two cars were vastly different. Not only was racial segregation incomplete, with white passengers routinely allowed to ride in the forward car designated for black passengers, but passengers from the rear car were also permitted to enter the forward car to smoke. Pierce determined that CO&S regulations were not evenly enforced and permitted behaviors such as "smoking and drunkenness" in the forward car that "reduced it below the grade of first-class," placing the carrier in violation of Tennessee law requiring the provision of first-class accommodations to both races. By forcibly ejecting Wells from the only first-class car provided by the carrier, CO&S employees had violated her rights, entitling her to five hundred dollars in damages.[17]

Although not directly addressed as a point of law, the crucial underlying question of *Ida Wells v. Chesapeake, Ohio, & Southwestern Railroad* was whether or not a black woman had the right to be considered a lady and enjoy all of the legal and social protections associated with that status. Conductors were permitted to employ reasonable force to remove objectionable persons, including women of low social status, from first-class carriages, but force could not be used against respectable ladies.[18] As Wells testified in the case, if Murry "wished to treat me like a lady, he would leave me alone" in the ladies' car.[19] Both the plaintiff and defendant confirmed that the "rear coach was for the best passengers" and served as "the only first class coach" on the train, while the forward coach was a second-class smoker that was "no fit place for a Lady."[20] Judge Pierce recognized Wells as "a person of lady-like appearance and deportment, a school teacher, and one who might be expected to object to traveling in the company of rough or boisterous men, smokers or drunkards." To compel a lady to sit in a second-class carriage was, according to Pierce, "an act of cruelty."[21] Although her victory could have set an important precedent for truly equal accommodations, Wells's case did not question the railroad's right to segregate passengers by race. Instead, Wells validated her rights as a middle-class lady.[22]

While waiting for her first suit to be heard, Wells had another altercation with CO&S officials. Having been advised by her attorney, Thomas F. Cassels, that conductors on the CO&S line would no longer refuse to admit her to the ladies' carriage, Wells continued to patronize the line on her visits to Woodstock after she passed the city school examination and relocated to Memphis. On May 4, 1884, Wells was refused entry into the ladies' car on a journey from Woodstock to Memphis. Having boarded the train through the forward coach, Wells attempted to transfer between cars to take a seat in the rear coach. The conductor, C. E. Clark, placed his hands on Wells and stopped her between cars, insisting that she surrender her ticket and return to the forward car. Wells refused. Clark signaled the engineer and stopped the train approximately a quarter mile from the station, where he put Wells off the train, leaving her to find her own way home. Wells sued for additional damages as a consequence of refusal of service and lost wages, winning a second judgment from Judge Pierce for two hundred dollars.[23]

Wells continued to encounter "the usual trouble about the first-class coach" when traveling, but she and many other middle-class African Americans of the period frequently "conquered" in their disputes with rail conductors. Until racial segregation laws began to trump company regulations regarding gender segregation, middle-class black women could ride in ladies' cars if seats were plentiful and the conductor and passengers were tolerant. As Terrell reflected, before racial segregation laws took precedence over those based on class and gender, "colored people who bought first class tickets could get first class accommodations if they insisted upon their rights, without violating the State law."[24]

Wells's legal victories proved short-lived, however. The CO&S appealed Judge Pierce's verdict in the Tennessee Supreme Court. Railroad representatives employed delaying tactics and used blackmail to undermine Wells's reputation in an effort to force her to abandon her claim for damages. Wells struggled to pay her lawyers' fees and defend her honor as her case dragged through the court system. The Tennessee Supreme Court eventually reversed the lower court's decisions and ordered Wells to pay court costs, claiming that she had refused to cooperate with CO&S officials with the express purpose of instigating a lawsuit.[25] Her legal battle to be recognized as a lady ultimately failed, but it reinforced her understanding of the importance of dismantling segregation to allow middle-class African Americans to enjoy the benefits of their achievements.

Although the reversal diminished Wells's hopes for fighting injustice through the courts, the experience created new outlets for her activism. Wells's transfer to the Memphis city school system provided her with additional opportunities to participate in the city's black cultural and literary community. She joined a lyceum, experimented with dramatic writing and speaking, and began her career in journalism with an account of her court battles published in the *Living Way*, an African American religious periodical.[26]

By 1887, Wells had established herself as a prominent member of Memphis's black literary circles. She was elected to edit the local literary magazine, the *Evening Star*, and under the pen name Iola became a regular contributor to the *Living Way*, the *New York Freeman*, and other African American publications.[27] In 1889, Wells bought a one-third share of a Memphis newspaper, the *Free Speech and Headlight*. Wells continued to teach to support her siblings, but her passion remained with black intellectual, political, and literary life. Wells used her journalism to combat injustice, a tactic that eventually ended her teaching career. She was fired after she denounced the conditions in Memphis's black schools and the quality of teachers they employed, forcing (or freeing) her to focus on making journalism a paying profession, a difficult task for even accomplished black editors in well-established markets such as Memphis in the late nineteenth century.[28]

Wells's journalistic success provided her with an outlet for both her intellect and her pugnacious disposition. The first female representative in the National Afro-American Press Association, Wells quickly became a favorite at the group's convention and was elected its secretary in 1889. As her career progressed, she became known nationally for her outspoken editorial attacks against injustice. Many of her *Free Speech* editorials were reprinted in black newspapers throughout the country, and some of her more controversial pieces were reprinted in or commented on by the white southern press. Her editorials often stirred strong reactions, at times including slanderous personal attacks by white newspapers. Yet even her notoriety brought Wells further success as an editor and a journalist.[29]

THE LYNCHING AT THE CURVE

Wells's activism covered a wide range of issues until the March 1892 lynching of three African American businessmen in Memphis focused her attention on lynching. Thomas Moss, Calvin McDowell, and Henry Stewart owned the People's Grocery Company, a successful store located in the Curve, a black neighborhood on the outskirts of Memphis where the streetcar line curved sharply. A white store owner, W. H. Barrett, had enjoyed a monopoly before the People's Grocery opened, and he responded to the appearance of a competitor by trying to destroy the business. Moss, McDowell, and Stewart stood their ground, but after a physical altercation, Barrett secured a grand jury indictment against the grocers. Knowing that white deputies would be going to the store to serve warrants for the arrest of Moss, McDowell, and Stewart, Barrett started a rumor that a white mob was preparing to attack. Living beyond the city limits without police protection, the owners of the People's Grocery recruited several of their black neighbors to stand guard. When the deputies attempted to enter the building, the guards mistakenly believed that the white men were a mob, opened fire, and wounded three deputies. White citizens used the incident as an excuse to loot black homes and arrest and beat more than thirty black men. Moss, McDowell, and Stewart were imprisoned. When the Tennessee Rifles, a black militia, attempted to guard the prison from mob attack, their guns were confiscated by white authorities. After four days, a group of white men entered the jail, took Moss, McDowell, and Stewart outside the city limits, and shot them, leaving their bodies in a field, partly covered with brush. McDowell had struggled with the lynchers and seized one of their guns. His hand had been shattered by a bullet, and perhaps in retaliation for his resistance, his eyes had been gouged out.[30]

The Memphis lynching was uncharacteristic of the city, which, despite disfranchisement and segregation, had developed a reputation for calm race relations and had experienced relatively little racial violence since Reconstruction. The event was both shocking and personal for Wells, who knew two of the men and was godmother to the daughter of one of the victims. Before the murder of her friends, Wells claimed, she had accepted southern excuses that mob violence was a necessary response to the rape of white women by black men. Wells claimed that she, like many other middle-class African Americans, had believed that the subjugation of the black race was a temporary response to the moral weakness of the race as a whole and would be remedied by educational and economic improvements in the black community. But Wells's mind was changed by the lynching of her friends to appease the jealousy of their white business rival. The fact that the men she knew had committed no crime against white women "opened my eyes to what lynching really was. An excuse to get rid of Negroes who were acquiring wealth and property and thus keep the race terrorized and 'keep the nigger down.'"[31] Wells concluded that lynching was designed to prevent African Americans from achieving social, political, and economic equality with white Americans.

Wells channeled her personal outrage over the "Lynching at the Curve" into her editorials and investigative journalism. She gathered statistics on lynching from white newspapers to demonstrate that assaults on white women were not the primary motivation for lynching. Her investigation revealed that rape was alleged against the victims of only one-third of all reported lynchings, and in some cases, those lynchings were precipitated by revelations regarding clandestine but consensual sexual relationships between white women and black men. In other words, lynch mobs had transformed voluntary interracial relationships into rape to justify the murder of black men who defied social mores. Wells publicized her findings through increasingly incendiary editorials in the *Free Speech*.[32]

On May 21, 1892, Wells penned an editorial that propelled her into the national spotlight and changed the course of her life. "Nobody in this section of the country believes the old threadbare lie that Negro men rape white women. If Southern white men are not careful," she warned, "they will overreach themselves and public sentiment will have a reaction; a conclusion will then be reached which will be very damaging to the moral reputation of their women." Wells's implication that white women were attracted to black men infuriated local whites. An angry editorial in the *Memphis Daily Commercial* encouraged leading citizens to take action against the "black scoundrel" who uttered such "obscene intimations" about the racial purity of white women. Assuming that the author of the offending editorial was a man, the *Memphis Evening Scimitar* reprinted the *Commercial's* editorial and warned, "If the Negroes themselves do not apply the remedy without delay, it will be the duty of those whom he has attacked to tie the wretch who utters these calumnies to a stake . . . brand him in the forehead with a hot iron, and perform upon him a surgical operation with a pair of tailor's shears." The *Free Speech* had finally exhausted the white community's patience and only the torture and castration of the editor could appease its indignation. A mob organized by local businessmen responded by destroying the newspaper. Fearing for his life, Wells's coeditor, J. L. Fleming, fled the city. Wells had departed for a conference in Philadelphia before the editorial went to press, but mob leaders vowed to kill her if she dared return.[33]

Less than a year later, Henry Smith's lynching in Paris, Texas, inspired two British women, Catherine Impey and Isabella Fyvie Mayo, to invite Wells to become the spokesperson for a nascent transatlantic antilynching movement.[34] Unsettled by the dissonance between British beliefs about American lynching as a form of "frontier justice" and the harsh reality of the Smith lynching, British audiences were ready to hear Wells's critique of American lynching.

TRANSATLANTIC REFORM NETWORKS
IN THE NINETEENTH CENTURY

The framework for Wells's transatlantic reform campaign existed long before her exile from the South propelled her into the international spotlight. Wells joined a long tradition of African American activists who turned to the British public for assistance. Although Frederick Douglass was perhaps the most celebrated of these activists, numerous African American men and women journeyed across the ocean seeking refuge, sympathy, or financial support from British philanthropists and reformers from the late eighteenth to the mid-twentieth centuries.[35] The antislavery movement in particular demonstrated the saliency of British moral indignation for African American activists in the struggle for black equality. However, Britons also took up the cause of former American slaves beginning shortly after the 1863 Emancipation Proclamation and continuing through Reconstruction. Unable to meet the needs of millions of freed slaves, American reformers appealed for British assistance. The British public responded with local and national collection drives to provide clothing, farm implements, and funds. By 1866, approximately fifty separate British associations provided assistance to former slaves in the United States. Armed with correspondence from white American missionaries decrying the deplorable living conditions, ignorance, and lack of adequate food and clothing among African Americans in the South, these associations first directed their aid to refugee camps for former slaves claimed as seized property or "contraband of war" by the Union Army. General Rufus Saxton, an officer ordered to take charge of fifteen thousand former slaves who had attached themselves to General William T. Sherman's military campaign in Georgia, warned Britons that the situation was dire. The liberated slaves "were all *utterly destitute of blankets, stockings, or shoes*"; among the first wave of refugees, "there were not *fifty* articles in the shape of pots or kettles, or other utensils for cooking, no axes, very few coverings for many heads, and children wrapped in the only article not worn in some form by the parents." In his opinion, the dislocation and destruction of war, compounded by the moral and intellectual deprivations of slavery, had created an acute need for outside intervention. Nevertheless, the mission to help former slaves needed to go beyond food and clothing for refugee camps. "Even when the physical wants of the Freedmen are supplied," an appeal from the Society of Friends explained, "the more difficult task remains of imparting the elements of Christian civilization to a race so long kept down by slavery, and, without fault of theirs, in a state of forced ignorance and social degradation." Adequate relief efforts would need to prepare the newly emancipated to become self-sufficient so that they could reenter American society as citizens.[36]

While the British public responded to moral, religious, and emotional appeals for support, the most successful petitions capitalized on British economic concerns. The British textile industry depended on southern cotton; the cotton industry claimed nearly one-tenth of Britain's investments and directly or indirectly supported roughly one-fifth of the British population. The American South provided approximately four-fifths of Britain's raw cotton imports. Not only businessmen but also factory workers suffered as a result of the Civil War's disruption of cotton exports. In Lancashire, wartime cotton shortages left two million British citizens without support, demonstrating that the U.S. and British economies had become inextricably entwined. By promoting "the well-being and diligence of the cotton-cultivating Negroes of the South," aid societies promised to get African Americans back into the fields and thus restore the cotton industry's health in both countries.[37]

In April 1866, recognizing that one coordinated campaign might be more successful than many overlapping individual appeals, the majority of British aid organizations pooled their resources and created the National Freedmen's Aid Union of Great Britain and Ireland. The National Union coordinated shipments of supplies and transferred funds from the various local associations to American relief agencies. The Union and its predecessors did not directly distribute the donations they collected but funneled goods and money into established American religious missions and philanthropic organizations, which handled the "practical and unpopular" work on the ground. This approach avoided the duplication of resources as well as accusations of British interference in American affairs. Although British funds remained welcome in the United States, British social and political intervention did not. Tensions between the United States and Great Britain ran high during and immediately after the Civil War. The freedmen's aid movement provided an opportunity to unite a wide variety of British and American reformers, long separated by political and philosophical differences, into a common, apolitical cause.[38]

Increasingly close social and economic ties defined relations between the United States and Britain at the end of the nineteenth century as Britain became isolated from other European nations. At the same time, industrialization had ended American dependence on manufactured goods from Europe, allowing the United States to compete with European powers for stakes in the emerging trade markets in Asia and Africa.[39] Americans increasingly concentrated on economic and industrial growth and sought to ease lingering tensions between the North and South. By 1877, the U.S. government abandoned Reconstruction to normalize relations with southern states and refocus its energies on continued industrial growth.[40] With the growth of transnational business, marriages between wealthy Americans and members of the British social and political elite became increasingly popular. Likewise, international exchanges of social reform leaders and philanthropists became more frequent. Economic and social ties, not political ideology, became the focus of transatlantic relations between America and Britain. Wishing to maintain positive relations, British reformers remained hesitant to interfere unnecessarily in American politics.[41]

As British and American philanthropic interest in helping former slaves dissipated during the 1870s, British public fascination with African Americans and American race relations continued to flourish. Although often more attracted to myths and stereotypes than to realistic portrayals of black people, the British public craved experiences with people of African descent. During the mid-nineteenth century, blackface minstrelsy became a popular and socially acceptable form of polite public entertainment. British fascination with the stereotypes, music, and dance of the minstrel shows continued into the early twentieth century. The stereotypes presented by these white performers were reinforced by serious errors in biological science, including scientific racism and social Darwinism, and British frustrations with the process of colonial emancipation. A rebellion in Jamaica underscored the potential dangers of eradicating slavery without adequately providing for the welfare of those released from bondage. Following the abolition of West Indian slavery in 1833, Jamaica had suffered from economic stagnation and government mismanagement, and conditions there worsened when drought and Civil War–era trade disruptions created shortages and significantly elevated the price of imported food and cotton. A wave of religious revivalism, rising crime rates, personal feuds, and the inflammatory rhetoric of politicians and missionaries created social instability. When rumors that slavery was going to be reintroduced to the island began to circulate in 1865, the black population rebelled. The island's governor, Edward Eyre, implemented martial law to put down the rebellion, using harsh methods of questionable legality.[42] Although Eyre's actions were initially denounced throughout Britain, as the 1860s progressed, members of the British upper and middle classes began to side more closely with white planters.[43] Many white Victorians believed that people of African descent were inherently less fit for competition in human societies than those of European ancestry. The belief in the superiority of white, Anglo-Saxons over the rest of the world's population became a justification for colonization, which was celebrated as a means for the world's salvation. Charles Dilke praised the United States in an 1868 book, *Greater Britain*, arguing that "by ruling mankind through Saxon institutions and the English tongue," the United States assisted England in shaping the world in the British mold.[44]

Despite the growth of damaging stereotypes, British philanthropists continued to support black schools in the United States, especially those that promoted industrial education, a philosophy that resonated with Victorian images of the self-made man. Britons subscribed to fund-raising tours by African American choirs, among them the world-famous Fisk Jubilee Singers. The Fisk troupe performed for a wide spectrum of the British population at venues that included large working-class audiences, revival meetings led by Dwight L. Moody, and private concerts for members of Britain's elite society, including Queen Victoria, Prime Minister William Ewart Gladstone, the Prince and Princess of Wales, and the Duke and Duchess of Argyll. The choir raised funds through admissions and collections from their concerts, private donations, and the sale of books depicting their travels, history, and songs. Sales of these books demonstrated the group's enduring popularity; between 1873 and 1900, the Fisk Jubilee Singers sold more than sixty thousand volumes in Britain. As support from Fisk University's sponsor, the American Missionary Association, dwindled in the mid-1870s, the choir faced great pressure to raise money to sustain the school. They repeatedly returned to Britain, where they could raise as much as ten thousand pounds per tour.[45]

The Fisk Jubilee Singers' tours provided a marked contrast to the images offered by blackface minstrelsy. The choir was credited with fighting racist stereotypes by providing an example of the moral and spiritual heights to which African Americans could rise. Introducing the performers during their 1875 British tour, Lord Shaftesbury announced, "They have returned here, not for anything in their own behalf, but to advance the interests of the coloured race in America, and then to do what in them lies to send missionaries of their own colour to the nations spread over Africa. When I find these young people, gifted to an extent that does not often fall to the lot of man, coming here in such a spirit, I don't want them to become white, but I have a strong disposition myself to become black." Actual contact with the performers tended, in other words, to belie the claims of social Darwinists concerning essential qualities of people of African descent. "If I thought colour was anything," Shaftesbury resolved, "if it brought with it their truth, piety, and talent, I would willingly exchange my complexion to-morrow." By demonstrating admirable qualities, the Fisk Jubilee Singers caused their privileged hosts to question artificial color barriers. More than twenty other choirs sought to duplicate the Fisk troupe's success in the 1870s.[46]

Despite waning interest in the antislavery movement, related transatlantic reform networks continued to strengthen. Former British and American abolitionists turned their attention to other social reform causes, including the temperance movement, tenement house projects, prison reform, religious revivalism, and women's suffrage. These reform networks offered opportunities for exchanges between British and American representatives. Frederick Douglass lent his support to many of these issues and used his influence to assist reform efforts on both sides of the Atlantic. As Douglass's protégée, Wells also became linked to this tradition of transatlantic reform. Although neither the first nor the last African American who traveled to Britain to gain support for abolition and reform programs, Douglass was certainly the most celebrated, and he retained that high profile until his death in 1895.[47] His life and work provided a continuous link between British and American reform communities.

One of the British reformers with whom Douglass collaborated was Catherine Impey, a member of the Society of Friends. Impey worked as an activist in both British and American reform circles and published an antiracism newsletter, *Anti-Caste*, in which she routinely denounced lynching as well as other forms of mistreatment of people of color throughout the world. Impey began publishing *Anti-Caste* in 1888 as an outlet for her reform work after a political dispute over reunification with segregated American branches in the Independent Order of Good Templars compelled her and a number of other Quakers to leave the temperance organization. These dissenters formed the core of *Anti-Caste*'s initial audience. Impey had been deeply involved with the Templars' Mission among the Freedmen of America (later renamed the Negro Mission Committee) for nearly two decades and had traveled to the United States as its honorary secretary.[48] She used her contacts among prominent African Americans and concerned white Americans to find support and sources of information for her new endeavor. Impey maintained correspondence with Frederick Douglass, Judge Albion W. Tourgée, and General Samuel Chapman Armstrong, founder of Hampton Institute, a leader in industrial education whose most famous graduate was Booker T. Washington.[49] She received copies of African American and sympathetic white American newspapers from which she reprinted articles in *Anti-Caste*. She denounced not only lynching but also electoral fraud and segregation in the Americas, slavery in Africa, and the caste system in India.

After her split with the Templars, Frederick Douglass encouraged Impey to continue her reform work and bring her activism to America.[50] While Impey began her independent work with the publication of *Anti-Caste,* she also hoped to create a new British organization, modeled after the antislavery movement, to combat American racial discrimination. Impey believed that "the evil" of lynching and race hatred was "so *glaring, so terrible* in America . . . Outside influences *must* be brought to bear." Faced with criticism that "British interference" might be unwelcome or ineffectual, Impey sought reassurance in the precedents set by British antislavery organizations. She marveled at the audacity of the Glasgow Emancipation Society, whose members had openly agitated for "the Universal extinction of Slavery wherever it exists—particularly in the United States of America." Such actions, she declared, constituted "'British interference' with a vengeance."[51] Impey believed the lack of widespread British interest in African American rights was merely a symptom of ignorance. "The chief difficulty over here is that people *don't know* & therefore *don't care* about the matter. If they knew of the wrong, if they *believed* it was a real solid standing evil, not a mere occasional freak of wrong doing," the "philanthropic and thoughtful classes" of England "*would* care, & would nearly *all* be true & right & high principled about it."[52] As reports of American lynchings appeared more frequently in

British newspapers and reinforced Impey's message, she began gathering allies.

Isabella Fyvie Mayo, a Scottish widow and popular novelist who wrote under the pen name Edward Garrett, had been a longtime advocate for colonial reform in India.[53] Impey heard about Mayo's interest in the problems of racial caste (understood as segregation) and began sending free copies of *Anti-Caste* to her Aberdeen home. Intrigued, Mayo corresponded with Impey "on the subjects dealt with in Anti-Caste, expressing so strong a desire to help in the movement for race-equality & justice, that . . . we agreed to meet for a few days conference."[54] Excited by the prospect of such a powerful new supporter, Impey reported to her friends, "I think an event has occurred. A Mrs. Isabella Fyvie Mayo (Scotch) whom I have never seen—a literary lady of something above mediocre ability & fame—has taken such a hold of *our question*—that I am going to travel some 400 to 500 miles to meet her." Mayo seemed "resolved to *do* something."[55]

When news of Henry Smith's lynching in Paris, Texas, broke in England, Impey began receiving letters from people "feeling that we in England &c ought to *do something* to stem this torrent of lawless violence & wrong." Reports of the Smith lynching were picked up by the Reuters News Agency and reprinted across Great Britain, eliciting feelings of anger, confusion, and disgust among many Britons.[56] Taking advantage of this heightened public attention, Impey and Mayo joined forces to create the Society for the Recognition of the Brotherhood of Man (SRBM) to combat American racial prejudice and violence. They sought to create an organization with international enrollment, enlist Frederick Douglass as president to gain credibility and clout with former British abolitionist networks, and court other notable reformers, including T. Thomas Fortune, militant editor of the *New York Age* and founder of the Afro-American League; abolitionist William Still; and Judge Albion W. Tourgée, president of the National Citizens' Rights Association.[57] But first they needed to present an alternative narrative about American lynching and race relations to the British public.

To that end, the two women collaborated on a letter inviting Ida B. Wells to come to England to recount the horrors of lynching before British audiences.[58] On a recent visit to the United States, Impey had heard Wells speak against lynching.[59] Wells had relocated to New York, where she received support and temporary employment at Fortune's *New York Age*. Relating the story of the lynching of the owners of the People's Grocery as well as the threats she faced for speaking against mob violence, Wells provided powerful personal testimony.[60] Her speeches brought her to the attention of a growing public, including Douglass, who recognized in Wells's critique the seeds of a successful antilynching movement. White audiences had interpreted black men's protests against lynching as a defense of rapists and had therefore dismissed those arguments as self-serving. As a woman, however, Wells could more freely argue that lynching was a racist act of violent oppression designed to support white supremacy, potentially removing the issue of black male criminality from the discourse. Wells received the British invitation while visiting Douglass's home, where she had been invited to discuss the possibility of organizing a protest against the exclusion of African Americans from the 1893 World's Columbian Exposition in Chicago. According to Wells, Impey wrote "that they knew Mr. Douglass was too old to come, and that if for [some] reason I could not come, to ask him to name someone else. I gave him the letter to read and when he finished he said, 'You go my child; you are the one to go, for you have the story to tell.'"[61] However, the only extant draft of Impey's letter says nothing about her desire to have Douglass come but instead delicately suggests that if Wells "cannot *possibly* come at present,—and Mr. Fortune *could*, do so *please* be so very kind as to hand on our request to him . . . I have never ceased to plan & hope for the time he could come and tell the story of wrong himself, & we should do our utmost to make his visit useful."[62]

The version of events that Wells presented in her autobiography contains other inaccuracies as well. Writing at the end of her life, three decades after her British speaking tours, Wells had a strong desire to legitimate her career as an activist. Moreover, she wrote in the preface that she had embarked on an autobiography because she had been forgotten by history. She had been pushed out of many of the civil rights and reform organizations she helped establish, including the National Association of Colored Women's Clubs and the National Association for the Advancement of Colored People. Although her passion and skills made her a valuable contributor to the black struggle for equality, her uncompromising attitudes proved incompatible with strategies designed to achieve gradual change. In preserving her legacy, Wells would not have wanted to privilege Fortune at such a seminal moment of her career, particularly because he, unlike Wells, abandoned his radicalism in the late 1890s to support Booker T. Washington's accommodationist tactics for African American advancement. More significantly, Wells's version of the invitation emphasized her ties to Douglass and positioned her as the logical heir to his reform legacy, a mantle stolen by Washington after white southern leaders anointed him as the leading spokesperson for African Americans following his

"Atlanta Compromise" address to the 1895 Cotton States Exposition. Despite Wells's debt to Fortune, who had offered her employment during her exile and had published her first pamphlet, *Southern Horrors*, the image of Douglass's blessing better legitimated her career as an activist. Moreover, in 1894, when factional disputes within the SRBM left Wells without a reliable sponsor during her second tour of England, Douglass's mentorship lent continued credibility to her campaign.[63]

Regardless of the exact wording of the invitation, Wells fit Impey's vision for a speaker to launch her new reform movement. Since the establishment of *Anti-Caste*, Impey had hoped to "arrange for the visit to [England] of a deputation consisting of one or two negroes or persons of negro descent (possibly ladies) competent to address our friends and others, on the present difficulties and struggles of their people, consequent to the system of caste separations which have gradually become established in America."[64] Impey believed that "a *woman* would perhaps find a *readier* hearing, among those who are densely ignorant of the whole situation."[65] As an African American woman, Wells fell outside of Great Britain's complex class and gender politics. Consequently, she might appeal not only to various British women's reform organizations but also to mixed-gender audiences from varying socioeconomic classes throughout the country, following a path trod by African American abolitionists before her.[66] Furthermore, as the female victim of mob violence, Wells could represent the innocence and vulnerability of her race while providing powerful personal testimony about the horrors of lynching.

Impey was eager to have Wells begin her tour as quickly as possible so that British moral indignation could be roused before tourists departed to attend the World's Columbian Exposition.[67] Wells had already begun working with Douglass on a pamphlet denouncing the exclusion of African Americans from the exposition, but she abandoned that effort and departed for England on April 5, 1893.[68]

LAUNCHING THE ATTACK
ON LYNCHING

After spending a brief time organizing letters, announcements, and membership forms, Wells began her British speaking tour with a drawing room meeting in Mayo's home on April 21, 1893. As a result of that meeting, the SRBM's first chapter was formed. Membership in the society was secured by signing a declaration or verbally agreeing to "make it our aim and study, as we have opportunity, to secure to every member of the human family, FREEDOM, EQUAL OPPORTUNITY, AND BROTHERLY CONSIDERATION."[69] Organizers extensively debated what to call their new group, considering Society for the Furtherance of the Brotherhood of Man and Society for the Recognition of the Universal Brotherhood of Man before settling on Society for the Recognition of the Brotherhood of Man on August 11, 1893. Despite the uncertainty regarding the official moniker, public meetings followed a standard format: a prominent local citizen chaired the meeting; a sponsor introduced Wells and her mission; Wells delivered her address; another local citizen proposed a resolution denouncing American lynching, which the audience passed; and appeals were made for voluntary subscriptions and membership. Wells's tour included speaking engagements in Huntly, Kirkliston, Edinburgh, Glasgow, Liverpool, Manchester, Newcastle, Darlington, Birmingham, Street, London, and Portsmouth, "at all of which meetings the 'Society for the Furtherance of the Brotherhood of Man' & its objects were introduced, & members enrolled."[70]

Impey's interpretation connected the antilynching movement to both the antislavery movement and a wider critique of imperialism. "In these days of frequent travelling and wide-spread emigration," Impey warned, "the whole question of the right relations between white and coloured races is rapidly becoming one of world-wide importance."[71] She asserted that the cruelty of lynching resulted from extreme alienation between the races brought on by racial segregation. Discussing a recent string of lynchings, Impey explained to readers of *Anti-Caste*, "In both South and North the motive is one—the maintenance, namely, of A BARRIER IMPASSIBLE AS IRON, HOWEVER GILDED, between Americans whose colour betrays an ancestry of slaves, and the free unbranded world of white men."[72] American segregation was the product of lingering racial prejudice and resentment from the Civil War and the end of slavery. Therefore, lynching was also a product of the lingering moral corruption of slavery: "The laws are administered solely by white men—who are *corrupted*—not by bribes, but by a fierce and terrible prejudice—the outcome of slavery."[73] By extension, Impey's narrative offers an anti-imperial critique of race separation and race hatred generally. The unnatural and immoral separation on the basis of an imagined difference (color) infected the moral integrity of whites throughout the world, much as slavery did.

The content of Wells's speeches altered subtly through her association with the SRBM. A published copy of a Boston oration delivered on February 12, 1893, differed significantly from the reports of her speeches in Britain.[74] In both cases, Wells's narrative declared lynching to be a violent act of racial oppression stimulated by lingering racial animosity from slavery, white jealousy over black prosperity, and white women's moral depravity. However, when appearing before British audiences, Wells spoke at length about racial segregation in the South and the unfinished work of bringing true equality to African Americans.[75] These additions tempered her assertion that rape accusations often were invented to conceal consensual interracial relationships and bolstered her claims that maintaining white supremacy, not punishing black licentiousness, constituted the true motivation for lynching.

Both Wells and Impey argued that the new antilynching movement was necessary because African Americans still lacked the right to enjoy equality. "Slavery was not only a monster but a tyrant," Wells claimed; "The *very same forces are at work now as then*."[76] Although many Britons "thought that the freeing of the slaves gave to the negroes in America all the liberties which others enjoyed to make men and women of themselves . . . that was not true." White southerners who lost their property and their livelihood when they lost their slaves bitterly resented African Americans.[77] True emancipation required an end to the system of race hatred that supported lynching and the oppression of all people of color.

Newspaper reports echoed the comparisons between British involvement in the antislavery movement and in the antilynching movement, thus carving out a historical and cultural legacy for Wells's campaign within a ready-made discursive space for British reform. The *Aberdeen Daily Free Press* explained that Wells sought "an expression of British sympathy" with the plight of African Americans and came "highly commended by the foremost men of her race," including "Douglass, whose name will be well remembered by that older section of our community which took a share in anti-slavery work."[78] In 1892, Douglass had provided a brief letter of support for Wells's analysis of lynching, and copies of that letter were printed as a preface to her first antilynching pamphlet, *Southern Horrors*; reprinted in her British pamphlet, *United States Atrocities*; and served as an important endorsement of her activism in Britain. Her campaign appealed to "the principal survivors of the old antislavery movement" and reportedly received "their warm approval and support."[79] Wells railed against the hypocrisy of southern Christianity in allowing and even supporting lynch law "to maintain [white] supremacy at any cost." "The tyrant slavery had gone to work under a new name and a new guise. Having destroyed the citizenship of the coloured men it . . . now sought to destroy their manhood" through segregation and lynching. In a modern society, at "the close of the 19th century this was being done, and by a Christian nation," no less. Legislation had not been enough to achieve the ideals of the antislavery movement because slavery had seriously damaged American morality; without "a strong public sentiment in favour of what was right and just towards every human being," the democratic ideals of freedom and equality could not be realized, and black economic and social progress would remain stunted.[80] By invoking the memory of the abolition movement and wrapping their work in its legacy, Wells and her sponsors hoped to both rally the support of the remaining members of the antislavery movement and claim legitimacy for their campaign.

Wells's decision to incorporate a broader discussion of segregation and discrimination also had practical considerations. Wells needed to create a specifically British campaign for a British audience. British newspapers were often more conservative in their reporting of sensational topics than were their American counterparts. Wells probably would not have received positive press coverage in Britain if she had not added a lengthy discussion of segregation and racial prejudice to her speeches. British reporters consistently glossed over her discussions of actual lynching cases, perhaps considering them too graphic or disturbing to print. If she had delivered her Boston speech without modifications, British newspaper conventions would have permitted the inclusion of very little of her material. Moreover, codified racial segregation was a recent and fast-moving development with which the British public would have been unfamiliar, so Wells's exploration of racial segregation would have provided necessary background information and placed her arguments in context for British audiences.[81]

The focus on segregation also allowed Wells's audiences to support the SRBM on Christian grounds. Audiences were appalled by the un-Christian sentiment of American segregationist policies, which excluded African Americans from the nation's moral institutions but allowed mixing with whites in low places such as bars. Wells explained, "The doors of the churches, the Young Men's Christian Associations, the temperance halls, and every avenue to influences tending to the higher development of men and women were closed against the negro."[82] Believing that their disapproval might instruct and improve their American brethren, British Christians enthusiastically passed resolutions denouncing these segregationist policies and the frenzied violence of lynch mobs. As one of Wells's supporters explained, "Although Englishmen could not alter the laws of the States, they could at least bring the moral sentiment of this country to bear upon the moral sentiment of the United States," just as they had done during the antislavery movement. He believed "they would find in the future, as in the past, that moral force was more powerful than swords and cannons, and that kind feeling expressed here would have the best influence upon the race on the other side."[83]

Through her personal appearances and the publication of her British pamphlet, *United States Atrocities: Lynch Law*, Wells inserted an alternative narrative into British discourse on American lynching. Her interpretation differed fundamentally from those that the British public had previously encountered because it did not excuse mob violence. Rather than claiming that a certain type of extralegal violence was justified, she asserted that all lynching was immoral and detrimental to American society. By focusing on the rising number of African American victims of mob violence, Wells brought attention to the racial aspects of lynching rather than the tortured logic of the popular sovereignty narrative or the romance of frontier justice. Wells worked within the limitations of the existing discourse on lynching but deconstructed existing white supremacist rhetoric and the excuses offered by lynching apologists. In the process, she subverted their underlying mythology and provided Britons with viable reasons to question those assertions.

Wells reassured Britons that their discomfort with the lynching for rape narrative was justified since that narrative was based on flawed logic. "The thinking public," she wrote, "will not easily believe freedom and education more brutalizing than slavery, and the world knows the crime of rape was unknown during the four years of civil war, when the white women of the South were at the mercy of the race, which is all at once charged with being a bestial one."[84] It was illogical to believe that African Americans' morality could have fallen so far so quickly after the end of the demoralizing system of chattel slavery. In his introduction to the pamphlet, S. J. Celestine Edwards, an Afro-Caribbean lay preacher and editor of *Lux*, a Christian newspaper published in London, argued that lynching revealed not the depravity of African Americans but "the evil effects of race hatred in the South," where white men could kill African Americans "with perfect impunity" on "trumped-up stories of rape and outrage." Former slaveholders, Edwards believed, leveled these false charges against black men out of "pure spite" resulting from the loss of status and property and in hopes that the day would come when whites could "once more enslave or exterminate the Negro."[85] The lynching for rape narrative, Wells and Edwards argued, had not adequately explained the events in Paris, Texas, because it was a fabrication designed to cover up the mob's real motivation: terrorizing and intimidating African Americans.

Wells employed popular new techniques of social science research to lend objective and verifiable support to her observations. In addition to the statistical data she compiled from white newspaper reports, she highlighted the cases of female victims of mob violence to demonstrate the falsity of southern assertions that lynch law was applied only against rapists. From exposés following the New Orleans lynching, Britons understood that the most commonly alleged offense in lynching cases was murder, not rape.[86] But many Britons continued to believe that even if the proportion of lynching for rape cases had been exaggerated, lynching was justified by the victims' presumed guilt, which was often reinforced by reports of confessions. Wells countered by using white newspaper reports to demonstrate that extralegal violence had been used in cases where no offense was even pretended: in one instance, a boy and girl had been hanged and shot when a Jonesville, Louisiana, mob could not catch their father. How could lynching be considered anything but murder when even the members of the mob did not believe the victims had committed crimes?[87]

Wells's investigations of individual lynching cases further called into question the veracity of the charges leveled against African American men. She insisted that consensual interracial sexual relationships between African American men and white women would have been unthinkable under slavery but had developed as a product of emancipation, when black men rose in stature and consequently became desirable to a "certain class" of white women. With this argument, Wells attacked the core assumption that white women could not consent to sexual relations with African American men: "The truth remains that Afro-American men do not always violate white women without their consent." When presented with unmistakable evidence of these interracial relationships, such as the birth of a child, however, the women involved came under intense pressure to save their reputations by claiming that they had been raped. Wells cited the case of Lillie Bailey, a Memphis woman who gave birth to a biracial child. Community leaders demanded that she divulge the name of the baby's father; when she refused, the white community ostracized her for her "fearful depravity" in consenting to sexual relations with a black man. Wells explained that in the 1892 Texarkana lynching that had generated great publicity in Britain, the white woman who had been "raped" by Edward Coy had been his lover, not his victim. After the two had conducted an extramarital affair for more than a year, their relationship had become public knowledge. Under intense pressure from the white community, the woman, Mrs. Jewell, declared that Coy had raped her. A lynching was planned, as many as ten thousand spectators traveled to Texarkana for the event, and perhaps fearing that she might become the mob's next target, Jewell lit the fire that consumed Coy. As she approached, witnesses heard Coy ask how she could "burn him after they had 'been sweethearting' so long." Wells believed that white newspapers often fabricated the details of lynching cases to make the alleged crimes more shocking and thus the resort to extralegal violence seem more justifiable. According to Wells, the "white Delilahs" who engaged in consensual sexual relationships with "Afro-American Sampsons" repeatedly betrayed and brought their lovers to ruin.[88]

Wells argued that lynching, like slavery, had demoralized white Americans, leading them to abuse their power and authority. The popular sovereignty narrative revealed white southerners' despotism rather than their bravery as activist citizens. White southerners controlled the political, legislative, judicial, and executive machinery, Wells explained, yet continued to claim that they needed to circumvent the legal system because the outcome of due process was inadequate or uncertain. "With the judges, juries, and prosecuting attorneys all Southern white men," she alleged, "no Negro has ever been known to escape the penalty of the law for any crime he commits." Any failure to convict would have been the fault of "those who make such inoperative laws, or the officials who fail to do their duty, and not the criminals." Echoing the sentiments expressed by British authors during the New Orleans crisis, Wells contended that those negligent white officials, not the alleged criminals, should be the object of the mob's retribution.[89]

The hearts of white Americans had been hardened by the cry that African Americans were a bestial race. As a result, "men who stand in high esteem . . . for Christian character, for moral and physical courage, for devotion to the principles of equal and exact justice to all, and for great sagacity, stand as cowards who fear to open their mouths before this great outrage." Just as abolitionists had claimed that lynching demonstrated that southern thinking had invaded the North, Wells argued southern lynching had insidiously demoralized the entire nation by making it impossible to voice dissent without appearing to support the violation of white women. The silence of these good Americans, "their tacit encouragement, their silent acquiescence," had allowed "the black shadow of lawlessness in the form of lynch law" to spread "its wings over the whole country." According to Wells, as northerners became accustomed to reading reports of lynchings in the South, they stopped questioning the difference between the reality and the rhetoric and began to imitate the actions of southern mobs. As a result, she concluded, mob violence was spreading.[90]

Unlike Americans, however, the British public had not been seduced by the lynching for rape narrative. Edwards reminded his readers that British colonial experiences did not support the wild assertions of southern lynching apologists. "We do not find similar charges brought against the West Indian Negroes," he asserted; nor did the missionaries in Africa complain of black licentiousness, although they worked with "Negroes who are much more savage than those in the South." Even "if it is true that Negroes thus misconduct themselves," Edwards demanded, "what right have white men to withhold a fair trial in a Court of Law, or brutally Lynch men who could be easily convicted, if the charges are true?" But Edwards felt encouraged that the "ruthless barbarity" of white Americans "will not go on for ever."[91] As the world became more aware of the racist system of oppression that underlay lynching, Edwards hoped the excuses of American lynching apologists would lose power and mob violence would become less tolerated. And with the decline of public tolerance would come a decline in lynching.

Wells and Edwards encouraged the British public to refuse to accept these fallacious lynching narratives and to undertake lynching as a transatlantic reform issue. Whether through emigration, boycott, armed resistance, withholding capital and labor, or using the press to investigate and publicize the truth about lynching, African Americans needed to push back against this overwhelming tide of racist oppression. But doing so would require outside assistance. Further, Wells reminded her British readers, lynch law was not purely an African American problem. Although most lynching victims were "coloured people who are [U.S.] citizens," the New Orleans case had demonstrated that foreign citizens, too, could be lynched and that the U.S. government would not prosecute those involved. No one, not even British travelers, could be truly safe in the United States until the curse of lynch law had been lifted. "The Negro asks for nothing more than justice," Edwards insisted. African Americans did "not require another Civil War to settle the vexed racial question" but wanted the expression of "a strong public feeling against injustice." Wells and Edwards sought to "awaken the love of fairness in the mind of every Englishman, so that influence—moral and religious influences—will be brought to bear upon the American Government" to uphold its own laws.[92]

The particular historical moment when Wells traveled to Britain was essential to the success of her campaign. By 1893, the temperance movement on both sides of the Atlantic had firmly established an acceptable public space for women as reformers. Thirty years after emancipation, the British public sought evidence of black progress yet remained sympathetic to African Americans and retained the antislavery movement's image of free black women as "ladies."

The persistence of this image, one not available to African American women at home, offered Wells an opportunity to move within the same spheres as white lady reformers overseas. While the Columbian Exposition in Chicago drew the world's attention to American progress, the 1891 New Orleans and 1893 Paris, Texas, lynchings had focused British attention on American failings. These incidents undermined accepted American lynching narratives, leaving British ideas about lynching and American race relations in flux. The severity of these attacks prompted British fears that American lynching was increasing in frequency, intensity, and viciousness. Wells and her supporters seized this opportunity to produce a compelling campaign against American lynching. Her explanation of lynching as racist oppression better answered the British public's concerns and helped transform British disapproval into the moral indignation needed to create a transatlantic reform campaign.

Chapter 3

THE STRUGGLE
FOR LEGITIMACY

By grounding their campaign within existing political and rhetorical frameworks and positioning British antilynching activism as the logical heir to the antislavery movement, Ida B. Wells and her supporters mobilized a valuable base of support. As the legitimacy of a British antilynching movement grew, Wells had the opportunity to build her own personal reform credentials in Britain through her association with the Society for the Recognition of the Brotherhood of Man (SRBM). By the end of her first campaign, she had met influential people, received positive press coverage of her activism, and been groomed for British public appearances. Nevertheless, for her antilynching rhetoric to win acceptance among the broader British public, Wells needed to establish herself as both a legitimate public figure and a credible source of information on the problem of lynching. Doing so required her to claim a position in British society that conformed to established social and gender norms, demonstrate her personal authority on the issue of lynching, and gain the support of her audiences, influential public figures, and the press.

ESTABLISHING WELLS'S
PERSONAL LEGITIMACY

For much of the nineteenth century, strict codes of propriety had discouraged respectable middle-class women from participating in public reform activism. Women in the antislavery and temperance movements justified the expansion of women's roles in the public sphere by claiming that the desperate moral crises facing society demanded their womanly influence and attention. Even under the best of circumstances, life in the public sphere at midcentury was difficult for women of both races. Victorian sexual politics questioned the legitimacy of any woman who chose to forsake her "natural" domestic role to enter public life. For the first half of the nineteenth century, women were not allowed to speak in public or take leading roles in reform organizations. Meetings of women's abolitionist organizations were traditionally "chaired by men while the women sat silently on the platform."[1] Even celebrated American author Harriet Beecher Stowe had to negotiate "the tightrope of feminine modesty in public life, leaving speeches to her brother or her husband throughout" her 1853 tour of England, sitting "silently while others spoke" for her.[2] Nineteenth-century women who demanded roles in the public sphere risked being dismissed as selfish aggrandizers or criticized as unfeminine. Nevertheless, they used the moral crises of slavery and later intemperance to insert their voices into transatlantic reform movements, embracing the conventions of domestic morality and claiming a moral obligation to enter the public sphere to protect vulnerable women and children from dangers created by men.[3]

African American women who attempted to enter the public sphere faced the additional complication of damaging racial stereotypes. The ever-present stereotype of the black Jezebel posed a serious obstacle for these women's attempts to claim the status of ladies in the United States. American pro-slavery advocates consistently portrayed black women as unfeminine and thus ideally suited for slavery. Yet in Britain, African American women's foreign status allowed them to occupy unique roles unavailable to them in the United States or to black British women at home.[4]

Black abolitionists gained British public sympathy and counteracted damaging American stereotypes by embracing cultural stereotypes of idealized womanly behavior. The antislavery movement held up respectable African American women to highlight the failings of American democracy and civilization. Visual representations and slave narratives encouraged benevolent British reformers and philanthropists to respond with sympathy and moral indignation to the cruelties of American slavery that robbed black women of the chance to fulfill their potential as wives and mothers. But midcentury gendered social conventions prevented African American women from articulating their own needs, leaving them largely voiceless in the world of British abolitionism. Although African American men were encouraged to produce powerful slave narratives and were welcomed on the British lecture circuit, their female counterparts rarely had such opportunities. Ellen Craft, a celebrated escaped slave who joined the British antislavery lecture circuit in the early 1850s, frequently appeared on stage next to her husband, William Craft, and William Wells Brown but was never permitted to address the audience. Although she played an essential role in her and her husband's daring escape, disguising herself as an infirm white gentleman so that her husband could pass as a servant, and although she was quite popular at private functions, decorum required Ellen Craft to appear in public as a silent and demure "specimen of Victorian femininity."[5]

Nevertheless, abolitionists used these feminine displays to depict African American women as black ladies, an image that contrasted starkly with American racial norms that proscribed black women from claiming respectability. This image was then reinforced for the British public by the appearances of African American female performers such as singer Elizabeth Greenfield and elocutionist Mary Webb in the mid-1850s. Greenfield toured Britain in 1853, partially under Harriet Beecher Stowe's sponsorship. Although Greenfield's tour was a commercial venture, her ethnicity, skill, public reception, and poise offered "a challenge to the images of African Americans dispensed in proslavery texts." Three years later, Stowe selected Webb to perform *The Christian Slave,* a dramatization of *Uncle Tom's Cabin,* for British audiences. Webb had great success, demonstrating her "femininity and good taste" and "conforming to notions of bourgeois respectability as well as womanliness." Reviewers complimented the "grace and dignity" with which she delivered a reserved and ladylike performance: she stood behind a lectern, did not dress in costume or wear blackface, and avoided masculine gesticulations. She was allowed to speak in public, but only because her words were not her own. Nevertheless, her performances helped establish a space for African American women in the transatlantic antislavery movement and reinforced the British public image of the black lady.[6]

Like Webb, abolitionist Sarah Parker Remond demonstrated poise and was "praised for being 'a lady every inch.'"[7] Remond came to Britain in 1859 as an antislavery agitator, not a silent exhibit of African American female potential. Although women had served as public speakers in the American antislavery movement, British constraints on female public behavior remained more severe. Remond used the desperate moral crisis of American slavery and its exploitation of black women as justification to cross the boundaries of Victorian gender roles and appear as a spokesperson for her race. As an African American woman, Remond moved outside the traditional middle-class British feminine role, with its emphasis on women's public silence. Unlike her African American contemporaries, however, Remond was a middle-class free black woman who came to Britain not for safety, dignity, or monetary assistance but to raise British moral indignation against the interconnected systems of American slavery and racial segregation that denied her the enjoyment of her freedom. She demanded the right to be considered a lady and to speak, forcing British reformers to choose between vilifying her as unladylike for using her voice politically or granting her a special status as a lady who also spoke. Although the men who chaired her speaking engagements felt obliged to defend her presence, her groundbreaking public lectures were the first delivered by a woman of any race to mass mixed-gender British audiences on the question of slavery, and her activism eased the way for white women's increased participation in the British antislavery movement.[8]

By the 1870s, women reformers maintained a delicate balance within the narrowly defined bounds of life in the public sphere. Echoing Remond, Woman's Christian Temperance Union (WCTU) activists argued that the crisis of intemperance forced them to enter the public sphere to protect innocent women and children from harm. Yet discomfort with the changing role of women in society lingered. Those female reformers who did not stray too far from traditional feminine characteristics received praise, while those who were seen as rejecting their womanhood were ridiculed in the press.[9] Frances Willard, president of the WCTU, pioneered the creation of an unimpeachable female public persona, the role of the "lady reformer." Understanding that women who maintained an outward appearance of conformity to their private, domestic roles were less likely to be criticized for attempting to expand the scope of those roles, Willard cautioned WCTU members to remember, "Womanliness first—afterward what you will." By dressing modestly and eschewing makeup and elaborate hairstyles, WCTU members disarmed would-be critics and opened doors for women's participation in subsequent reform movements.[10]

Wells claimed legitimacy for her activism and built her public identity in Britain on these foundations. Wells entered Britain in the guise of a lady reformer, capable of articulating and representing African American interests. Employing many of the same tactics used by temperance women to legitimate her role as a public speaker and activist, Wells presented her activism as a selfless concern for her race. Wells invoked these traditions by providing personal testimony of her near-lynching and exile to demonstrate that the mob, not her ambition for personal celebrity, had driven her into the public spotlight. The *Aberdeen Daily Free Press* described Wells as "an American negro lady-journalist, who, for her devotion to the cause of her race, has herself suffered at the hands of a Tennessee mob, and still remains, for the safety of her life, in exile from the Southern State where she laboured as schoolmistress and editor."[11] If Wells's suffering had been caused not by any wrongdoing but by her personal integrity ("her devotion to the cause of her race"), bringing her complaints to the public constituted an acceptable extension of that morality. Many reports of her 1893 speeches noted her former career as a schoolteacher—traditional employment for respectable educated single women. Wells had tried to live in a traditional female role but had been prevented from doing so by the mob's actions. Wells's personal testimony served the dual purposes of establishing herself as an authority on the subject of lynching and emphasizing the vulnerability of innocent black women to the outrages of mob violence. Her arrival in Britain represented a critique on the subversion of traditional values in the South: racial oppression and lawlessness had driven Wells out of her traditional feminine role as a nurturer (schoolmistress and provider for her orphaned siblings) and onto the public platform, where she spoke against the sexual and social immorality that surrounded her in the South.

However, the violence of lynching and the scandal of illicit interracial sexual relationships were inappropriate topics for a young, single woman to describe on the public platform, especially in front of mixed-gender audiences. Respectable unmarried women were not supposed to have knowledge of sexual relations. For an unmarried woman to speak publicly of either sexual assault or consensual sexual relations would imply an inappropriate level of personal sexual experience.[12] Wells needed to legitimate her claim to speak about these salacious topics in public. "It is hateful in the extreme for me to have to discuss this," Wells confessed, "but I have come to England for the purpose . . . of letting daylight in upon the dark charge which is preferred against my people." Acknowledging her discomfort with the topic, Wells argued that the immoral conduct of white southerners, her sense of duty, and the *strength* of her morality forced her to leave her home and testify against these wrongs.[13]

Wells had success in portraying herself as both appropriate and ladylike. The *Scottish Pulpit* reported that "Miss Wells was quietly, but neatly, attired, and the white flower which adorned her breast contrasted well with the dark dress and dark features." *Lady's Pictorial* similarly praised Wells's "attractive manners" and "pleasant voice."[14] Such published assessments assisted audiences in categorizing and evaluating the acceptability of women who assumed public roles, providing reassurance that although women might appear to be entering new arenas, they were still walking the fine line between traditional feminine values and the new, conservatively defined role of women in the public sphere.[15] Observers also praised Wells's preparation and skillful yet feminine manner of speaking. Although her "strong American accent" might sound harsh to some British ears, reporters admired her "educated and forcible style."[16] She offered humble apologies "for being compelled to use manuscript, on the ground that she had not much practice in public speaking. The notes, however, did not in any way interfere with her delivery, but rather enhanced it, because she seldom referred to them."[17] Such claims were disingenuous—Wells was an experienced public speaker and had studied elocution.[18] However, by appearing uncomfortable with making a public address, Wells demonstrated the important feminine quality of vulnerability. She addressed meetings "in a quiet and highly-cultured manner. Her statement was excellently prepared, and there was a reserve of dignity about its delivery which added much to its charm and value."[19] Despite delivering addresses of "considerable length," Wells "was listened to most attentively and sympathetically, and her remarks were very lucid and cultured."[20] Wells thus skillfully played the role of lady reformer.

Struggling to categorize Wells's presence, British reporters fell back on images of African American women as tragic figures left over from the days of the antislavery movement. In Glasgow, one author described her as "a young lady, not more than thirty, with the tragedy of her race inscribed in every lineament of her face—the sad, sorrowful look begotten of centuries of serfdom, of physical and mental slavery."[21] But thirty years after emancipation, such images of the helpless, abused wretch could produce only a limited amount of compassion; African American reformers needed to demonstrate strength, progress, and independence to gain the respect of British audiences. Wells thus also needed to demonstrate intelligence, competence, and dignity. She surprised some observers with her sophistication: a reporter for the *Scottish Pulpit* remarked that Wells was "educated and speaks admirably. There is a pathos in her voice which catches the auditor and thrills him."[22]

Acknowledging African American women as ladies may not have challenged such patronizing sentiments but had always provided Britons with an opportunity to rattle nineteenth-century American observers. White Americans, especially southerners, were uncomfortable with displays of social equality between African American and British ladies and gentlemen. Eliciting negative reactions from American onlookers became a sign of victory for British reformers. British antislavery activists employed "tried-and-true strategies of deracinating" African Americans when they promenaded together at the 1851 World's Fair in London as social and intellectual equals.[23] One of the participants was pleased that the mixed-race and -gender promenade caused obvious discomfort among American observers: "To see the arm of a beautiful English young lady passed through that of 'a nigger,' taking ices and other refreshments with him, upon terms of the most perfect equality, certainly was enough to 'rile,' and evidently did 'rile' the slaveholders who beheld it . . . Probably, for the first time in their lives," he posited, "they felt themselves thoroughly muzzled." Much to his disappointment, southern slaveholders refrained from comment, daring "not even to bark, much less bite."[24]

Exhibitions of interracial social equality were no less irksome to American observers forty years later. When British newspapers identified Wells as a lady and granted her the accoutrements of respectability, they both reinforced the image of the black lady and invoked a long-standing tradition of ridiculing American shortcomings through demonstrations of superior civilized behavior. Likewise, the two British gentlemen Wells met on her return journey to the United States in 1893 reveled in the indignant stares and complaints they received from white Americans when they publicly doted on Wells. Feting African American women not only decried the hypocrisy of American liberty and democracy but also declared "the moral victory of monarchical England over its upstart colonial nemesis."[25]

To incorporate the specific needs of her campaign, Wells effectively combined the images of the black lady and the lady reformer to create a space for herself as a black lady reformer, a separate status that allowed her to move within respectable British circles while stretching the boundaries of Victorian conventions of feminine propriety to speak publicly about graphic violence, rape, and illicit interracial sexual relationships. Wells's unusual position was not lost on her sponsors, who thought her "possibly the first Afro-American negress who had spoken on a British platform."[26] Though this assertion overlooked Remond's efforts thirty years earlier, it was a useful advertising strategy and highlighted the novelty of African American female speakers in Britain. White curiosity about the exotic Other had certainly contributed to the popularity of Craft, Webb, Greenfield, Remond, and the Fisk Jubilee Singers, but a public career built solely on exoticism would have had a short life span, as Remond experienced firsthand.[27] To this end, Wells presented statistical evidence of the apparently epidemic rise of mob violence in the United States to demonstrate the immediate and vital necessity of her activism.

The danger surrounding Wells's activism and her personal sacrifices to testify about the horrors of lynching made for good copy and recalled the thrilling narratives of escaped slaves. The *Newcastle Daily Leader* told readers how Wells was "compelled to leave her home in Tennessee . . . and has been threatened that if she returns in twenty years she will be shot on sight."[28] The *Huntly Express* described "how the whole of the populace determined to get rid of the *Free Speech*" and resolved to lynch Wells. Disappointed to discover that Wells was already beyond the reach of the mob, "a leading white lady . . . expressed the earnest wish that there might be some way by which she (Miss Wells) could be brought back and lynched."[29] The intrigue of Wells's escape might have thrilled audiences in much the same way as Frederick Douglass's flight from slavery decades earlier. Her continued exile from the South made Wells a living martyr for her cause and tied her campaign to the noble history of antislavery reform. Although curiosity about Wells's exotic status in Britain certainly increased attendance at her lectures, her role as a lady reformer legitimated her campaigns.

Coverage of the audiences at Wells's speaking engagements provided important signals for British readers about how to interpret the legitimacy of her campaign. Newspapers reported that Wells was met by "a large and sympathetic audience," "a large and representative attendance," and "a large audience, consisting mostly of ladies."[30] The presence of respectable men and women offered another endorsement of the appropriateness of Wells's conduct. Following a speech in Birmingham, reporters noted that "amongst those present were several ministers, members of the Society of Friends, and ladies and gentlemen interested in local philanthropic work."[31] Prominent local citizens and clergy who endorsed Wells's campaign were also frequently mentioned, as were the positive responses she garnered: she was "listened to attentively, and loudly applauded," "was warmly welcomed," and was "awarded a cordial vote of thanks."[32] Wells's thrilling delivery of her material prompted audiences to listen "with rapt attention."[33] If her speeches were well attended, well received, and "listened to with close attention," readers might rest assured that they too should pay attention to her claims.[34]

Moreover, the numerous press reports allowed readers who could not attend in person to participate; when they agreed with the audiences' reactions, their personal views were legitimated. British audiences repeatedly expressed outrage over the failings of American Christian morality. Cries of "Shame" rang out when a Birmingham audience learned that although a "coloured man might be employed as a janitor or to ring the bells . . . he would not dare to walk into the church simply to hear the preacher." Another chorus of "Shame" followed Wells's assertions that segregation made it illegal for whites and blacks to ride in the same railway carriage and prevented Christian ministers from administering "the sacrament to a negro side by side with a white communicant." Descriptions of mob attacks and of Wells's own threatened lynching provoked similar indignation: an account of a man burned alive while "20,000 people looked on and cheered" was met with "cries of 'Shame.'" The flimsy excuses for lynching were underscored by the case of a Tennessee man who was hanged for being "drunk and 'sassy' to white people," making the news that "over a thousand black men and women and children had been lynched" since 1882 even more shocking. Audiences answered each point with shouts of "'Shame,' and cries of 'Abominable.'"[35] These choruses of protest and their repetition in newspaper reports allowed British listeners, reporters, and readers jointly to participate in expressions of public disapproval.

Through their applause and comments, British audiences also expressed support for the principles of justice and groups that stood up against lynching. A Birmingham audience applauded the *Chicago Inter-Ocean* as the only American newspaper with "the courage to publish articles in denunciation of the crimes" of lynching. In Aberdeen and Huntly, "loud applause" erupted when Wells declared that "the only remedy" for lynching was for "all supposed or accused criminals [to] be tried and punished by the due process of law, and not by mobs." A chorus of "Hear, hear" ran through a Birmingham audience when Wells argued that "the Southerners appeared totally unable to realise the common humanity of the negro with themselves, and that was why it was desirable that they should learn the views of Englishmen, whom they regarded as equal, and whose good opinion they valued." Other listeners responded approvingly when Wells asked "where the Christian sentiment of the world was" while her race was "being punished as scapegoats for the crimes of others."[36] The declaration and recording of these sentiments reinforced the legitimacy of Wells's message by demonstrating respectable British citizens' sympathy and support for her campaign.

Wells built her personal credentials as a black lady reformer in Britain under the sponsorship of the SRBM, which provided her an institutional network within which to operate and assisted Wells in sculpting her antilynching appeal specifically to address the concerns and court the sympathy of British audiences. Her affiliation with a credible British reform organization conferred presumptive legitimacy and respectability on someone who would otherwise have been an outsider. That endorsement and her ability to meet or exceed all expectations resulted in positive press coverage, which in turn reinforced her personal legitimacy.

Wells's first British antilynching campaign lasted six weeks and generated only modest success. While the audiences to which she spoke reacted with suitable indignation over the horrors of lynching atrocities, they constituted only a small segment of the British population accessed through Catherine Impey's and Isabella Fyvie Mayo's personal and religious affiliations. Wells's speeches failed to cultivate sufficient publicity to appeal to the broader British public. Coverage of her speaking engagements remained limited to reports in local newspapers and rarely received editorial support. The *Birmingham Daily Post* briefly discussed Wells's mission after printing her rebuttal to a letter to the editor complaining that appeals to British social leaders were an inappropriate and ineffective means of addressing American social problems. The *Liverpool Daily Post* offered its support to Impey's activism with the SRBM but referred to Wells only in passing. Although the *Lady's Pictorial* granted Wells a personal interview, other journals largely ignored her campaign.[37] And because her audience was limited to Impey's and Mayo's networks of personal affiliation and obligation, any conflict between the SRBM's cofounders had the potential to disrupt the nascent movement and threaten Wells's efforts.

THE PERSONAL COST
OF ILLEGITIMACY

Many of the difficulties Wells faced in broadening her audiences resulted from a personal dispute between Mayo and Impey over the potential romantic intentions of a mixed-race dentist from Ceylon (now Sri Lanka), George Ferdinands. Although Wells was not directly involved in the matter, it seriously threatened her personal reputation, her financial security, and the success of her campaign in Britain because her legitimacy rested on that of her sponsors.

　　Impey devoted her life to social reform and advocating the rights of people of color through her work with the Independent Order of Good Templars' Negro Mission Committee, the British and Foreign Anti-Slavery Society, and *Anti-Caste*.[38] In the process, she met and befriended several prominent African Americans, including Frederick Douglass, Henry Highland Garnet, and William Wells Brown.[39] Through her work with the Templars, Impey hosted Brown in her Somerset home and stayed as a guest in Brown's home while touring the United States at a time when "social visitation between coloured and white" was typically "regarded as a flagrant breach of propriety." These experiences led her to conclude that the unnatural separation of the races led to racial prejudice and discrimination. Impey was horrified by racial segregation: "It is almost incredible that cultivated and noble men and women, who are devoting their lives to the elevation of their race, should, equally with the most degraded, be excluded on account of their colour from all social intercourse with their white neighbours."[40]

Impey's desire to perpetuate true social equality between the races inspired her to advocate legalized interracial marriage. Impey hoped *to* dismantle the "artificial and unnatural gulf set between even educated *white* persons with whose blood a drop of ancestral negro blood may mingle, and the *pure whites*."[41] In 1890, General Samuel Chapman Armstrong, founder of Hampton Institute, reassured Impey that "we wish the same end—absolute equal chance for both races." Although he agreed with Impey's assessment of the importance of this issue, he did not agree with her tactics. While Impey pursued open "agitation of the marriage question," Armstrong sought to bring equality "by quietly fitting [African Americans] so far as possible for intermarriage."[42] Nevertheless, Impey's social interactions with African Americans encouraged her belief that only through the removal of all social barriers would black and white Americans learn to embrace each other in the spirit of human equality. She fondly remembered Garnet's compassion in calming her stage fright during her first public speech and delighted in finding herself part of "an interesting mixed family, as to colour" when she visited the home of Frederick Douglass and his second wife, Helen Pitts, who was white, in 1892.[43] Impey viewed these experiences as powerful evidence that only true social equality could dispel fallacious racial stereotypes and end racial oppression in America.

While visiting Mayo's home, Impey met and became infatuated with Ferdinands, who lived there. With the formation of the SRBM, Impey confessed, she found herself "swept along rather faster than my senses were prepared for—& not *quite* sure whither?"[44] She later recalled that Ferdinands was "so tender & watchful & loving to me that though he was many years my junior, I at last believed that in very truth he *loved* me." Knowing Ferdinands to be poor and "self-distrustful by nature," Impey chose to take the lead, writing to Ferdinands to propose marriage "in the course of a letter on some trivial matters of business."[45] According to Wells, Impey's letter "declared that she returned the affection she felt sure he had for her; that she was taking this advance step because she knew he hesitated to do so because he was of a darker race; that she had written to her family acquainting them with the state of affairs, and telling them to prepare to receive him as her husband and that she rejoiced to give this proof to the world of the theories she had approved—the equality of the brotherhood of man."[46] Marriage to Ferdinands might well have seemed like the perfect completion to her mission; moreover, at forty-five years old, Impey might have seen him as her last hope for marriage.

Impey nevertheless understood that it was not socially acceptable for a woman to initiate a marriage proposal. "The letter was no sooner posted" than she "was overwhelmed with embarrassment" that she had acted so indiscreetly over "a romantic & exaggerated view of what was really on both sides a warm & unconventional friendship." Not only had her proposal admitted her infatuation with Ferdinands, but her letter also provided written evidence of her indiscretion and unwomanly behavior. Staying together as guests at Eliza Wigham's house in Edinburgh, Impey consulted Mayo regarding the offending letter. "*With her concurrence,*" Impey sent a telegram and a second letter beseeching Ferdinands to "*burn my letter as unread,*" but her plea either arrived too late or was ignored.[47]

Having no interest in the proposed marriage and not wishing to jeopardize the trust of his benefactor, Ferdinands forwarded Impey's letter to Mayo in Edinburgh, where the two women met with Wells to discuss its impact on their campaign. Mayo's reactions to the letter and to Impey were less than charitable. According to Impey, Mayo "in her blind fury could see no other course than my extermination." Mayo "demanded with violence & threats that I should instantly cease from public work" and "declared me either a foul character or a monomaniac."[48] Mayo went on to label Impey a "nymphomaniac" and demanded that Impey withdraw from the campaign. In addition, Mayo announced that if Wells wanted to continue her work in Britain, she would have to break all contact with Impey. Wells refused to denounce Impey "after all these years of faithful, honorable service before the public in our behalf"; Mayo responded by casting Wells and Impey "into outer darkness."[49]

As a professional woman who had repeatedly chosen career over marriage, Wells may have held some sympathy for Impey's plight and the apparent desperation that drove her to make such an impulsive gesture. Courtship patterns for middle-class women at the end of the nineteenth century could be difficult to navigate. The decision to accept a marriage proposal often came with great sacrifice, since women were expected to withdraw from public life after marrying and to limit their personal interactions with male friends. Nevertheless, women could delay marriage for only a limited period of time before their desirability as potential mates waned or their choice to pursue a career at the expense of their "natural" destiny as wife and mother brought their credibility into question. During a period in which there were few reliable methods of birth control and fatal complications in pregnancy remained distressingly common, women who married for the first time after the age of thirty also faced increased risk of death in childbirth. Wells had struggled to maximize her career opportunities, repeatedly resisting her suitors to retain her freedom and independence, yet cultivating sufficient interest from potential suitors to keep the possibility of marriage open. In 1886, Wells had chastised herself in her diary for allowing one of her potential suitors to kiss her in a moment of weakness. "I feel so humiliated in my own estimation at the thought" of this momentary lapse in propriety, she lamented, "that I cannot look any one straight in the face."[50] Wells was frustrated by Impey's decision to allow a romantic entanglement to disrupt her antilynching mission, but the apparent desperation that drove Impey to make such an impulsive gesture made her an object of pity. Impey's life may well have served as a cautionary tale for Wells, who agreed to marry Ferdinand L. Barnett in 1895, within a year of her return from her second British campaign.[51]

More important, however, Impey's long-standing relationship with Frederick Douglass and decades of service for African American progress made it impossible for Wells to accede to Mayo's demands. The manner in which Impey's affections were expressed had clearly been inappropriate. However, Douglass certainly would not have denounced Impey for the target of her affections since he had married across the color line in his second marriage. Wells relied on Douglass not simply as a mentor but also as her protector against outside criticism. As long as Wells retained the public support of the most influential African American leader of the nineteenth century, her transatlantic activism might be able to continue despite Impey and Mayo's scandal. If Wells had made Impey's indiscretion a public matter without Douglass's consent, her relationship with him almost certainly would have ended, and she could not afford to lose it.

Only two weeks into the campaign, Wells had lost more than half her potential financial and organizational support in Great Britain. Mayo not only withdrew her own support but undermined Impey's efforts on Wells's behalf. Mayo refused to compensate Impey for her promised share of the expenses of Wells's campaign (leaving Impey, a woman of limited financial means, to cover the remaining balance of more than thirty-seven pounds from her personal funds) and used her influence to splinter the campaign into two factions. Wells appealed to Mayo to reconsider; Mayo never responded, but Ferdinands sent a condemning reply.[52]

Mayo may indeed have felt deeply concerned that any romantic involvement—or even the hint of its potential—between a white woman and a man of color in the campaign might bring dishonor or disrepute to their mission.[53] To have such an occurrence involve a member of her household would undoubtedly have caused scandal and hurt Mayo's standing in both local and international social and reform circles. Interracial marriages were not widely accepted in the 1890s, even among liberal reformers. Douglass's marriage to Pitts prompted outrage from both white and black social leaders.[54] Mayo may have found the idea of a white woman's desire for a sexual relationship with a man of color, particularly a man who was significantly younger, distasteful or even disturbing. Many British reformers viewed African Americans as pets or projects rather than social equals. Although they might be worthy of friendship or playful, curious affection, black men were not considered potential life partners.[55] By British standards at the time, South Asians and African Americans were considered equally black. Therefore, marriage to a "half-Indian" man would have been just as taboo.[56]

The incident also raises questions about the nature of the relationship between Mayo and Ferdinands. Ferdinands was well known to Mayo's closest friends and continued to live in her Aberdeen home at least as late as 1910, tending to her medical needs and accompanying her to social events.[57] Although it is possible that their mutual affection exceeded the bounds of platonic friendship, it is unlikely that Mayo's attack on Impey was prompted by mere jealousy. Mayo lived as a widow most of her adult life and found comfort in Ferdinands's companionship. She viewed herself as a wife, even though she had been separated from her husband by death for thirty years. Over that time, Mayo believed, her husband had accompanied her "every step of the way," and her love for him had grown "because there is more of me to know how to love!"[58] Mayo appears to have embraced Ferdinands as her helpmate, adopted son, protégé, or some combination of all three.[59] Mayo would have wanted to protect Ferdinands, her household reputation, and her community position as a respected widow from any hint of impropriety. By claiming that Impey's interest in Ferdinands was the result of mental illness, Mayo deflected responsibility for the incident away from her household.

Nevertheless, even by contemporary standards, Mayo's response to Impey's marriage proposal was harsh. She passed Impey's offending letter among her friends within the British reform community, rallying them to her side. She used her influence to protest Impey's public appearances in connection with the SRBM and sent telegrams to Wells's hosts warning them of Impey's insanity. Mayo arranged to have medical experts examine Impey's letter: they concurred that she was unstable. Mayo wrote to Impey's influential American supporters, including T. Thomas Fortune and Albion W. Tourgée, attempting to persuade them of Impey's immorality. Mayo also threatened to expose Impey's indiscretion to London social leaders if she accompanied Wells to the influential annual May Meetings of British religious and reform organizations. As Tourgée commented in a letter to Fortune, "For a 'secret' it seems very badly kept considering the number that are engaged in holding it down."[60] By the end of Wells's first British tour, Mayo had forced Impey to retire from public life.

Accusations of female mental illness were very serious charges in Victorian England. Moreover, any "deviance from socially accepted behavior" might lead to charges of "moral insanity." Despite growing public tolerance of women's participation in reform movements, women who rejected a domestic life to participate in the public sphere were still considered with a degree of suspicion. Female hysteria or mental illness, for which "uncontrolled sexuality seemed the major, almost defining symptom," was believed to come from "unsatisfied sexual and maternal drives." Contemporary observers would certainly have considered Impey's interest in a man of color more than fifteen years her junior unnatural and out of control. And even rejecting marriage and motherhood in favor of intellectual endeavors was considered evidence of mental illness. Although younger women might acceptably delay marriage for a time, women who reached menopause without fulfilling their womanly nature were regarded as failures. The sexual desires of menopausal women, especially those who were unmarried, "were considered ludicrous or tragic."[61] Tourgée feared that Impey "may be insane"—"no doubt overwrought with the great endeavor" she had undertaken in her quixotic mission. "Very good men and women," he regretted, had been driven insane "by less heroic endeavor than hers." Judging "from her apparent age," Tourgée presumed Impey had also been debilitated by menopause, "that time when woman's nature is the weakest." Thus, Tourgée did not blame Impey for her indiscretion: her "unceasing thought and labor for others" was simply too much for a woman weakened by menopause to handle.[62]

The accusations of moral insanity also prompted Impey's local branch of the Society of Friends to call her before a hearing.[63] Had the charges been found to have merit, Impey might have faced expulsion, and her family would have been shamed for their association with her immorality. In addition, without a male relative to take responsibility for her, Impey could have been committed to an asylum if she were found mentally unstable. Expulsion cases were "discussed and decided . . . in the absence of the accused," with no opportunity to defend herself. Impey would have had to rely on those members assigned to investigate the allegations to present her case sympathetically before the Monthly Meeting. Victorian Quakers' desire "to preserve their public reputation at all costs" would have meant that Impey's indiscretion could have effectively ruined her life.[64] In the end, however, the meeting dismissed the charges against her, expressing "'surprise' that 'any honourable person' should not have destroyed my letter as so immediately requested to do."[65] Impey felt vindicated when the members of the meeting "kindly allowed the charges of my assailants to be fully laid before them & having heard everything, *indignantly dismissed the case as in 'no way'* calling for their action."[66] But this decision did not restore her community standing.

After Impey finally acquiesced to Mayo's demands that she distance herself from Wells's work, Mayo paid for a German woman to chaperone Wells in London but offered no assistance in obtaining an audience for Wells at the numerous May Meetings being held there. As a result, Wells was denied valuable opportunities to speak before representatives of international reform organizations and members of Parliament and chose to leave the country at the end of May 1893 to continue her work assisting Douglass's protest against the Chicago World's Fair.[67]

May 1893 also saw the emergence of S. J. Celestine Edwards as a leader in the SRBM. He joined Wells's speaking tour, became involved in the publication of the final issue of *Anti-Caste* devoted to the society, and provided a third, neutral force in the divided movement. He published and wrote the introduction to Wells's British pamphlet, *United States Atrocities*, copies of which were distributed to influential individuals in advance of Wells's speaking engagements and sold at various SRBM meetings to raise money to cover her campaign's expenses.[68] A West Indian Methodist evangelist who seemed capable of holding the two factions of the SRBM together, Edwards was chosen as the pro tempore secretary of the society.[69] He helped broker a tentative truce between Impey and Mayo in which each confined herself to her local sphere of influence. As the proprietor of a publishing house specializing in religious tracts and a weekly Christian newspaper, *Lux*, Edwards was a desirable addition to the SRBM. He became the editor, manager, and principal author of the group's new publication, *Fraternity*, and agreed to take financial responsibility for it until the SRBM was able to secure sufficient advertising "to take it off his hands." Edwards's new role allowed the SRBM to move away from its dependence on Impey's *Anti-Caste* accounts and personal networks.[70]

Edwards's leadership ushered in an era of growth and stability for the British antilynching movement. His authority as a male leader appears to have calmed the SRBM's existing membership and his background allowed him to travel within various reform networks that had remained closed to Impey and

Mayo. As a black British man, his leadership appealed to and helped create an emerging pan-African community. As an evangelist for the Christian Evidence Society, Edwards was well known across England. A British evangelical ecumenical Christian organization, the Christian Evidence Society used large open-air meetings, public lectures, and published pamphlets to explain the fundamental principles of Christianity to a largely working-class Anglican audience. Edwards's political connections also encouraged a number of prominent political reformers to join the SRBM's executive committee, including members of Parliament such as Irish Home Rule advocate Alfred Webb and Indian rights campaigner Dadabhai Naoroji. Using his skills and connections as a journalist and publisher, Edwards increased the circulation of *Fraternity* to more than seven thousand.[71]

In September 1893, apparently pleased with the progress of the SRBM under Edwards's leadership, Mayo wrote to Wells on Edwards's behalf, inviting her to return to England the following spring. According to Mayo, Edwards "could arrange *a perfect tour through the country.*" Wells's expenses would be paid, and this time she "would *not be asked to work for absolutely nothing.*" Adding reassurance that she approved of the proposal, Mayo concluded, "Of course, *I* wish you would come back: because I fully believe Mr. Edwards' arrangements would do you justice,—and you would work *unblighted!*"[72]

Convinced of Mayo's sincerity, Wells accepted the invitation, negotiated terms with Edwards and the SRBM Executive Council, and prepared to return to England. In December, however, Mayo complained to Wells that Impey "was still giving trouble" and declared that "there must be no secresy but the whole truth be told." When Wells again refused to reveal Impey's indiscretion, Mayo accused Wells of sympathizing with Impey and "thought I had better not come over, as she would have nothing to do with me if I had anything to do with Miss I."[73] Wells wrote to Edwards to determine whether Mayo's letter represented the position of the SRBM. Reassured that the Executive Council would honor its agreement and did not expect her to speak against Impey, Wells sailed for England and arrived in Liverpool on March 9, 1894.[74] Furious that the Executive Council had sent for Wells over her objection, Mayo resigned her position, withdrew her funding for Wells's campaign, and convinced the Scottish branches of the SRBM to form a separate organization under her leadership.[75] Rather than allow Wells to tour in Scotland, this Northern Federation of Branches invited an African American politician, former Ohio state senator John P. Green, for an alternative speaking tour from April to June 1894.[76]

Although certainly an undesirable outcome, the withdrawal of Mayo's support for Wells's campaign would not have been an insurmountable obstacle on
its own. But Edwards became incapacitated by influenza and rheumatic fever,
effectively leaving the SRBM without leadership by the time of her arrival.[77]
Overworked and unwilling to reduce his commitments, Edwards maintained
a grueling schedule of speaking engagements evangelizing on behalf of the
Christian Evidence Society, wrote for and edited both *Lux* and *Fraternity*, and
tried to organize Wells's tour and maintain control over the splintering SRBM.
Financially dependent on his lectures and refusing to rest until *Lux* became a
paying venture, Edwards sent appeals for subscriptions from his sickbed.[78] By
the end of March, a fund was started to send Edwards back to the West Indies
to recuperate.[79] Without Mayo's financial backing or Edwards's charismatic appeals for subscriptions at Wells's speaking engagements, the SRBM lacked the
money to adequately fund Wells's campaign. In addition, without Edwards's
leadership, the SRBM was in disarray: according to Wells, "The Council is not
a strongly organized body because of the withdrawal of Miss I's friends who
feel that she has been ill-treated." Unwilling to expose Impey's "weakness" to
win back Mayo's support and with no practical support from the SRBM, Wells
was left to her own resources.[80]

Befriended upon her arrival in Liverpool by her sympathetic host, the Reverend Charles F. Aked, Wells attempted to salvage her campaign. Because she
was stranded in Britain without a sponsor to promote her work or provide her
with credentials, Aked encouraged her to appeal to Douglass for help. Aked
believed that Wells needed letters of support and introduction from a prominent American "vouching for my testimony and character" and asserting that
she represented the interests of African Americans rather than her own personal agenda.[81] Although Aked gave Wells "a hearing in his church and felt
there were others who would do the same thing . . . from knowing of me last
year," without Douglass's help, she would be plagued by questions about why
she no longer had the support of the organization that had invited her to the
United Kingdom.[82] As the preeminent African American statesman of the
era, Douglass could provide her with a public endorsement that would separate her from the stigma of personal scandal and open access to higher-level
political and reform circles.

Douglass responded with suspicion to Wells's appeal for assistance. He demanded that Wells "oblige me by telling me frankly who invited you to spend
three months in England" and questioned whether Wells had misrepresented
her mission to him and had instead "gone to England on your own motion and

for your own purposes."[83] Although Douglass understood that Wells bore no personal responsibility for the quarrel between Impey and Mayo, the continuing scandal of female immorality had tainted her. Wells despaired at Douglass's response: "I have never felt so like giving up as since I received your very cool and cautious letter this morning, with its tone of distrust and its inference that I have not dealt truthfully with you . . . For without knowing anything about these people and their invitation," she chided Douglass, "you *did* know me and had never had cause to doubt my truthfulness." Over the next few weeks, Wells implored Douglass to give her the letters of support and introduction she needed to continue her campaign.[84]

When Edwards died on July 25, 1894, at his brother's home in Barbados, the SRBM's future became even more uncertain. Edwards's death created a power vacuum, and Impey and her supporters rushed in to try to gain control. Impey suspected Edwards of having participated in "double dealing & 'back-stair' intrigues" against her under Mayo's influence and hoped that his death might finally end the problems "brought about by Mrs. Mayo's hard & distorted view of my unhappy mistake." Dr. W. Evans Darby, secretary of the English Peace Society, became the SRBM's new honorary secretary, and the Executive Council was filled by members sympathetic to Impey. Allowed to play an active role in the society once more, Impey believed that Mayo's "spiteful attacks" had finally lost their potency and might have even "driven many to me more closely in their sympathy & indignation at the unmerited nature of the assault." Impey believed that the SRBM could finally accomplish "greater things than have yet been possible."[85]

Mayo retaliated against Impey's attempt to reenter public life by attacking her in the pages of *Fraternity*. In an unsigned article, "The 'Female Accusation,'" Mayo discussed the rise of "certain morbid peculiarities" of the female mind. The article compared Impey's offending letter to Ferdinands with imagined rape accusations in the American South. Mayo claimed that "morbid" women "who will 'fancy' anything" will "imagine that men 'fall in love with them.'" Hinting that Ferdinands's perceived interests in Impey were merely mistaken deference to a woman of "manifest infirmity," Mayo accused Impey of being "elderly, dowdy, and disappointed."[86] Mayo claimed that in cases where white women indulged their "imaginations" about black men in the South, those assertions would cost the men their lives. While in Great Britain, such accusations might only result in the disruption of philanthropic work, Mayo warned that "sensible women, for the sake of all parties, will entirely refuse to work with [such women] in co-operation with men."[87]

Printed alongside Wells's account of her second campaign, "The 'Female Accusation'" echoed and reinforced Wells's arguments about the complicity of white women in the lynching deaths of black men. Although Wells asserted that consensual interracial sexual relationships, not imagined assaults, lay behind many lynchings, Mayo's explanation offered an alternative interpretation for those who could not conceive of the idea of consensual interracial sex. Both explanations rested on the moral weakness of white women: either they imagined black male sexual interest and violence, or they lured black men into inappropriate sexual relationships and then forfeited their lovers to mobs to avoid public disgrace. Mayo believed that people who knew these unstable white women had a duty to prevent them from harming the lives of men of color. "If the women of the South were all 'pure of heart and sound in head,'" Mayo supposed, "we should hear of fewer lynchings; and if British philanthropy, whenever forewarned, gently set aside the dubious help of these diseased imaginations . . . many good works which now flag and falter, would go on apace."[88]

Mayo continued her public assault on Impey in a signed announcement, "The Present Position of Our Society." Mayo and her fellow signatories pointedly attacked Impey's morality, mental stability, and suitability as a reform worker and called for reformers to defect from the current SRBM leadership. Glorifying her role in the society's formation, Mayo claimed she had invited Edwards to join to protect it from "a prominent English helper" whose "mental or moral unsoundness" threatened the group's mission. She charged that a "small clique" working within the society was grappling for power and attempting to "force upon the society's councils a person of admitted mental instability—the victim of 'hallucination.'" Mayo left little doubt about the identity of the object of her scorn. Rejecting the authority of the Executive Council, she announced her election as the SRBM's new president and of Ferdinands as vice president.[89]

The final schism in the SRBM and the personal vendetta that prompted it not only destroyed Impey's public reputation but also eroded an important source of consolidated British support for Wells's antilynching campaign. Struggles for control of the SRBM name prompted Mayo's Scottish-led faction to become the International Society for the Recognition of the Brotherhood of Man in early 1895.[90] The new group's focus turned increasingly away from the issue of American lynching; however, its leaders encouraged members to support the work of the London Anti-Lynching Committee, an unaffiliated organization spawned during Wells's second campaign that occasionally worked in coordination with the SRBM. The London Anti-Lynching Committee included many influential social leaders and politicians who pressured southern governors to investigate and prosecute lynchers.[91] Nevertheless, the new organization's shift in emphasis on problems in India and Africa reduced the amount of British social pressure on American politicians, law enforcement officials, and religious and social leaders.

Nineteenth-century women reformers operated in a volatile world of gendered discourse. When navigated successfully, this powerful discourse could provide legitimacy; if overreached, the same gendered conventions could drive women out of the public sphere. Mayo pursued a vigorous public and private campaign against Impey at least in part to protect Mayo's own reputation, and Impey's reputation never recovered from Mayo's attacks. When Darby welcomed an alliance with Joseph Malins, grand chief templar, Impey fell into despair. After all, her frustration with the Templars' tolerance of segregated branches had prompted her to resign in protest and help to found the SRBM. Feeling betrayed, Impey closed her SRBM Minute Books over the same issue that had prompted her to open them; she retired from public life in 1895.[92] In contrast, by successfully conforming to British gender roles, Wells secured her personal legitimacy and weathered the storm of Impey's scandal. As the conflict between Impey and Mayo came to a head, Wells extricated herself from the SRBM and launched a transatlantic antilynching campaign using the public support of Frederick Douglass and Charles Aked's circle of religious reformers.

Chapter 4

BUILDING A TRANSATLANTIC DEBATE ON LYNCHING

Lured back to Britain for a second campaign in 1894 by a tentative truce between the founders of the Society for the Recognition of the Brotherhood of Man (SRBM), Ida B. Wells quickly found herself caught once more amid her benefactors' heated conflict. The dispute between Catherine Impey and Isabella Fyvie Mayo that had stifled Wells's first campaign and threatened to undermine her legitimacy as a reformer reignited with Wells's return to England. This time, however, a more complete breakdown of SRBM networks allowed Wells to escape the oppressive confines of Impey and Mayo's narrow moral reform circles. She was free to make full use of her talents and intuition as an activist, and her second campaign sparked an explosion of British public interest in American lynching.

Wells's second British campaign had two elements: an overt attack that she led, and a covert attack fought on her behalf by British supporters. As a young, single, outspoken, and controversial African American woman, Wells could not enter every British circle. Therefore, she needed a way to introduce her ideas without alienating British audiences. While she strove to gain publicity as the public face of a transatlantic antilynching movement, Wells recruited British supporters to introduce her ideas into conservative forums from which she was excluded. In this way, her arguments against lynching appeared in mainstream and conservative British journals and secured antilynching resolutions from prominent religious organizations. Making full use of her networking skills, Wells's second British antilynching campaign mobilized a vibrant alliance of British reformers who pressured American social and political leaders.

The nature of this dual strategy makes it impossible to gauge the impact of Wells's British antilynching campaigns on the United States without first evaluating their effects on the other side of the Atlantic. Only by assessing the extent to which Wells's rhetoric penetrated British circles is it possible to measure the transfer of those ideas from Great Britain to the United States. Doing so, in turn, calls for a closer examination of the transatlantic political, social, and reform networks that existed in Wells's day.

CHARLES AKED AND THE BATTLE
FOR RELIGIOUS NETWORKS

Ida B. Wells arrived in Liverpool on March 9, 1894, to discover the SRBM in disarray. Not only had the conflict between Impey and Mayo reignited, but the organization's neutral leader, S. J. Celestine Edwards, had been incapacitated by severe illness.[1] Without a strong leader, the SRBM splintered along factional lines of personal loyalty to the two founding members. Mayo withdrew from the national SRBM organization and claimed Scotland as her personal sphere of influence. Angered by Wells's consistent refusal to expose Impey's impropriety, Mayo withdrew her financial support of Wells's campaign and forbade her from touring Scotland. Although they remained active in the local branches, Impey's closest supporters had resigned from the central leadership of the SRBM to protest what they viewed as her continued mistreatment at the hands of Mayo's allies. Without the leadership of Mayo, Impey, Edwards, or their loyal supporters, the SRBM's Executive Committee was left adrift and ineffectual.[2]

Wells found herself stranded in England without a credible sponsor or organizational structure to support and promote her campaign. Without Mayo's backing, access to the coffers of Impey's *Anti-Caste* accounts, or Edwards's fund-raising skills, the SRBM was unable to provide any significant financial support. Edwards had arranged Wells's initial speaking engagements and accommodation in Liverpool, and he made at least one appearance there, but his illness prevented him from traveling with Wells to vouch for her activism.[3] Mayo's private attacks made it impossible for Impey to organize an effective national campaign on Wells's behalf. Assured that she would be reimbursed by the SRBM, Wells had borrowed money from Frederick Douglass for her passage to England. With the disintegration of the SRBM's Executive Council, Wells did not receive the promised funds. Without even the money to return to the United States, Wells was left to her own devices.[4]

Edwards had arranged for Wells to stay as a guest in the home of the Reverend Charles F. Aked, a radical Baptist minister. His leadership had saved the previously dwindling congregation of Pembroke Chapel and transformed it into Liverpool's largest congregation. Young, handsome, passionate, and charismatic, Aked drew crowds of more than fourteen hundred to his sermons. His plainspoken style and emphasis on social and political reform appealed to his middle- and working-class congregation. Accused by more conservative Baptists of employing sensationalism and theatricality in his ministry, Aked prided himself on bringing practical Christianity to life from his pulpit. "If they mean that I do not read my sermons in a husky wheeze and dolorous hum, with my nose in my manuscript, and my chin on my chest," Aked declared triumphantly, "that is perfectly true . . . The people in our day just need some honest man to get up and speak as a living man to living men; and whether I succeed or not, that is what I shall try to do."[5] Aked used his pulpit to promote temperance, raise money for relief projects, fight prostitution, and denounce injustices throughout the world. In the struggle "against war, against drink, against vice, against poverty," he praised the members of his congregation for their steadfast loyalty to the causes he championed.[6]

Allowing Wells to air her grievances before his congregation was not unusual for Aked. During his tenure at Pembroke Chapel, Aked invited numerous speakers to bear witness to international crises from his platform. Notable guests included American investigative journalist George Kennan, who revealed the harsh conditions in Russian political prisons; Kate Marsden, the English founder of a Siberian leper colony; and Armenian Christian rights activist Madame Thoumaian. Wells's style of activism and socioeconomic critique of American race relations would have complimented Aked's vision for Pembroke and his congregation's concerns.[7]

Finding herself abandoned by the SRBM and in desperate need of assistance, Wells took a calculated risk and revealed to Aked and his wife, Annie, the entire story of the dispute between Impey and Mayo, Edwards's invitation and illness, and the SRBM's failure to fulfill the financial terms of its agreement.[8] Although they might have shied away from association with the unpleasant scandal, the Akeds were sympathetic to Wells's situation and agreed to help salvage her antilynching campaign. Providing Wells with shelter, friendship, and access to their personal networks, the Akeds became invaluable supporters of her activism.

Aked played an essential role in the success of Wells's campaign that historians have not fully appreciated.[9] Their relationship served both Aked's ambition and Wells's immediate need for assistance. As a white British clergy-man, Aked could access venues that remained closed to Wells; he used such opportunities to promote her agenda, and his allies in the ecumenical move-ment provided Wells with a network with which to continue her campaign while she sought alternative avenues of support. Their combined activism was instrumental in generating a true transatlantic debate on American lynching.

Yet Aked was aware of the limitations of his personal influence; he did not believe that Wells could launch a successful campaign on the basis of his spon-sorship alone. He immediately encouraged her to ask Douglass for letters of support and introduction. Wells followed Aked's advice and appealed to Dou-glass to write a general letter of introduction and endorsement for her work, a letter of thanks to Aked "in the race's name for the help he has already given the cause," and "if you wish for the splendid success of the work to write let-ters to all your friends in Great Britain commending me to them." Douglass needed to act quickly, "as it will take the letters nearly a month to reach here."[10]

Aked and his friends in the religious community came together to pro-vide Wells with a temporary network for her campaign while she waited for Douglass's letters to arrive. A close friend of Aked's, the Reverend Richard Acland Armstrong, enthusiastically lent his support to Wells's campaign, and she addressed a large crowd at his Unitarian Hope Street Church. She also ap-peared at a large demonstration in Hope Hall, where Sir Edward Russell, an influential Liberal political figure and editor of the *Liverpool Daily Post*, pre-sided. Russell endorsed Wells's campaign, introducing her as a "distinguished lady . . . adorned by every grace of womanhood and justified by her abilities the public duty which she had undertaken, having been provoked into appealing to the public opinion of this country by acts which they must all deplore, and of which they should be glad to make some people ashamed."[11] In the absence of a credible sponsor, such a powerful endorsement from a respected social leader helped bolster Wells's public legitimacy.

Nevertheless, Aked's support could not launch Wells's campaign into Lon-don's most influential circles. Despite his political aspirations, Aked never held office and lacked the connections to assist Wells in securing endorsements from members of the British government.[12] Aked was only a midlevel player in British religious circles, including his own Baptist Union. His friendships with influential clergymen from other dissenting religious orders made him a valu-able resource for Wells but also limited his reach, as national religious organi-zations shunned the emerging ecumenical movement. His support alone could not guarantee either Wells or her arguments a hearing at the important annual May Meetings of national religious and reform organizations in London.

Aked did have connections with the religious press, and he exploited those ties to promote Wells's campaign. He published articles on her activism in the *Christian World*, Britain's leading religious newspaper, and in his own ecumenical journal, the *Liverpool Pulpit*.[13] Coedited by Aked; Charles William Stubbs, an Anglican dean; and Armstrong, the Unitarian minister who opened his church to Wells, the *Liverpool Pulpit* promoted "spiritual unity amid intellectual diversity" by reprinting sermons from local clergy of various denominations.[14] Through the pages of the *Christian World*, Wells's campaign came to the attention of churches of all denominations throughout Britain. It promoted her activism and provided Aked with a forum to lobby in favor of antilynching resolutions.[15]

As the press coverage of her activism increased, the need for Wells to secure proof of Douglass's endorsement grew more urgent. When it became clear that the SRBM's support would fall short, Aked began advertising Wells as Douglass's protégée. In the *Liverpool Pulpit*, Aked claimed that Wells was "accredited to the friends of popular progress in this country by the Hon. Frederick Douglass, and is one of the recognised leaders of her Race." In the *Christian World*, Aked declared Wells "a personal friend of the old slave orator" who had "come direct from the veteran's house at Washington, urged to this mission by him and his colleagues." Douglass scolded Wells when he learned that she was "already advertised as accredited to England by me." Suspicious of Wells's complicity in these advertisements and her abandonment by the SRBM, he refused to grant his endorsement without a satisfactory explanation of how Wells had come to need his support. Wells tried to distance herself from Aked's assertions, claiming that she "did not know Mr. Aked had put it in the paper . . . until it appeared. I told him it was not true altho you knew and approved of my coming." Believing that a letter of support would arrive soon, she explained, Aked had used Douglass's name to justify supporting her activism when "a wealthy American had asked [Aked] in church after service who I was." Attempting to appease Douglass, Wells maintained, "I am not to blame for that; it is too unlike me to sail under false colors." Nevertheless, in light of such questions, the need to affirm Wells's legitimacy as a representative of the African American community became increasingly urgent.[16]

Similarly, Wells's request for a letter of thanks from Douglass to Aked "in the race's name" was not a mere formality. Part of the strategy she developed with Aked necessitated Douglass's validation. Aked proposed using his interdenominational personal connections to introduce antilynching resolutions at the annual meetings of various religious organizations. Although his close friendships with progressive clergymen from other denominations provided

Aked with avenues to pursue this plan, it also marginalized him and limited the power of his personal influence. In a letter to Douglass, Aked explained, "I have given notice of a resolution for the forthcoming meeting of the Baptist Union of Great Britain in London. I do not know whether I shall be allowed to move it; the Baptist Union is not very fond of me, because I am a heretic and associate with Unitarians!"[17] Without the added legitimacy of Douglass's endorsement, Aked realized that his reputation for sensationalism in the pulpit and nonconformity in his ecumenical focus would stymie his efforts at these important national meetings.

Following one of Wells's speaking engagements, Armstrong sent a letter to the editor of the *Christian Register*, America's leading Unitarian publication, containing a strongly worded resolution against lynching passed by his Liverpool congregation. Learning "with grief and horror of the barbarities of lynch law as carried out by white men on some of the colored citizens of the United States," the Hope Street Church called on "all lovers of justice, of freedom, and of brotherhood among our kinsmen in the States to determine that these things shall be no more." Armstrong urged Americans to "save the good name of your nation" from the disgrace of mob violence by denouncing "the seizure of untried men and women, their execution with every device of torture, the acquiescence of all the guardians of the law, the instilling into the boys and girls of the United States of the lust of cruelty and callousness to murder." Armstrong bemoaned the futility of the international declaration of "a world-wide human brotherhood" made by the 1893 World's Parliament of Religions held in conjunction with the World's Columbian Exposition in Chicago, when "the Negro on your own soil—nay, the mulatto in whose veins flows as much Anglo-Saxon blood as African—can find beneath your national flag no security against the brutality of lawless mobs and the nameless horrors of the amateur scaffold, the branding-iron, and the stake."[18]

In anticipation of the upcoming National Triennial Conference of Unitarians, Armstrong sent copies of his letter to the *Liverpool Daily Post* and the *Inquirer*, Britain's leading Unitarian publication. Working with Armstrong, the Reverend S. Alfred Steinthal, a respected Manchester minister, proposed a similar antilynching resolution at the Triennial Conference:

> That the members of this National Conference of Unitarian and other Non-subscribing and Free Christian Churches have learned with grief and amazement (from Miss Ida B. Wells) of the prevalence of Lynch Law in the Southern States of the United States of America, especially as practised against the co-

loured population: that they regard the execution of men accused of a crime without due trial as an abandonment of the first principles of justice and liberty; that they contemplate with horror the barbarities with which these executions are perpetrated, and the corruption of the white population which must result from familiarity with such excesses, and that a copy of the resolution be sent to the *Christian* [*Register*].

In support of the resolution, the Reverend Charles Roper read a "lengthy letter . . . from Miss Ida B. Wells" on the subject of lynching, "asking that a protest should come from the conference against such outrages." Armstrong seconded the resolution, declaring "public opinion" to be "the most potent factor in putting an end to these atrocities" and urging his fellow Unitarians to do "their part to arouse the conscience of their American brethren . . . to save their Christian faith from this great blemish."[19]

Although Armstrong's words were greeted with applause, the Reverend Brooke Herford quickly raised a protest against Wells's assertions and the proposed antilynching resolution. Although he acknowledged that "it was impossible to exaggerate the horrors of the Lynch law," Herford believed "it was a terrible misrepresentation for Miss Wells to say, as she did in her letter to the conference, that these crimes had the encouragement of the Southern Press and the pulpit, and the connivance of the legal authorities." Herford's objections were supported by a series of speakers. The Reverend W. Reynolds proposed an amendment to soften the language of the resolution, which "suggested that the churches were not taking steps against this lawlessness." He asked the members to consider their reactions if Americans passed resolutions condemning British societal shortcomings. Women's rights advocate and social-purity activist Laura Ormiston Chant objected to the resolution on the grounds that it did not give credit to those American Unitarians who were working to end lynching. She concluded, "The two nations should not irritate each other in the great work each had to do." Claiming that Britons had "no right to send a message across the sea condemning a special evil resulting from a state of society of which we had nothing like it in this country," the Reverend Charles Hargrove proposed a final amendment: "That the conference desired to express to their brethren in the States their deep sympathy with them in their protest against atrocities of the Lynch law so frequently perpetrated in the Southern States, and trusted that they might be encouraged in their efforts to suppress them." Trying to regain control, Steinthal "reiterated that the authorities of the towns, the pulpit, and the newspapers of the great cities of the South had spoken in defence of Lynch law." He argued that the conference "should not send a message of sympathy to those who were not doing their duty in this matter." Armstrong stood to protest these changes, but was ruled out of order and not allowed to speak. Despite their objections, the eviscerated resolution was passed.[20]

The persuasive power of Herford's objections demonstrated that Wells and her supporters needed to rally broader support for their cause if they wanted future national conferences to pass resolutions. Roper believed that Herford "spoke as he did at the Conference because he had been to America, had occupied a leading Boston pulpit & had not himself done what he might & ought to have done in the matter . . . In speaking as he does of the North he is excusing himself." Chant also had connections to the United States and had recently participated in a Boston meeting of Unitarians that passed a resolution condemning lynching.[21] Regardless of Herford and Chant's personal motivations, their arguments against the resolution struck a chord with the assembly. As long as British religious leaders remained reluctant to anger their American counterparts or afraid of receiving admonishments for British cultural failings, Wells's campaign would lose an important opportunity to stimulate transatlantic debate through national and international religious governing bodies. Without a way to weaken Herford's position or persuade him to recant his objections, it would be difficult to overcome the precedent of noninterference in American domestic affairs established by the Triennial Conference.

In early May 1894, Wells sent another plea to Douglass for letters of support for her campaign and the efforts of her English supporters. This time, however, she had evidence of her need: she enclosed a letter from Unitarian minister Ambrose N. Blatchford "so you may see for yourself how much they wish for a letter of approval from you. The first Unitarian Conference at Manchester defeated the resolution of condemnation of lynching thro the efforts of Dr. Brooke Herford. Rev. Armstrong & Dr. Steinthal are going to try again at a conference to be held June 14, and it is for this that the writer wishes you [would] write a good strong letter." Frustrated by Douglass's reluctance to endorse her activism, Wells concluded, "In it you can say whether I speak for my race or not and endorse most strongly the effort to pass the resolution. It will hold up their hands against their opposers."[22]

As she waited for Douglass's response, Wells received a boost from another American source, Samuel J. Barrows, editor of the *Christian Register* in Boston. Although Armstrong's letter to Barrows was not printed in time to influence the proceedings of the Triennial Conference in Manchester, his lengthy editorial response flew in the face of the sentiments expressed by Herford and Chant.[23] Barrows welcomed Armstrong's denunciation of both lynching and the silence of American Christians that perpetuated its existence: "Every justice-loving American will blush for his country that any such protest is necessary," yet British reformers "are simply telling the truth when they call our attention to the fearful and barbaric atrocities . . . committed against colored men in the South." Americans had failed to live up to their democratic ideals and could not simply ask England "to mind her own affairs." British reformers had every right to speak out against this horrible failing of American civilization, for "wherever . . . deep wrong exists, it is the business of every lover of humanity to raise his voice against it." Barrows went on to accuse "the religious press in the South" of being "culpably negligent in ignoring the barbarism" of lynching. "There is an international standard of civilization and justice which every enlightened nation is expected to maintain," but southern society "has been rude and barbaric, and falls far below the standards of decency, order, toleration, and justice" expected of less developed nations. Barrows believed the situation could be remedied only "as public sentiment is awakened in the South," so he implored "the clergy and journalists and educators of the South" to openly denounce "the degradation and lawlessness and race hatred which now make the Southern States a reproach to the civilized world."[24]

Barrows's editorial was powerful and timely, almost anticipating the heated debate at the Triennial Conference. Stirred by Barrows's vigorous words, the editor of the *Inquirer*, the Reverend William George Tarrant, offered Wells an opportunity to respond to the accusations of misrepresentation leveled by Herford and his supporters. Quoting verifiable statements made by prominent American clergymen in leading American publications, Wells reiterated her attack on the American pulpit's and press's complicity in lynching. Even without such statements, Wells believed the fact that many lynchings occurred "in broad daylight and in the leading towns" justified her assertions, "for if the Press and Pulpit had exerted the power which we are led to believe they possess, some of the lynchers would have been punished for these murders, or the lynchings would have been prevented in the many cases where the mob's intention was known beforehand." "It is because of the moral cowardice shown by the Christian bodies of my own country," she concluded, "that I come to England and ask them to do what Unitarian along with other Christian bodies in America have failed to do—speak out against this great evil . . . and put a stop to it."[25]

Tarrant was quickly won over, reasoning that "if our people become per-

suaded that the case is anything like as horrible as it is understood to be by
Mr. Steinthal and Mr. Armstrong... there will be no lack of indignant protests and urgent appeals from them to our American brethren." He concluded
that "unless some very strong counter-evidence is supplied" to refute Barrows's
harsh words, "we shall have no other course than to concur in the most strenu-
ous remonstrances" against lynching.[26]

Barrows's editorial and Tarrant's conversion to Wells's antilynching movement placed Herford in a difficult position. Roper assumed that "Barrows'
confession in the *Christian Register* must have roused [Herford] rather
roughly. I think that, altogether, he feels cornered." Wells's supporters continued to pressure Herford to recant his charges against Wells and support her
position. Roper believed "Tarrant is 'right,' & will not likely allow the matter
to drop. Moreover, if I judge Herford aright he will veer round still more; &
we shall have him supporting our protests unconditionally."[27] Wells vowed to
pursue a chance to speak and secure a successful resolution "at whatever cost
to myself," but she feared the impact of another defeat on her campaign: "I
cannot recover from the set-back given the work in this public manner and by
so large and representative body... It will neutralize & paralyze further effort
in other bodies, taking this as a precedent." At Blatchford's encouragement,
Wells eventually met with Herford to plead her case directly. With the cumulative influence of her supporters, Wells won his cooperation and was invited
to speak to his congregation in London.[28]

Meanwhile, Aked submitted an antilynching resolution at the annual
meeting of his denomination, the Baptist Union of Great Britain and Ireland.
"Having learned with grief and horror of the wrongs done to the coloured
people of the Southern States of America by lawless mobs," Aked called on
"all lovers of justice, of freedom and of brotherhood" to restore American
honor by demanding "a proper trial in the courts of law" for any citizen accused of a crime.[29] Because his progressive theology and acceptance of Unitarians as equal members of the catholic church marginalized him, he solicited
the support of Dr. John Clifford, a leading member and former president of
the Baptist Union. Clifford was sympathetic to the style and goals of Aked's
ministry, remaining "open to new directions in theology" and advocating "the
primitive Christian faith as a social gospel," including support for labor strikes
and liberal social and political reform programs.[30] Aked considered Clifford
"the greatest of living Baptists" and "an intimate friend." Promising to second
Aked's resolution, Clifford ensured that the issue would be heard and brought

to a vote. Aked was confident that the resolution would "be heartily carried if I can so break through officialism as to get a hearing."[31]

With Clifford on board, Aked advertised his antilynching resolution in the *Christian World* to drum up support in advance of the meeting. The article quoted a letter from Douglass to Aked to bolster support for the resolution. "The side of the American mob," Douglass lamented, "has been told to England by a hundred Presses; the side of the negro has been hushed in death." Sent in response to Wells's initial request for support, Douglass's letter of gratitude to Aked was tempered by suspicion and caution. Nevertheless, even a lukewarm letter of support from Douglass legitimated Aked's appeal. Passing Aked's resolution, the *Christian World* "earnestly . . . hoped," would enable "the voice of England [to] help the better feeling of America so to assert itself as to bring to a speedy end a state of things which, if the published reports be correct, would disgrace a nation of cannibals."[32]

A. E. Fletcher, editor of London's influential *Daily Chronicle*, offered words of encouragement on the morning of the hearing. The problem of lynching concerned all humanity, Fletcher argued, and the Baptist Union had a "plain duty" to give "a moral nudge" to American Christians to end this system of extralegal violence and racial oppression. Fletcher concluded that British religious leaders must play a crucial role in transforming American public sentiment. "The hope for the negro," he explained, "is that in the 'new South' which is growing up, and which is beginning to affect seriously the political situation, a class is rising to power which is more open than the older Southerners to moral appeal." "Lynching may be stopped—may perish in the atmosphere of a better ethical feeling," if this more progressive class could be reached. This transformation would require the moral leadership of "the Christian Churches of the United States," and Fletcher believed that British religious leaders had a duty "to provoke those Churches to such a good work."[33]

By drumming up publicity and support in advance of the meeting, Wells's backers increased their chances of success. Aked had more time than did Steinthal and Armstrong to build the case for his resolution. Barrows's timely editorial helped to neutralize the precedent of noninterference established by the Triennial Conference. Clifford's endorsement strengthened the resolve of Baptist Union members who were sympathetic to the antilynching appeal but had reservations about taking action as a national body. Consequently, the Baptist Union greeted Aked's resolution enthusiastically and passed it on April 25, 1894.[34]

This victory opened the possibility of securing additional resolutions from other national organizations. It provided momentum for Wells's campaign and set a precedent for other religious and quasi-religious organizations to follow. Unlike her campaign the preceding year, Wells received invitations to speak at several influential annual May Meetings in London, including women's reform and religious organizations. There, her powerful, impassioned speeches consistently won support. Reassured by Douglass's endorsement, the British Women's Temperance Association (BWTA) invited Wells to speak at its national meeting. Through the intervention of Lady Somerset and popular Woman's Christian Temperance Union leader Frances Willard, Chant, one of the opposition leaders at the Unitarian Triennial Conference, was persuaded to support Wells's appeal and the adoption of an antilynching resolution. "Having heard the statements of Miss Wells . . . concerning the burning and lynching of her countrymen," the BWTA felt "constrained by the dictates of common humanity to express our sympathy with her." Not even the most heinous crimes, the resolution concluded, could "justify the infliction of such forms of retribution." The BWTA's statement ignored Wells's assertions that lynching was not motivated by rape; nevertheless, receiving even "sympathy" from the organization constituted a major victory for Wells, who had come under fire in Britain for criticizing Willard's acceptance of the lynching for rape narrative.[35] Supported by several Quakers connected with local branches of the SRBM, Wells's campaign was warmly embraced by the Women's Yearly Meeting of the Society of Friends. The meeting "heard with much concern of the cruel and unjust treatment of the coloured people" in the United States, who "have been barbarously put to death without judge or jury, while the perpetrators of these murders are allowed to go uncondemned." "No human being," the meeting members declared, "should suffer for a crime until proved to be guilty," and "race prejudice" should not "be allowed to set aside this fundamental law of liberty." The Women's Yearly Meeting called on American Christians "to use their powerful influence on public opinion to put an end to this great injustice" and urged them not to rest "until they have secured equal rights to all, without respect of colour."[36]

Although she gained the support of these influential women's networks, Wells found it difficult to secure an audience with mixed-gender organizations. Despite the recommendation of both the Women's Yearly Meeting and Bristol and Somerset Quarterly Meeting for Sufferings, Wells was not permitted to speak before the London Yearly Meeting, the national governing body of the Society of Friends. Although her initial appeal was hotly debated, her second request for a hearing was quickly dismissed, and the issue of an anti-lynching resolution was never put to a vote.³⁷

Wells suffered a further disappointment when the Congregational Union Assembly passed a weak antilynching resolution in her absence. Lacking influential allies within the Congregational Union, Wells was unable to secure a hearing before the assembly despite repeated appeals.³⁸ Expressing only prayers and sympathy for American Christians "who feel the scandal and shame" of lynching, the resolution proposed by Dr. Robert F. Horton did not call for Americans to take action to end mob violence. Horton, who like Herford had recently returned from the United States, accepted apologists' assertions that lynching was used as a response to black criminality. Horton expressed these beliefs in his address to the assembly, acknowledging that "excited and indignant" mobs might seize the wrong man but also asserting that "some of those negroes deserved to be lynched." Horton expressed greater concern for the demoralizing effects of lynching on the members of the mob than on their victims and urged the Congregational Union to pray "that this reproach may be removed from our common humanity."³⁹

Though far from the desired outcome, the Congregational Union's weak resolution still generated interest in Wells's campaign that filtered back to the United States. "In view of the resolution introduced by the Rev. Dr. Horton," the *Columbus (Georgia) Enquirer-Sun* reported, "a representative of the United Press had an interview today with Ida Wells . . . who is here on a mission to arouse British public opinion" against lynching. And Wells took advantage of the publicity to challenge the Congregationalists and by implication all religious bodies to prevent their meetings from closing "without doing justice to her cause."⁴⁰

The Baptist Union resolution pushed through by Aked, the public pressure campaign, and behind-the-scenes negotiations also began to pay dividends when Wells was seated on the platform with Herford, who withdrew his objections and lent his support, at the meeting of the British and Foreign Unitarian Association. Invited to speak in support of the resolution, Wells relayed "some terrible facts and figures as to lynching" and "sickening stories of torture of men and women, often for offences of which they were quite innocent." After hearing the horrific details of Henry Smith's lynching in Paris, Texas, the association unanimously passed the resolution on May 15, handing Wells's campaign a major victory. The resolution denounced the "increasing frequency of lynching in the Southern States of America" and called for "the Churches and all lovers of order and good government to raise such a protest of public opinion as shall make such outrages impossible." Although one member questioned whether the resolution fell within the association's purview, the chair concluded that the association's support of the antislavery movement had established sufficient precedent for the issue to be heard. Another participant praised the chair, W. Long, for his bold decision, noting that only recently "a proposal to bring political subjects within the purview of the rules met with a very decisive defeat." The resolution was later published as a circular for distribution to newspapers and persons of influence. The victory was important not only for the British antilynching movement but also for the reputation of Unitarians as moral leaders: declared one participant, "We quite made amends to Miss Wells for our lack of sympathy at Manchester."[41]

The letters of thanks and support Wells and her supporters had waited so long to receive from Douglass finally arrived in early June. Coupled with the antilynching resolutions from the Baptist Union, British and Foreign Unitarian Association, BWTA, Aborigines Protection Society, Protestant Alliance, Women's Protestant Union, and the Society of Friends, these letters brought Wells's campaign to the peak of its influence.[42]

TRANSMITTING WELLS'S MESSAGE
INTO BRITISH PUBLIC DEBATES

While Aked and his network of friends fought to gain the support of the national religious networks, Wells worked to gain the support of the British press. As in the first campaign, her speeches attracted favorable local newspaper coverage. This time, however, Wells used her experience as a journalist and editor to court the support of her British counterparts. If she won their support, she reasoned, she might stimulate a sustained British and then transatlantic debate on American lynching that might in turn pressure the United States to end the practice. While favorable reports on her activism were beneficial, editorials in support of her campaign and denouncing lynching were more powerful.

Despite the coverage of Wells's campaign in the *Liverpool Pulpit, Inquirer,* and *Christian World,* secular British journals remained reluctant to join the emerging public debate. Wells needed a new strategy. Victorian journals often commented on, reprinted, or responded to articles from other publications. If her message could break into even one respected journal, she might start a conversation that would spread to other publications. She turned to Aked's reputation to try to get her foot in the door.

In June 1894, the *Contemporary Review* published "The Race Problem in America," in which Aked combined his experiences of American lynching with Wells's rhetorical arguments. He reiterated many of her statistics about the extent of lynching as well as the assertion that mob violence was both increasing and spreading. He repeated Wells's accounts of the lynching of women and children, debunking lynchers' claims that they were retaliating against rapists. Again borrowing from Wells, Aked asserted that only one-third of lynch victims were accused of "criminal assaults" (a frequent code phrase for sexual assault, specifically rape) and that many of these incidents were in fact consensual relationships. At base, Aked asserted, "the demand of the negro is for the most elementary justice." Refining a quotation originally given by Wells in a personal interview to represent the voice of the African American community, Aked declared, "Make your laws as terrible as you like against that class of crime; devise what tortures you will; inflict death by any means you choose; go back to the most barbarous punishments of the most barbarous ages if you think you must; but prove your criminal a criminal first. Hang, shoot, roast him, if you will—if American civilisation demands this—but give him a trial first!"[43]

Aked did not overtly acknowledge his use of Wells's rhetoric and ideas. However, their mutual respect and close working relationship, plus the fact that Wells later named her firstborn son after Aked, indicate that he was not attempting to plagiarize Wells's work. Instead, Aked apparently lent his name, reputation, and white British male identity to give credibility to her ideas. Aked separated the politics of Wells's identity from her message, thus defusing controversy and bringing her arguments before an audience that would otherwise not have heard them.[44]

Free to examine lynching without discussing or supporting Wells, both the *Spectator* and the *Economist* responded to Aked's rebranding of Wells's arguments by publishing articles denouncing lynching. The *Spectator* asserted that there was "no room for doubt" in Aked's indictment of lynching. The only reason that could "account for the determination of the white population of the South not to allow negroes to take their trial, is the race-feeling that what is good enough for the white man is too good for the black man." Although the *Spectator* asserted that such white supremacist beliefs were immoral and unfounded, the *Economist* labored to denounce lynching while reaffirming its support of white supremacy. "Be it understood that we do not write as friends of the negro. The equality of the races does not exist." Nevertheless, although blacks should be subordinated, they should not be subjected to "capricious and insulting cruelty." The *Economist* did "not ask good Americans to interfere for the sake of the negro, but for that of their own countrymen, who cannot be good Republicans with Lynch Law in their midst."[45]

Any journal that would go to such lengths to assert the validity of white supremacy would not knowingly support the arguments of a controversial black woman. Thus, without Aked's efforts to disguise Wells's antilynching rhetoric, neither the *Economist* nor the *Spectator* would have condemned lynching. In fact, the *Spectator* continued to enthusiastically denounce American lynchings until William McKay, a Presbyterian minister from Macon, Georgia, sent a letter to the editor accusing the *Spectator* of supporting Wells's campaign. "Credulity appears to be epidemic in England," he wrote, as "proved by the success of the Ida Wells Crusade, and the unmistakable evidence we have that any contradiction of her false statements will not be even considered. Your article about lynching," McKay admonished, "was evidently based upon this state of feeling, and your usually calm and considerate judgment of men and things was certainly under eclipse."[46]

Stung by allegations of bias and gullibility, the *Spectator* quickly backpedaled from its outspoken criticism. Quietly siding with Wells's facts, the *Spectator* stated that, "making every allowance for exaggeration and misrepresentation, there remains a substantial mass of testimony" that cannot be ignored. "The case for the outraged negro is a strong one." Nevertheless, the *Spectator*'s editor concluded that British interference in this American domestic issue was wholly unwarranted. Such a quick reversal suggests that had the *Spectator* been aware that American readers would view an editorial stance against lynching as support for Wells's campaigns, the editors would not have engaged so enthusiastically in the debate. Yet while the *Spectator* might have viewed Aked's article as deceptive, Wells's message had finally broken into mainstream British journals.[47]

Meanwhile, Wells also used her experience in journalism to cultivate editors of British newspapers. The press responded with renewed coverage of her activism and granted Wells her sought-after personal interviews. When she finally made her mark as a minor celebrity, it was as the public face of the antilynching movement. No longer hindered by her sponsors' heated conflict or forced to temper her rhetoric to appeal to Impey and Mayo's strict sense of propriety, Wells revealed herself as a strong and independent crusader.[48]

Wells seized the opportunity to direct her interviews to highlight the brutality of lynching. For the first time, British newspapers described Wells's accounts of the shocking cases of cruelty and torture committed by lynch mobs against women and children. She told of a woman wrongly accused of poisoning her employer who was "dragged out of gaol, every stitch of clothing torn from her body, and . . . hanged in the courthouse square in sight of everybody." A black man who refused to confess to the murder of a white man was forced to watch as a mob hanged first his son and then his young daughter. The ingenuity and cruelty of lynch mobs, she declared, "can scarcely be believed." In Texas, a "mob laid hold of" a woman accused of poisoning, "took a barrel into which they drove nails and spikes, thrust her in and fastened her in, then rolled the barrel down the hill. After half a mile of this rolling, the mob howling furiously after the barrel as it bumped down the hill and men vieing with each other to give it a kick as it rolled, they knocked it open again, dragged off the spikes a mass of ragged skin and bones and bloody clothes, hanged it—for there was little semblance to a human being then—upon a tree and shot it as it hung."[49]

Wells took a great risk by bringing the terrible reality of lynching into British homes through the pages of the morning newspapers. For a young, single woman of good standing to publicly recount such horrific stories was inherently scandalous. Even though the task sickened her, Wells insisted that she had no choice. "It is frightful," Wells admitted, "that I should have to discuss such things as these." But the dire state of American race relations compelled her to testify. "My people are being flayed, scourged, hanged, shot and burnt, and the sympathy of the world is being turned aside by the hideous charge that we are a bestial race, in whose presence womanhood is never safe, nor childhood sacred, that our men are unclean brutes, into whose vile nature even fire cannot burn respect for law, and shall I not tell the world the truth?" As long as American Christians remained silent, Wells believed, the moral power of Great Britain remained African Americans' last hope. "America will not listen to us. She despises us as an inferior race . . . But she will be obliged to listen to a nation which she owns as her equal, if not her superior."[50]

Wells's efforts gradually won the editorial support of an increasing number of British newspapers. After weighing her testimony, the *Bradford Observer* determined that "there seems to be nothing irrational or impossible in the plea that [African Americans] ought not to be branded and burned alive and rolled in nailed casks, or even hanged on a tree, at the whim and sport of a mob." The *Newcastle Daily Leader* sneered at America's "boasted forwardness in civilisation," which in reality amounted to a "chamber of horrors" for African Americans. The *Daily Chronicle* did not pull its punches in its denunciation of the South: "Race prejudice, and even a slight mixture of cruelty, is one thing; the horrible tortures, not only described by Miss Wells, but admitted and almost gloried in by the Southerners themselves, are quite another." Such actions "outrage the most elementary rights of humanity." "When we read of such atrocities," the editor concluded, "we ask ourselves whether the Southern States are really fitted for self-government." Such powerful declarations from British newspapers increased public sympathy for Wells's campaigns, brought her message to a wider British audience, and fostered the emerging transatlantic debate on lynching.[51]

Wells won the friendship and support of two influential London newspaper editors, A. E. Fletcher of the *Daily Chronicle* and Peter William Clayden of the *Daily News*. In the aftermath of the Henry Smith lynching, both editors had accepted American assertions that black criminality led to lynching. Although Fletcher and Clayden disapproved of the torture inflicted by the mob, the strength of the lynching for rape narrative had tempered their responses. Unwilling to attack lynching directly, they instead expressed their concern for the demoralizing effects of mob violence on the members of the white community.[52] By offering a more satisfying explanation of American mob violence, Wells persuaded both editors to adopt her interpretation of lynching as racist oppression; as a result, Wells secured two powerful allies in her struggle to stimulate a transatlantic debate on American lynching.

Wells's contention that lynching was a racist act of violent oppression used to maintain a system of white supremacy provided the moral justification Fletcher needed to freely attack lynching. He denounced the "cruel passions which have reached such a terrible climax in America." Reflecting the comments of midcentury British travelers, Fletcher viewed southern lynching as "a part of the brutal spirit prevailing throughout the South which manifests itself otherwise in duels and blood feuds." Granting Wells a lengthy personal interview, Fletcher highlighted the barbarity of lynching. He asked Wells about the possibility that Henry Smith had been guilty of the crime of which he had been accused. "Yes, suppose he were," Wells responded, but how could they be certain? At the very least, "try your criminal before you roast him."[53] Fletcher embraced Wells's argument, later proclaiming that even though "negroes are undoubtedly sometimes guilty of infuriating crimes . . . this does not remove in the slightest degree the overwhelming reproach which these recurrent horrors constitute for American civilisation."[54] Fletcher's remarks were reprinted in the *Chicago Inter-Ocean*, which employed Wells as a correspondent and closely followed her British antilynching campaign, and were thus brought to the attention of newspapers and social leaders throughout the United States.[55]

Although the *Daily News*, London's second-largest daily newspaper, provided detailed coverage of the antilynching resolutions proposed at the May Meetings, Clayden's greatest support for Wells came when his wife, Ellen, invited Wells to stay as a guest in their home and made their domestic staff available to assist in her campaign. The Claydens were well connected in London's Liberal nonconformist political and social reform circles; by hosting Wells, the Claydens granted her legitimacy within and increased her access to these circles. After each of her speaking engagements, they "purchased not less than one hundred copies of whichever paper had the best report. The next morning's work" in the Claydens' home "was to gather around the table in the breakfast room and mark and address these newspapers . . . to the president of the United States, the governors of most of the states in the Union, the leading ministers in the large cities, and the leading newspapers of the country."[56] Wells was a prolific speaker during her time in London and became the subject of numerous reports; over a short period of time, such a consistent barrage of British press clippings would have certainly increased American leaders' knowledge about Wells's activism.

As Wells moved through London's social reform circles, she began to attract the attention of British politicians. She was invited to visit the Houses of Parliament at Westminster twice, once for an interview with James Keir Hardie, founder of the Labour Party and editor of the *Labour Leader*, and later for a dinner sponsored by William Woodall, a member of Parliament and financial secretary of the War Department.[57] Before she left London, Wells was invited to a Parliamentary breakfast at the Westminster Palace Hotel sponsored by Sir Joseph Whitwell Pease, another member of Parliament and president of the London Peace Society.[58]

The growing currency of antilynching reform and Wells's passionate appeals for outside intervention inspired the formation of a second independent British antilynching organization, the London Anti-Lynching Committee, on June 5, 1894. Through letter-writing campaigns, the committee pressured American governors to investigate lynchings committed in their states. It also sent a delegation to the United States to investigate lynching and race relations. The committee attracted the support of several distinguished British gentlemen, including Woodall and Pease, Sir John Eldon Gorst, member of Parliament Justin McCarthy, philanthropist John Passmore Edwards, and George Douglass Campbell, the eighth Duke of Argyll. They were joined by Aked's cohort of liberal nonconformist clergy and several influential editors, including Fletcher and Clayden as well as William E. A. Axon (*Manchester Guardian*), Percy Bunting (*Contemporary Review*), and Sir Edward Russell (*Liverpool Daily Post*).[59]

Although most of the group's members had been drawn to the issue through her activism, the London Anti-Lynching Committee did not promote Wells's campaign directly or coordinate its actions with her original SRBM sponsors. Impey approached leaders of the London Anti-Lynching Committee shortly after its formation to discuss a possible merger, but although they were willing to maintain a friendly and cooperative relationship, they wanted to remain independent of Impey and Mayo's fractured organization. Nevertheless, the committee's activities provoked harsh rebukes from several American political leaders, including Alabama governor Thomas Goode Jones (1890–94) and Arkansas governor William Meade Fishback (1893–95). Undaunted, the committee continued pressuring American leaders to end lynching well into 1895.[60]

Wells's speeches also inspired local British communities to act. Members of London's Eccleston Square Church petitioned the U.S. ambassador to Great Britain, John Milton Hay, "to use his best efforts with the American authorities to put a stop to the terrible atrocities practised in the Southern States." The ambassador's private secretary, Lloyd C. Griscom, reassured the congregation that the ambassador "shares fully your abhorrence of cruelty and injustice in all its forms and everywhere, and will be very glad to use any influence he may possess to secure every human being a fair trial before condemnation or punishment."[61] Although the embassy's response was carefully worded to avoid singling out any particular section of the United States, an important American diplomat had officially taken a position against lynching. Such actions might appear small, but when combined with other local efforts, their cumulative power became substantial.

Wells was an astute campaigner. Although she could have severed her ties completely with the divided SRBM, she did not choose to do so. Rather than rely on its crippled national structure, she turned to the organization's local branches. The Bristol chapter provided funding for Wells's campaign, arranged a reception in her honor, and distributed more than one thousand copies of English newspaper articles critical of American lynching to influential persons throughout the United States. The West of England branch also donated funds to Wells's campaign and distributed more than eighteen thousand copies of *Fraternity*, the SRBM's official publication, worldwide. These branches' efforts ensured that American religious, social, and political leaders were aware that

Wells was receiving publicity in the British press, thereby applying a wide-spread, direct moral pressure that Wells could not have generated on her own.[62]

By the end of May 1894, British newspapers had begun to report on the American impact of Wells's campaign. According to the *Daily Chronicle*, "Miss Ida B. Wells, the young coloured lady who is conducting in England such a plucky campaign for the rescue of her people from the brutalities of the Southern States of America . . . seems to be accomplishing by her indirect attack what direct efforts have hitherto failed to effect." The editor was happy to announce that "some of the American papers have noticed the comments of the British Press with great magnanimity . . . Miss Wells may congratulate herself that her gallant efforts are already bearing this fruit, and that her words are already echoing from continent to continent." The *Anglo-American Times*, a British newspaper devoted to American issues, took notice in mid-June: "The role this coloured lady is playing is producing an effect in America." However, the editor warned, "Americans can never be persuaded that an ordinary gathering of Englishmen really understand and know anything about" the United States. As one incredulous American journal complained, "Judging by the resolutions adopted at some of her meetings, there are Englishmen who believe that Judge Lynch is a member of the Supreme Bench." Yet every American protest against English ignorance or interference demonstrated the power of British moral authority in American culture. Wells's supporters were passionate in their disapproval; one even pronounced, "Every time the blood of an untried coloured person flows the American flag is trailed along the dust of criminality." The American press and political leaders found it increasingly difficult to ignore the flood of condemnation that rose higher after each of Wells's speaking engagements.[63]

Wells's antilynching campaigns permanently altered the way in which the British public understood and discussed American lynching. Henceforth, British journalists discarded romantic notions of frontier justice and accepted Wells's assertions that lynching was a racially motivated act of violent oppression. By June 1894, even the conservative *Economist* concluded that "race hatred," not rape, remained at the heart of American lynching.[64] Perhaps the most impressive evidence that Wells's rhetorical arguments influenced the British public debate on lynching is the fact that several journals accepted the existence of consensual relationships between black men and white women and acknowledged the possibility that such relationships might lie at the heart of rape accusations in some cases of lynching. Of all Wells's assertions, this

was the most divisive, for it attacked the Victorian image of white women as
the embodiment of chastity and moral purity. Wells was acutely aware of the
power and volatility of this issue; after all, her editorial on precisely that topic
had prompted a furious Memphis mob to send her into exile. By repeating the
idea that such consensual relationships existed, the British press granted Wells
a major victory.[65]

Wells's second British antilynching campaign attracted a broad and influential base of support. Her alternative interpretation of lynching as a violent
form of racial oppression was widely adopted by the liberal British press and
began to shape British public discussions of lynching. Her supporters began
to focus their expressions of moral indignation on American social, religious,
and political leaders, and this outspoken British public disapproval made her
efforts increasingly difficult to ignore.

Chapter 5

AMERICAN RESPONSES

TO BRITISH PROTEST

Ida B. Wells's second British antilynching campaign initiated a far-reaching and contentious transatlantic debate on the issue of American lynching. British religious, social, and political leaders pressured their American counterparts to denounce lynching and mob violence. While some Americans accepted British criticism, many resented what they viewed as foreign interference with American domestic problems.

Southern leaders in particular felt the strain of British antilynching activism, in part because it disrupted their efforts to end mob violence in their states. Just as Texas governor James Hogg called for legislation to grant him the authority to prosecute the leaders of the Paris, Texas, mob in 1893, other progressive southern governors had pushed to rid their states of lynch law since the early 1890s, arguing that mob violence disrupted the smooth functioning of American society by reducing public respect for law enforcement. Their goals were prompted by a mixture of religious or moral objections to their constituents' participation in mob violence and a desire to promote the South's economic development to northern and European investors, who expected certain social, economic, and political standards. Although minor deviations might be forgiven, southern leaders needed to demonstrate the general respectability of their states to be treated as trusted business partners. As the pressure from British scrutiny increased, these moderate voices promoting "law and order" were quickly overshadowed by more incendiary rhetoric supporting the lynching for rape narrative. Seeing their efforts to stamp out mob violence unravel as their constituents rallied around white supremacist rhetoric in defense of lynching, southern leaders searched for ways to negate the impact of Wells's campaign. However, Wells's success at rallying a broad coalition of influential British supporters and the cultural divide between British and American discourses about lynching caused unexpected difficulty for white southerners in their attempts to control or redirect the lynching debate.

THE STRUGGLE FOR LAW AND ORDER
IN THE MIDST OF DEPRESSION

As the global economic crisis that became known as the Depression of 1893 developed, southern leaders struggled to balance domestic and international interests in an increasingly transnational society. When Wells's campaign elicited expressions of British moral outrage, the complex social, political, and economic landscape placed southern leaders in a difficult position—needing to uphold white supremacy yet simultaneously suppressing the mob violence it inspired to court outside investment.[1] After maintaining this precarious balance became untenable under British scrutiny, southern leaders were forced to choose whether to embrace the rhetoric of white supremacy to please their white constituents, seek to impose law and order to reassure prospective international investors, or generate a viable strategy to abrogate Wells's campaign.

Protecting the South's national and international reputation became an important priority for southern leaders intent on courting potential investors. Following the devastation of the Civil War and the social and political upheaval of Reconstruction, southern politicians hoped not only to transform the South's economy but also to restore traditional race, class, and gender hierarchies by embracing white supremacy. "New South" leaders sought to move away from dependence on cotton exports to develop diversified agricultural and industrial centers fully integrated into transatlantic markets. The efforts of southern politicians and businessmen took on a new sense of urgency after widespread agricultural failures in the late 1880s thrust the South into yet another economic decline, several years ahead of the rest of the nation. Even without wartime losses, the South's infrastructure had lagged far behind that of the North and Midwest. Southern leaders believed that the key to the South's development lay in attracting outside investment for infrastructural improvements and industrial production, including the creation of new railroads, textile mills, and mines, as well as tempting desirable immigrants to move to the South.[2]

The need to cultivate investment capital placed Georgia's William J. Northen (1890–94) and other New South governors in a difficult position. Like much of the rest of the region, Georgia desperately needed to attract investment capital from the Atlantic economy that integrated Atlanta markets with those of Bristol, Birmingham, Liverpool, and London.[3] As the global panic and Depression of 1893 took hold, the pool of available capital shrunk precipitously, dramatically increasing the competition for investors. British capital, which accounted for approximately three-fourths of all foreign investment in the United States, evaporated as new capital issues dropped by two-thirds during the height of the economic crisis.[4] With fewer resources to invest, British businessmen might perceive the region as a high-risk investment unless southern communities could demonstrate their ability to maintain law and order. Without renewed British investment, southern economic recovery would continue to lag behind the rest of the nation.

Recognizing that mob violence was bad for business, Northen worked to suppress lynching throughout his tenure as Georgia's governor. His attempts to curb lynching formed part of a broader vision for economic development. From his first gubernatorial address, Northen sought to make his state more desirable to outside investors via an improved public school system, property protection for individuals and corporations, and more rapid convictions in the criminal justice system to reduce mob violence.[5] He offered substantial rewards for the arrest and conviction of lynch mob participants, pressured local sheriffs to defend prisoners against mob attacks, and pushed for legislation to hold local law enforcement officials accountable for the safety and security of their jails. The *Elbert County Star* endorsed Northen's antilynching stance, arguing, "Capital that has been invested in land in Georgia is quietly being withdrawn from the state" as a consequence of the prevalence of lynching. "The laws of God, morality and peace are against it," but that had not been enough to end lynching. In an "appeal to our common sense and interests," the editor believed it was "for the good of the community and the county and the country at large to listen to the sage advice of our Christian governor."[6] While Northen's program was politically popular and won editorial support, it met with little practical success, for Georgia communities remained unwilling to break the wall of silence that shielded lynchers from prosecution.

Finding monetary rewards ineffective in reducing the frequency of mob violence, Northen proposed antilynching legislation modeled after the resourceful and determined efforts of Montgomery County sheriff George W. Dunham. Dunham had prevented the lynching of three black men accused of murder by enlisting the assistance of a conference of Methodist ministers to calm the growing mob, lodging the prisoners in a distant jail, arranging for a special session of court, and convincing a train engineer to skip the stop at the victim's hometown when transporting the prisoners to trial. While other progressive southern governors dispatched the state militia to protect prisoners in communities threatened by mob violence, Northen refused Dunham's requests for state assistance in hopes that his success would set a new standard for all local law enforcement officials. If the accused prisoners were brought to trial, convicted, and legally executed, Dunham could be held up as a role model throughout the South. If "outrages against society" were consistently met with "certain punishment," Northen contended, it might "satisfy the people that justice will be meted out by the courts," giving them the confidence to "remand into the hands of the law the punishment for crimes and thereby destroy all possible excuse for mob violence and awful lynchings in this state." Dunham succeeded, and Northen commended the sheriff for his "courageous and determined purpose in the enforcement of the law."[7]

Ironically, the possibility that the accused might be innocent of the charges never entered into Northen's deliberations. Northen, like many southern leaders, attempted to maintain law and order by encouraging perfunctory trials to record legal convictions of black defendants quickly followed by executions. Giving juries of white men the power to put black defendants to death seriously blurred the line between lynching and legal execution, in effect replacing mob violence with judicial murder (a tactic famously dubbed "legal lynching" by the International Labor Defense during the Scottsboro trials of the 1930s).[8]

On December 19, 1893, the Georgia Assembly passed the Act to Prevent Mob Violence. Establishing law enforcement officials' duty to protect prisoners and arrest mob participants, the new legislation permitted the use of deadly force in upholding the law. It authorized sheriffs to summon local citizens to assist in the defense of prisoners and made participation in a lynch mob a felony. The act also prescribed criminal penalties for sheriffs and deputized citizens who neglected to perform their duties.[9] Armed with a tough legal statute against lynching based on a proven model, Northen was ready to defend Georgia's image and lobby for foreign capital and immigration.

Other New South governors embraced similar law-and-order platforms to encourage outside investment. Alabama governor Thomas Goode Jones (1890–94) denounced lynching as a stain on Alabama's honor "and a great obstacle to our healthy progress and prosperity."[10] In his inaugural address, Jones argued that the maintenance of a state militia was essential: "Labor will not work, nor capital invest," he warned, "unless the laws are enforced and the peace assured." Moreover, when local authorities could not maintain the peace, Jones believed that they had a duty to call in the state militia. He praised the citizen-soldiers who offered "themselves a living sacrifice if need be against lawless commotion and violence."[11]

Like Northen, Jones believed that to suppress lynching, local sheriffs must be determined to defend their jails. While a colonel in the Alabama National Guard, Jones had vigorously protected the Birmingham jail against a drunken angry mob, and he had no sympathy for the "cowardice" of local sheriffs who refused to use force of arms to defend their prisoners.[12] When lynchings did occur, Jones investigated the circumstances, pressuring local sheriffs to explain their failure to safeguard their prisoners or request help from the state. In 1893, Jones even hired the famous Pinkerton Detective Agency to investigate when Pickens County sheriff J. T. Hamiter could not provide a satisfactory explanation for the lynching of three black men taken from his custody in the Carrollton jail.[13]

Similarly, Governor Charles T. O'Ferrall (1894–98) led the charge against lynching in Virginia by pressuring local officials to forestall lynchings and dispatching state militia units to areas threatened by mob violence. Elected shortly after an 1893 lynching riot in Roanoke left eight people dead and at least twenty-five wounded after clashes with the state militia, O'Ferrall was determined to prevent further incidents of lawlessness from disgracing the state. Shortly after taking office, he sent troops to Manassas at the request of the local sheriff, J. P. Leachman, to prevent the threatened lynching of James Robinson and Ben White in February 1894. O'Ferrall called out the militia again two months later to parade in front of the Staunton opera house at the request of Sheriff N. C. Watts to deter the lynching of Lawrence Spiller, a black man accused of raping and murdering a white girl. In both cases, armed soldiers ensured that the accused survived to stand a brief trial followed by a conviction and legal execution. Many southern governors saw such speedy "justice" as the only viable remedy for lynch law, for if conviction and execution were deemed certain, communities would have no reason to take the law into their own hands and financiers might have confidence in the security of their southern investments.[14]

In exchange for infrastructural and industrial investment, southern states promised to provide a steady supply of labor. The wave of violent strikes that stretched from Coeur d'Alene, Idaho, to Homestead, Pennsylvania, in 1892 had demonstrated the potential investment risks associated with organized labor. Southern leaders hoped to compete against the industrialized North and the rich mineral resources of the West by offering investors something those regions struggled to provide: a cheap, cooperative, English-speaking labor force to support new railroads, mines, and factories. The southern system of white supremacy could be used to discourage labor organization and biracial coalitions, limit Populist Party political challenges to the status quo, and reinforce strict class, race, and gender boundaries. When the southern racial hierarchy was challenged by successful African Americans such as the owners of the People's Grocery Company in Memphis, communities could use lynching to buttress white supremacy. The potential social, political, and economic benefits derived from white supremacy were considerable; nevertheless, its violent manifestation in the form of lynch law undermined legal protections for personal and property rights and risked deterring potential immigrants and investors. Therefore, southern leaders sought to suppress mob violence through appeals for law and order that remained largely uncritical of the white supremacist system.[15]

Since poverty, poor educational opportunities, rural isolation, and racial discrimination confined most African Americans to agricultural and domestic work, southern states sought to secure their industrial labor force by attracting northern white migrants and Western European immigrants. As with other indicators of development, the South lagged far behind other regions in attracting immigrants. Although the South accounted for approximately 30 percent of the national population, it housed less than 6 percent of the foreign-born population. New York alone attracted nearly three times as many immigrants as the fifteen southern states combined.[16] Given the widespread ethnic conflicts and labor strife plaguing the major immigrant centers of the North and West, British immigrants were highly valued for their ability to assimilate easily into America's largely Protestant, English-speaking society. Yet the supply of British immigrants contracted during the Depression of 1893–97. As the total number of immigrants dropped by more than half at the height of the depression, the proportion of British immigrants fell from approximately one in five before 1890 to less than one in twelve by 1894.[17] The southern states were locked in fierce competition with northern industrial centers and western mining and agricultural regions for British investment capital and immigrant laborers.[18]

As British reformers and newspapers increasingly turned their attention to the problem of lynching, New South governors and other advocates of southern immigration and investment began to fear the economic consequences of Wells's campaign. By casting the South as a lawless, violent, and uncivilized region, Wells might deter potential investors and discourage new arrivals.

As the *Christian Register* warned, "People will refuse to invest capital and to live in a country in which there is no adequate protection by law for life and property."[19] But beyond concerns that a violent reputation might frighten off squeamish investors, the black citizens of Memphis had demonstrated in the wake of the People's Grocery Company lynching that economic boycotts and selective migration could be effective tools in the campaign against mob violence. Wells advocated withholding capital and labor from the South to force American communities to end lynching because, as she cynically observed, appeals "to the white man's pocket" have "been more effectual than all the appeals ever made to his conscience."[20] The severe economic depression had already prompted migration out of rural southern districts and dramatically increased national competition for the limited pool of available investment capital; a black exodus from Memphis and other growing New South cities could cripple their economies. Recognizing that "the South owes its rehabilitation" to "Northern capital and Afro-American labour," Wells speculated that without a steady supply of labor, outside investment capital would be withdrawn and the South's economy would collapse.[21] As Wells's campaign gained momentum and she increasingly won the support of liberal British newspaper editors, the potential impact of British antilynching sentiment on the South's economy became a palpable threat.

Rumors circulated of a conspiracy launched by western land developers to use "the colored problem" to direct capital and immigration away from the South. As one visiting Englishman reportedly explained, "The excitement of immigration has to be kept up, or values will tumble... Immigration must not be diverted south, or anywhere else, until those interests in the west shall have saved themselves." Governor Northen feared that capitalist consortiums employed speakers such as Wells to turn people against the South. "The business of slandering the southern people, of impeaching their civilization," was, according to Northen, well organized. "Innocent, but meddlesome, people," Northen claimed, were lured together to hear a speaker. Resolutions were typed in advance and "a couple of talkative men primed to second them" so that they could be "passed with a rush" and sent out the same night. "By a curious coincidence," their recipients also "received by the same mail gorgeously printed maps and circulars describing the west as home for intending emigrants."[22] Northen bemoaned how such "malicious attacks upon the south" surfaced "whenever an effort is made to attract the attention of the world to the superior advantages of these southern states."[23]

No direct connections between Wells and her supporters with western land

developers have surfaced. However, J. L. Fleming, Wells's former coeditor, who
had been assaulted and driven out of Memphis in response to her editorial on
lynching, worked for an organization that promoted African American migration out of the South. After relocating the *Free Speech* to Chicago, Fleming became secretary of the North-Western Emigration Association, which catered
to African American emigrants interested in "more favorable opportunities"
in the North and West.[24] Lynch law remained a liability for southern leaders
as long as African Americans were willing to vote with their feet. Although focusing on conspiracy theories might have been easier and perhaps more satisfying than addressing the practical realities of lynching, southern leaders were
nevertheless forced to confront Wells's campaign if they hoped to reverse these
trends and win desirable immigrants and corporate investors in an increasingly competitive international market.

As British moral indignation against American lynching increased, white
southerners rallied around their belief in the white supremacist rhetoric associated with the lynching for rape narrative. That narrative so thoroughly
infused American debates on lynching that even Northen, Jones, and other
governors who held strong moral convictions against mob violence could not
allow themselves to consider Wells's assertions that lynching was a racist act of
violent oppression. Consequently, British public scrutiny made it increasingly
difficult for southern governors to advocate their law-and-order campaigns
to replace mob violence with a system of accelerated due process. Needing to
demonstrate the stability and security of their states to court desperately required outside capital in a tight international market while also maintaining
political power in the face of Populist Party challenges during a volatile election year, southern governors were left with an impossible choice: appear to
support lynching by embracing the rhetoric of white supremacy to curry favor
with their white constituents, thus alienating potential investors, or risk appearing to support Wells's campaign by continuing their law-and-order campaigns to reassure investors, thus alienating their white constituents. Southern
leaders quickly recognized that their only viable option was to find an effective
way to neutralize Wells's campaign in Britain.

THE AMERICAN BACKLASH

Through mass mailings of favorable British newspaper reports, Wells's British supporters efficiently promoted her to American leaders as the public
face of the transatlantic antilynching movement. Therefore, white southern-

ers initially focused their energies on attacking and discrediting Wells. If they could undermine her legitimacy, they might be able to avoid directly addressing Wells's critique of lynching. However, white southerners found it difficult to insert their voices into British public debates on American lynching. Conservative British publications such as *The Times* that had ignored Wells's campaign likewise ignored debates about the merits of her assertions. Consequently, most lynching apologists submitted rebuttals to the publications that expressed support for and publicized her campaign. This tactic met with little success for a number of reasons: the antilynching biases of British editors, strict British libel laws, and the strength of Wells's evidence and narrative, which made her detractors' claims unappealing to these sympathetic British publications.

Wells was skilled at cultivating relationships with British editors. Most of the newspapers that publicized her campaign and denounced lynching were run by editors who joined the London Anti-Lynching Committee or had close ties to Charles Aked.[25] Consequently, they were unlikely to be persuaded to print responses that attacked Wells's character, misrepresented her assertions, or attempted to defend mob violence without engaging with her socioeconomic critique of lynching's role in southern society.

The *Christian World*, Britain's leading ecumenical religious publication and one of the strongest supporters of Wells's campaign, became one of the prime targets for her American opponents. After the paper published an interview in which Wells repeated her assertion that some instances of supposed rape were in reality consensual affairs between white women and black men, the Virginia Baptist Preachers' Association appointed the Reverend J. J. Hall to write a response to these "grossly false," "infamous," and "reckless" accusations. Hall contended that lynchings were direct responses to the sexual assault of white women by black men, refusing to concede that black men (and women) were lynched for a variety of reasons. Because he insisted that all black men who were lynched were rapists, he could not comprehend Wells's statements: "I had fully believed that the terrible crime committed by" the victims of the mob was "committed by the most ignorant and depraved of her race, but if what she says be true I am mistaken, and it comes from those who are 'advancing in intelligence and position.'" Incredulous that any white women could or would choose to have relationships with black men, Hall continued to interpret Wells's statements through the lens of the lynching for rape scenario: "'These who outrage with a fiendish delight the virtue of women, caring not for age or condition, these becoming attractive to the white women of the South!' Horrible! And as false as it is horrible!" Hall sympathized with southerners who believed "lynching is an evil," but he maintained that "the very worst evil under the sun is the ruin of pure little girls by black demons." The only solution, he insisted, was to end rape by black men: "Let this evil stop and there will be no more lynching for it."[26]

The *Christian World* consistently refused to print rebuttals from lynching apologists. Hall's letter to the editor was declined without comment, "as all articles have been by that paper denying the slanders against the South."[27] "Similar communications from Governor Northen, of Georgia, and Governor [John Marshall] Stone, of Mississippi," Hall reported, "were similarly treated."[28] An Englishman by birth whose family continued to live in London, Hall believed himself an objective observer and took exception to being dismissed by the British press in the same manner as southern-born writers. "Having lived in the country of my birth (England) twenty-one years, and in the North fifteen years," Hall did not believe he was unduly "prejudiced in favor of the South." He had arrived at his position after spending "several months in gathering information" about the lynching of African Americans and the attitudes of southern social, political, and religious leaders toward mob violence. Hall insisted that he had found "abundant proof" to support "every statement" in his article defending the practice of lynching.[29] As with most protests from lynching apologists, however, Hall's lengthy response found a more eager audience in the United States, where the article was printed in full by the *Norfolk (Virginia) Landmark. In London, the Christian Commonwealth* finally agreed to print a synopsis of Hall's article after the persistent lobbying of his father, S. Hall Sr., but for the most part, white southerners' responses did not appear in Britain and consequently had little influence there.[30]

Armed with antilynching legislation, countless press clippings about mob violence in the North, and a vigorous personal disdain for outside critics, Governor Northen prepared to battle with the press to promote Georgia's economic potential to the world. He directed his first attack at "these people up north" who "keep hammering at us about the lawlessness at the South, and I expect to continue replying... by pouring some of their own rot into their own stomachs."[31] In April 1894, Samuel J. Barrows, editor of the *Christian Register*, invited Northen to respond to the antilynching resolution from Richard Acland Armstrong's Hope Street Church in Liverpool, which the Boston publication had endorsed. Northen used the opportunity to question Wells's credibility and highlight recent cases of lynching and mob violence in the North. According to Northen, the North's record of mob violence was far worse than that of the South because labor riots resulted in countless deaths, while "in lynching only one man is murderously killed."[32] Placing both regions on an equally immoral plane yet painting the South as a land of harmonious labor relations, Northen tried to tempt businessmen who were tired of strikes and riots to move away from the North and invest in Georgia.

Northen's response to the *Christian Register* won public and private accolades. One Georgia editor praised Northen's "Masterly Defense" of the South as the crowning achievement of "the best Governor that the state of Georgia ever had." The editor asserted that "nothing before has ever been said or published that so completely answered the implied charge that the white people of the South were not as good and as just in their treatment of the negro as the white people of the [North]." W. P. Turner, a Methodist Episcopal Church, South, missionary working in Japan, wrote to Northen, "There ought to be a million copies of your letter printed in pamphlet form and sent to every preacher and editor in the North and in England. It would be worth more to the South and to Georgia especially, than all the efforts of the combined Governors of the South to invite capital and immigration."[33]

Pleased with the reception of his tirade and encouraged by his friends, Northen produced a pamphlet, *The Negro at the South: Letters by Gov. W. J. Northen*, containing the unedited text of letters addressed to the *Christian Register* and *Home Mission Monthly*; he distributed the pamphlet to sympathetic newspaper editors and religious leaders. Turner requested several copies so that he might educate an English newspaper editor in Japan whose publications were trying his patience.[34] Frustrated by outside criticism of the South, Northen wrote to encourage a sympathetic minister to review his *Home Mission Monthly* response in a Baltimore newspaper. It was time, he believed, to "take these people by the napes of their necks and shake them a little to let them know that we have some little resistance." He hoped that his actions would initiate a southern backlash that might quell outside criticism. If more people would "take up the fight that has been begun, I think we can at least put them at some disadvantage."[35]

Encouraged by the success of his *Christian Register* article, Northen decided to confront Wells's British supporters. In response to an editorial and interview with Wells published on April 28, 1894, Northen wrote an indignant letter to the editor of the *Daily Chronicle*, who had asserted, "It would need a firm upright Governor in any Southern State to protect a coloured man" from lynching where public sentiment favored mob violence. This time, rather than push his recent record for reform or highlight the North's immorality,

Northen chose simply to attack Wells's credibility. He argued that the British press should obtain information from a "more generally accepted authority" than Wells's testimony and denied accusations that the people of the South were "unduly brutal and cruel above all nations."[36]

Even when southern leaders inserted their voices into the British debate, the substance of their message was not guaranteed to be published. For example, Northen's letter to the editor of the *Daily Chronicle* could not be printed in its entirety without violating British libel laws. While many newspapers might have edited Northen's letter without comment, A. E. Fletcher used the incident to reemphasize the *Daily Chronicle*'s denunciation of lynching. In an editorial note, Fletcher explained to his readers that he had been forced to remove "one brief paragraph" from Northen's letter. Out of deference to the governor's office, Fletcher rationalized Northen's inappropriate language by noting that English libel law differed significantly from Georgia's. Nevertheless, by gently highlighting the disrespectful behavior of an esteemed southern gentleman toward a lady of color, Fletcher reinforced for his readers Wells's assertions that the underlying race hatred that perpetuated lynching had permeated all levels of American society. Thus, although Northen's voice broke into the British debate, his words ultimately did not carry the meaning he intended.[37]

In the United States, where her race precluded her from being considered a lady, Wells remained vulnerable to vitriolic published attacks on her character. Confident that Wells had no effective legal recourse against him, W. D. Robinson, managing editor of the *Memphis Commercial*, distributed a letter attacking her character and credibility to newspapers throughout the United States and Great Britain. Claiming Wells was the "paramour" of her coeditor and "a notorious woman of ill-repute," the *Memphis Commercial* "repeatedly denounced her, and invited her to sue for libel ... in any State she sees fit." Robinson insisted that Wells must be guilty of these transgressions because "she has never dared to bring the suit."[38]

Wells had good reason not to pursue the lawsuit. She had attempted to sue the *Memphis Commercial* for libel after it made similar attacks in 1893 but abandoned her claim when it became clear that her race made her unlikely to win the court's sympathy. In the decade since her civil suit against the Chesapeake, Ohio, and Southwestern Railroad, the attitudes of southern courts had hardened in favor of codified segregation. Although black women continued to struggle against the constraints of Jim Crow, they found it increasingly difficult to demand the right to be considered ladies. A failed libel suit, which would have been interpreted by the public as official confirmation of Wells's immorality, would have been significantly more damaging than even the worst unsubstantiated accusations. As Wells explained to British readers, American courts refused to punish editors for "gross libels" when "directed against a negro."[39] Although the letter of the law granted African Americans equal protection, American judges consistently dismissed the claims of black plaintiffs in favor of white defendants. Moreover, the necessity of combating racist stereotypes that portrayed black women as inherently hypersexual beings placed an undue burden of proof on black female plaintiffs.

In Britain, however, strict libel laws deterred editors from publishing anything that might impugn the character of respectable men and women. Libel laws were also more likely to be applied equally to persons of color. The editor of the *Daily Chronicle* quietly rebuked Northen for his attack on Wells, explaining that Christian men of honor "should not permit themselves to attribute unworthy and sordid motives to a young negress who comes to this country to plead for her unfortunate fellow countrymen."[40] Wells's position as a black lady reformer granted her a higher degree of social and legal protection in Britain than she possessed in the United States. Consequently, American responses containing unsubstantiated attacks on Wells's character or the use of derogatory racial stereotypes and slurs were unlikely to be reprinted by any British newspaper, even those strongly opposed to her campaign.

Wells viewed Northen's attacks on her character as a victory for her campaign, claiming, "Outside agitation has done some good even in the South, when the governor of the great State of Georgia comes forward to defend her."[41] The attempts by Northen, Hall, and other white southerners to neutralize British antilynching sentiment by attacking Wells's character certainly demonstrate the importance of British public opinion and the dynamic nature of the transatlantic debate sparked by her campaign. Unable to undermine Wells's credibility, white southerners struggled to find an effective way to influence the British press.

Southern leaders were shut out of British public debates in part because they could not conceive of lynching in terms other than the lynching for rape narrative. Exposed to that narrative for considerably longer than British audiences, many Americans had internalized assertions made by lynching apologists that extralegal violence was necessary for the protection of white women. Pro-lynching advocates such as Rebecca Latimer Felton even demanded that southern white men defend the honor of white women through lynching.[42] As British antilynching sentiment grew, American debates on lynching increasingly privileged the tenets of the lynching for rape narrative. In a November 1894 survey of prominent southern religious, social, and political leaders, John Franklin Crowell, former president of Trinity College (later Duke University) in Durham, North Carolina, sought to determine the socioeconomic factors that contributed to the perpetuation of lynching as part of his graduate study in the sociology department at Columbia University. Instead of answering his questions about the impact of industrialization, deficiencies in the justice system, population change, and lingering social tensions from the Civil War and Reconstruction, however, his respondents repeatedly commented that the crime of rape was the single-most-important precipitating cause of lynching. Complained the Reverend Collins Denny, professor of mental and moral philosophy at Vanderbilt University, "I find I cannot give answers satisfactory to myself to the questions you ask, & I do not believe the answers I could give would be helpful to you. . . . [T]his leaves out of account the cause, & to my great surprise nearly all who touch this question ignore or deny the cause. Rape must cease, & then lynching will cease. Have you thought about studying 'Rape' as well as 'Lynching'?"[43]

Time and again, Crowell's respondents reiterated the lynching for rape scenario. Hall declared emphatically that "the cause of lynching is the *crime* which invokes it. Let that cease and there will be little or no lynching." Even Governor Northen insisted that Georgia "had no lynching at first except for rape." The Reverend E. E. Hoss, editor of the *Nashville Christian Advocate*, confirmed "that the spirit of mob law is kept alive by the one crime of rape. If that crime were ended, it would be easy to suppress the mob." But while rape "continues to be practised, the mob will maintain a more or less vigorous existence, & will punish men for other offenses also, such as house-burning or murder." According to Crowell's informants, lynching could not be eliminated until rape ceased to exist; nevertheless, as long as lynching existed, it might also be used to punish other crimes.[44] There was simply no longer room for law-and-order appeals amid the tensions created by British antilynching activism.

Despite sympathy for emotional appeals on behalf of victims of sexual assault by white southerners, British newspaper editors found Wells's statistical evidence more convincing. Wells had deliberately sought to complicate white southerners' task of refuting her claims by gathering her examples from white American newspapers. Furthermore, Wells's evidence lent credence to her assertions that the supposed chivalry of the lynching for rape narrative did not extend to the countless black victims of white rapists. Lynching was justified under the lynching for rape narrative as a chivalrous method for protecting white female victims of rape from the humiliation of facing their attackers and testifying in open court. The image of a white woman publicly confronting a black man who had raped her was particularly troubling for a society dedicated to keeping white women and black men separate at all costs. As Denny explained, "Almost always the only legal evidence [in rape cases] is in the keeping of the woman," who "has suffered bodily and mentally from the assault." White southerners simply would not permit white rape victims to be subjected "to the ordeal of cross examination," especially when it was "publicly conducted." Therefore, lynching could be defended by southern leaders as a necessary if regrettable evil because it presented the only viable way to punish rapists. If the crime of rape, not racism, was the true cause of lynching, Wells claimed, such acts of community justice would have been extended to defend the honor and virtue of all women—white and black alike. Instead, white southerners employed lynching only to reinforce white supremacy, denying black women the right to be considered worthy of protection from assault.[45] Finding Wells's evidence unimpeachable and her lynching as racist violence narrative more satisfying than the explanations offered by white southerners, the *Christian World, Daily Chronicle, and other British publications* had no reason to print rebuttals based on counterfactual assertions about the underlying causes of lynching. White southern opponents of Wells's campaign needed to employ new tactics if they hoped to participate in the British debate.

On the whole, British newspapers and journals printed only a small portion of the correspondence they received. British expatriates generally found it easier to break into the British debate on American lynching than did southern-born correspondents. The editor of the *Spectator*, Meredith White Townsend, published letters to the editor expressing a variety of opinions, but he privileged only British voices in the debate on lynching. On one occasion, the *Spectator* printed a letter from a correspondent claiming to represent "the few Englishmen resident in the country districts of this thinly settled State of Tennessee." Although the author insisted that he did not want to defend the practice of lynching, he sympathized with white southerners who believed "that the negro is not a human being in the same sense as the white man." Like many lynching apologists, he ignored the role white southerners played in maintaining the social, political, educational, and economic disadvantages African Americans faced, blaming the black community's failure to thrive on African Americans' inherent inferiority. "For nearly thirty years," he insisted, African Americans had "every opportunity" to improve themselves, but they had "signally failed to do so." According to the correspondent, African Americans remained "constitutionally dishonest, hopelessly lazy, and devoid of any idea of sexual morality." Without firsthand experience of the challenges white southerners faced in maintaining control over the black population, the correspondent believed Britons had no right to chastise.[46]

Even though he strongly disagreed with its contents, Townsend printed the letter, but he added his own editorial comment: "Our correspondent misses the point. Nobody argues that inferior races may not need severe disciplinary laws," but "they should be tried . . . heard in their own defence, and . . . convicted by Judges who intend to be *impartial*."[47] The *Spectator* viewed lynching as an unnecessary and demoralizing disruption to American social order. White Americans controlled the legal and political systems; therefore, they had the power to impose whatever legal punishments they deemed necessary and had no reason to fear that any guilty black criminal would escape conviction. "Lynching in the South is not the infliction of capital punishment on guilty persons," argued the *Spectator*, "it is the infliction of capital punishment on people whose guilt is still unascertained and who, therefore, may easily be innocent." The cruelty of American lynch mobs toward black men also disturbed the *Spectator*: "Race-hatred, apparently, blinds the white population alike to the wickedness and to the mischief of their actions. Their treatment of the accused negro would be brutal if the victim were not a man, but a dangerous wild beast."[48] The *Spectator* was willing to print dissenting opinions from British authors but answered them with editorial notes that contradicted the correspondents' assertions and reinforced the publication's stance against lynching.[49]

Failing to undermine Wells's credibility or win British sympathy and taking a cue from the 1893 Bakersville hoax, opponents of Wells's campaign attempted to deny the authenticity of particularly gruesome lynching reports circulating in British publications. One such attempt was made by the Reverend William McKay of Macon, Georgia, an Englishman who had moved from Manchester to the United States to do business as a cotton exporter. McKay reportedly "had a perfectly awful experience in 'Reconstruction' times." He attributed his business ventures' failure to the "impossibility of getting the blacks to work." Frustrated, McKay abandoned the cotton industry to pursue accounting and a ministry in the Presbyterian Church. Decades later, he still resented black laborers for failing to perform faithful service for his business. A regular reader of the *Christian World*, McKay would have been aware of Wells's campaign and the support it was gaining in Britain.[50] Upset by the *Spectator*'s harsh denunciation of a Georgia lynching in which the mob's victim was reportedly skinned alive, McKay sent a copy of the *Spectator* article to Northen.

The governor launched an investigation, and the alleged skinning was swiftly denied. Declared a work of "pure fiction" spread by "an imaginative young man at Waycross, who poses as a press correspondent," the "unauthenticated rumor" was picked up by the Reuters News Service and quickly spread overseas. McKay denounced the *Spectator*'s antilynching stance as evidence that it had been duped by the "Ida Wells Crusade." He also claimed that a "similar story was recently on record as having occurred in a Western State, but this also was denied by the Governor of that State, and denounced as a canard." McKay challenged the veracity of various examples recounted by Wells in her campaign: "The woman rolled in a barrel stuck full of nails, and the lynching of women and children, are exactly on a par with this Georgia skinning."[51]

Even though McKay's letter helped to convince the *Spectator*'s editor that British antilynching activism was unwelcome, he refused to modify his stance. The *Spectator* was "very glad to have this contradiction" and hoped that it was "absolutely true," but "American correspondents" were responsible for "supply[ing] this false information to the English newspapers." If McKay wanted to place blame for the perpetuation of such negative images of the South, he needed to look closer to home. Ignoring the implication that southerners were responsible for the images they presented to the outside world, the *Atlanta Constitution* later reported this exchange as an important victory for Governor Northen.[52]

British correspondents weighed in on McKay's tactic. The next issue of the *Spectator* printed a rebuttal from the Reverend S. Alfred Steinthal, sponsor of an antilynching resolution at the National Triennial Conference of Unitarians and a supporter of Wells's campaign: "Every one who had taken part in what Mr. McKay . . . calls 'the Ida Wells Crusade' . . . will rejoice in the official contradiction of such horrors as the skinning of a negro, or the rolling of a woman in a barrel stuck full of nails; but Mr. McKay gives us no evidence of the latter atrocity being an invention. He seems to wish us to doubt the common occurrence of lynching because one statement, made not on Miss Wells' authority, but that of Reuter, is contradicted."[53] A later correspondent concurred that "the inference to be drawn from the spirit of [McKay's] letter seemed to be that not only was that particular story a fable, but all such stories alike fables, and this is quite incorrect. Surely no one has yet forgotten the Paris-Texas affair, and many of the same kind!" Even if the Georgia skinning could be discredited, American mobs had committed other confirmed acts of unimaginable brutality that constituted "a national disgrace."[54]

If American lynching apologists wished to question the veracity of these lynching stories, they risked opening all lynching reports to scrutiny. This was a dangerous ploy. The validity of American lynching narratives, from frontier justice to the lynching for rape scenario, was predicated on the assumption that newspaper reports were reliable. When lynching apologists claimed that some American lynching reports were fabrications, they helped strengthen Wells's assertions that the American press invented rape accusations to justify lynchings of black men.

British lynching opponents were quick to point out the contradictions of lynching apologists. When an American woman, Elizabeth L. Banks, claimed in the *Sun* "that fully one-half the reported lynchings are purely imaginary," two incredulous rebuttals appeared in the London newspaper within three days. "If all the newspaper reports of lynchings are untrue," insisted Philip C. Ivens, "more shame to the American press, which circulates such calumnies against its own country." However, he continued, "I notice that Miss Banks admits that lynching does occur in the States." Ivens believed that all extralegal punishment was worthy of reproach because it denied due process to its victims, so he needed only this admission to continue to denounce lynching. Banks's attempt to defend lynching as an honorable expression of southern chivalry did not resonate with Ivens, who noted that "even the Inquisition gave a man some sort of a trial, and an opportunity to clear himself of an accusation, but 'Southern Chivalry' evidently does not see the necessity of giving a nigger a fair trial." Britons, he observed, had not found it "necessary to burn negroes alive to ensure due protection to white women," even in colonies with majority-black populations. Lynching's sole accomplishment was to inflict "the most dreadful tortures on men who may be quite innocent of any crime."[55]

Furthermore, British correspondents rejected Banks's "sweeping assertion" that half of all lynching reports were fabricated. As George Shute pointed out, "It is not likely that the responsible newspapers of the chief cities of such States as Tennessee, Georgia, South Carolina, Alabama, and Louisiana should have published full details of the revolting cruelties committed if they had not really happened." He continued, "If it could have been maintained that fully one-half of the reported lynchings were not facts, our countrymen would have been precisely and repeatedly assured of it upon the most indubitable authority."[56] Thus, questioning Wells's veracity proved ineffective. White southerners needed to find another way to neutralize her campaign.

The formation of a new British organization during the summer of 1894 provided southern leaders with a welcome opportunity to attack British antilynching activism without appearing openly to support mob violence or needing to devise a compelling response to Wells's rhetoric. The London Anti-Lynching Committee pressured American political leaders, particularly state governors, to investigate reported lynchings by attempting to shame them into taking action against these "outrages ... whose inhumanity, lawlessness, and cowardice cannot fail to compromise the reputation of Americans generally."[57] Committee members included prominent British politicians and social reformers such as the Duke of Argyll; former abolitionists Moncure D. Conway and Eliza Wigham; Welsh Home Rule advocate and Liberal Party Whip T. E. Ellis; historian and law professor Frederic Harrison; Irish Home Rule advocate Justin McCarthy; the first Asian member of Parliament, Dadabhai Naoroji; and educational reformer Professor James Stuart. Their influence was instrumental in the tactic's success. By focusing on the immorality of lynching and the disgrace such outrages brought—or should bring—on American communities rather than attacking the underlying causes of lynching, the committee divorced British antilynching activism from Wells's critique of southern race relations and made committee members' moral authority a central part of the debate.[58]

The *Spectator* cautioned British antilynching reformers that Americans "would be exasperated at the impertinence of another nation seeking to meddle in what, after all, concerns Americans primarily." The result might be "the exact reverse of that desired"—a backlash that would "lead the Americans of the Southern States to look upon the negro with greater hatred than before." Those Americans who had supported the use of lynching "would be more exasperated than before," while "those who had hitherto condemned such treatment of their fellow-citizens would come to look upon it with acquiescence, perhaps with approval." The *Spectator* feared that if British reformers were not careful, lynching might be transformed into an American institution to be embraced and vigorously defended from outside attack. Lynching, the editor warned, might become "in their eyes simply an assertion of their own nationality, of their right to deal with their own affairs as they thought best."[59]

In September 1894, the London Anti-Lynching Committee sent a delegation led by Sir John Eldon Gorst to the United States to investigate lynching, unleashing a wave of American indignation. The *New York World* telegraphed governors throughout the Midwest, South, and West asking for reactions to the British investigation. Eighteen responded by denouncing the impertinence of the British committee, and their reactions appeared in newspapers across the country.[60] Arkansas governor William Meade Fishback (1893–95) was outraged that England would "assume the role of a missionary to teach us our duty" and warned that "the officious intermeddling of outsiders" would only make it more difficult for "the better class of people to suppress" lynching. Virginia's O'Ferrall believed that it was "the quintessence of brass and impudence" to have "a lot of English moralists sticking their noses into our internal affairs," while Missouri governor William J. Stone declared it "an exhibition of superb cheek." Indiana's Claude Matthews regarded the committee's "meddlesome interference" as "wholly unwarranted, and not deserving of even courteous or tolerant treatment by our people." "We have no need for English committees in this country," South Dakota governor Charles H. Sheldon stormed, "when the purpose is to give peculiar emphasis to the English idea of English superiority."[61]

South Carolina governor Benjamin R. Tillman (1890–94) offered the British committee a chance to gain firsthand knowledge of lynching by visiting his state: "The Englishmen are welcome to come to South Carolina and learn the truth . . . I will afford them every facility to get at facts." Tillman's "invitation" could have been interpreted as a veiled threat, and southern newspapers picked up on this nuance and echoed his words with their own offers. The *Rome (Georgia) Tribune* invited the committee to "Come south and stay with us a while." The *St. Louis Republic* suggested "the way to cure the visitors is to take each one into an agricultural community in one of the black belts and bid him or her wait until something happens."[62] Such equivocal statements constituted an essential component of Tillman's political strategy. While he publicly championed beleaguered farmers and denounced black criminality, even famously pledging to lead a lynch mob if necessary to defend white women's virtue, "Pitchfork Ben" Tillman nevertheless strove to enforce law and order during his term as governor. Like Northen, Jones, and O'Ferrall, Tillman pressured local sheriffs to bring accused criminals to trial and repeatedly sent troops to prevent outbreaks of mob violence. In his 1890 inaugural address, Tillman asked that he be given the power to remove any sheriff who allowed a prisoner to be taken from his custody. If mob violence were eliminated, Tillman argued, "all classes and colors" might finally compete "with each other in friendly rivalry to make the State prosperous and happy." Like most New

South governors, Tillman promoted the cause of white supremacy to gain electoral support while simultaneously fighting to suppress lynching to maintain good relations with outside investors.[63]

The debate over American lynching quickly moved from the underlying causes of mob violence to the impertinence of British moral interference. White southerners convinced themselves that foreign investigators possessed no useful understanding of American society. "While we have irregularities at the South," Northen conceded, "and negroes are sometimes lynched, they are never slaughtered by wholesale, as Englishmen sometimes destroy them." O'Ferrall warned that the committee "had better sweep in front of their own doors before seeking to regulate us." "Possibly the English committee can do some good in the South," speculated Illinois governor John P. Altgeld. "If it does, then the Southern people should return the compliment and send a committee to Ireland to stop the outrages there." Unable to denounce mob violence while public attention focused on Wells's campaign and the committee's investigation, American governors abandoned their law-and-order campaigns to decry British hypocrisy. Domestic political concerns infused these responses. Attacks on British failings might court support from Irish American voters, who traditionally held strong anti-English sentiments, during a contentious midterm election season marked by Populist Party challenges. Similarly, Oregon governor Sylvester Pennoyer attempted to rally the support of Populists when he accused Britons of "running" the Cleveland administration by encouraging support of the gold standard, a financial policy favored by British banks but intensely unpopular with members of the Populist Party.[64]

For many governors, the committee's investigation stirred feelings of nationalism. According to Delaware governor Robert J. Reynolds and North Carolina governor Elias Carr, Americans had proven themselves "amply able" to manage their own affairs "without the officious intermeddling of a foreign power." West Virginia's William A. MacCorkle similarly regarded the investigation "as a piece of intermeddling... not to be excused," while Eli C. D. Shortridge of North Dakota bluntly declared, "America will not tolerate foreigners meddling with our home affairs." Responding as if the London Anti-Lynching Committee proposed imposing a new era of Reconstruction on the South, Northen cautioned, "We have already endured more outside interference in our local matters than we will submissively tolerate in the future." Similarly, Tennessee governor Peter Turney patriotically reminded Americans that when Britons tried to take over U.S. affairs in the War of 1812, they "went off worsted."[65]

Thus, the tactics of the London Anti-Lynching Committee, not lynching it-self, became the new focus of debate. Because the controversy surrounding the committee's tactics pushed Wells's arguments to the side, her opponents finally found room in the transatlantic debate for their voices. *The Times*, which had both ignored Wells's campaign and refrained from participating in the British debate on lynching, eagerly published Governor Jones's indignant rebuttal to the London Anti-Lynching Committee's request to investigate a lynching re-ported in Alabama. As "a sturdy foe of mob violence," Jones warned that there could be "no more formidable hindrance" to efforts to end lynching "than the attempt of a committee of British subjects to constitute themselves an interna-tional moral tribunal" and "arrogate the right to summon States to defend their civilization." "The laws, the efforts of the authorities, and the force of public opinion," Jones insisted, "are solving the problem and the good work can be re-tarded, but not hastened by your present method." Such impertinent interfer-ence could only generate resentment that would hinder progressive southern leaders' efforts to end mob violence.[66] Minimizing the importance of the an-tilynching campaign and demonstrating his paper's general disdain for liberal reformers, the editor of *The Times* ridiculed every aspect of the committee's protest, including the writing skills of the committee's secretary, Florence Bal-garnie: "It would be such a pity if Miss Balgarnie were lynched by a mob of en-raged grammarians." By infuriating white Americans with their sanctimonious-ness, *The Times* warned, the committee members' interference likely "multiplied the number of negroes who are hanged, shot, and burnt by paraffin ... through-out the Southern States."[67] The *Daily Telegraph* joined the debate, attacking the committee's lack of deference to the governor's office and expressing sympathy for southern white men who were "inflamed to madness by outrages on their wives, their sisters, or their daughters, committed by negroes."[68]

Expressions of conservative British disapproval for the London Anti-Lynching Committee's activities received enthusiastic coverage in the Ameri-can press. The London correspondent for the *New York Times* was delighted by *The Times*'s declaration that although it had "little or no sympathy for lynching," it had "none whatever with anti-lynching." The correspondent believed this was "almost the first expression ... of a big majority of sensible Englishmen who resent the meddlesome antics of a little and noisy minority." Similarly, the *New York Times* reprinted the *Truth*'s denunciation of British reformers "who take upon themselves to regulate the conduct of the whole world" and the *Saturday Review*'s praise for Jones's "very good snub" of the London Anti-Lynching Committee.[69] Finding supportive coverage in several

London newspapers, including *The Times, Pall Mall Gazette, Westminster Gazette, Globe, London Society, Sun,* and *Daily Telegraph,* the *Montgomery Daily Advertiser* was pleased to announce that Governor Jones's letter had "Cut to the Quick."[70]

Despite the tactical miscalculation that resulted in this sudden burst of negative British press, the supporters of Wells's campaign interpreted southern leaders' attacks as a sign of progress, much as Wells had done in the face of the assaults on her character. Balgarnie considered the appearance of Jones's letter in *The Times* "a herald of good tidings, for it evinces a certain hopeful sensitiveness to outside opinion which augurs well for the ultimate and universal suppression of lynching."[71] Her sentiments were echoed by William Lloyd Garrison Jr., son of the famed abolitionist, who claimed that "the very denunciation of foreign criticism by the Southern offenders demonstrates its potency." According to Garrison, Americans who recognized the evils of mob violence were no longer intimidated into silence. While only "a year ago the South derided and resented Northern protests[,] today it listens, explains, and apologizes for its uncovered cruelties."[72] By the following year, the committee's annual report celebrated the "changed attitude of the Southern Press" and the actions taken by several governors, judges, and state legislatures to denounce and ultimately suppress lynching.[73]

Wells had seized a valuable opportunity to critique the role of lynching in American society during a period when southern leaders were desperate to court international investment. As British scrutiny of American lynching increased, American lynching debates became more polarized and less nuanced and increasingly focused on the lynching for rape narrative. As British social leaders rejected southern excuses for lynching, southern governors struggled to avoid the appearance that they condoned lynching, giving new urgency to their efforts to suppress mob violence despite the increasing internal political pressure to embrace the rhetoric of white supremacy. Southern leaders found success in characterizing criticism of lynching as foreign meddling, enabling them to avoid addressing lynching's true purpose and nature. British reformers consequently lost valuable momentum, and the backlash against the London Anti-Lynching Committee's investigation eventually stalled the British antilynching movement. Nevertheless, by changing the way British reformers understood American lynching and encouraging them to hold southern leaders accountable for their constituents' lawless excesses, Wells's activism had increased the perceived international costs of lynching for the South during a critical period of social and economic upheaval.

Chapter 6

e ──

A TRANSATLANTIC

LEGACY

In less than eighteen months, Ida B. Wells mobilized an extensive network of British reformers, many of whom had close American connections through other transatlantic social, religious, and reform organizations. Despite their dedication and determination, however, no white American counterpart to these British reformers developed. In their absence, Wells called on African Americans to create an organization that would continue the momentum of her British campaign, "in appreciation," she recalled, "of what the English people had done for us." She promised to continue her program of reform in the United States if African Americans would contribute to the cause, but newspaper appeals for donations and other assistance went unanswered. "I waited in New York nearly a month for the response from the appeal," she remembered, "but somehow it seemed that the necessary funds were not forthcoming." Despite the difficulties she faced working with the Society for the Recognition of the Brotherhood of Man (SRBM), Wells was pleased that "every cent of the expense connected with the campaign had been met by the English friends; although they paid me no salary they had provided for every need." Wells expected no less from middle-class African Americans. She believed that the black community now needed "to show that we could do as much for ourselves as they had done for us." If she were going to devote her time and energy to this cause, she wanted African Americans to show their appreciation for her efforts by supporting her campaign financially.[1]

Wells had reason to expect African Americans to respond positively to her appeal. Before her 1892 exile from Memphis, Wells had experienced great success in canvassing parts of the South to increase the circulation of the *Free*

Speech. Traveling through Tennessee, Arkansas, and Mississippi, she had been cordially received by middle-class African Americans wherever she went. Wells had exploited her southern ties and status as a middle-class woman to court support. As she explained, "A woman editor and correspondent was a novelty; besides, Mississippi was my native state." Wells cultivated a broad readership, appealing equally to both middle- and working-class black communities. Wells cast a wide net, securing subscriptions from political meetings, church conventions, and Masonic lodges. Appearing before a meeting of African American lawyers in Greenville, Mississippi, she left "with the subscription of every man present." She cleverly printed the *Free Speech* on pink paper so that even illiterate African Americans would be able to identify and purchase it for friends or family members to read to them. Her proven ability to gather support from a broad cross-section of the black community led Wells to anticipate that African Americans would rally to support her antilynching campaign.[2]

Nonetheless, Wells's new endeavor failed. African Americans might have been unwilling to contribute financially to a campaign without evidence of its viability, might have been unable to contribute amid the ongoing economic crisis resulting from the Depression of 1893, or might have believed that Wells should work for free. Most likely, they did not wish to associate themselves with such a controversial figure. The white southern press had criticized Wells's activism and maligned her character, and her notoriety and the threats against her prevented her from traveling through or agitating in the regions most affected by lynching. Confined to the northern and western states, she could not directly court support from the same middle- and working-class black communities that had subscribed to the *Free Speech*. Nor could she protest lynching in the states with the highest rates of mob violence. Wells found it increasingly difficult to make an impact without the benefit of British moral authority to increase her public profile and force her message into the South.

In October 1892, shortly after the destruction of the *Free Speech*, Wells's ordeal had prompted the leading black women of Brooklyn and New York to present her with five hundred dollars to support her struggle. But they did not come to her aid this time. After two overseas tours, Wells had demonstrated that she was capable of taking care of herself. Her independent, outspoken style of activism shattered her image as a vulnerable woman in need of sisterly sympathy and support. Moreover, although the South's vitriol had rallied British supporters to her defense, two years of persistent attacks on her character had damaged her reputation in the United States. Her erstwhile sponsors—

middle-class, respectable black women—likely did not step forward again because they feared that they would be tainted by association with Wells.[3]

In response to the ongoing attempts to impugn the character of Wells and other black women, middle-class African Americans began to organize to defend their status as ladies. The National Association of Colored Women's Clubs (NACW) grew out of a national conference held July 29–31, 1895, in Boston. The conference was organized as a reaction to an inflammatory letter written by a southern newspaper editor, John W. Jacks, to Florence Balgarnie, one of Wells's supporters and secretary of the London Anti-Lynching Committee, that declared all black women to be unchaste and lacking in moral virtue. "The women are prostitutes," Jacks asserted, "and all are natural liars and thieves." Unable to rely on black men to defend their honor from the racist stereotypes that supported both lynching and the sexual exploitation of black women, middle-class African American women rallied to their own defense. As disfranchisement increasingly restricted the political influence of black men, the women of the NACW utilized their newfound solidarity to become race leaders, and the association adopted as its slogan, "Lifting as We Climb." Following the example of Wells's campaigns, black women began to argue for the protection of *all* women, not just white women, as ladies. In the process, they defended their own virtue and respectability and the legal rights of persecuted black men by demanding trials for all accused rapists—black and white—regardless of the color of their victims.[4]

Wells's rhetorical strategy caused a strong adverse reaction among her ideological allies, especially in the black community. African Americans were concerned that Wells's assertion that consensual relationships existed between white women and black men would exacerbate racial tensions. Before an interview with the *New York Sun*, Wells was approached by a delegation of black men who asked her "to put the soft pedal on charges against white women and their relations with black men." Wells refused, explaining "that wherever I had gone in England I found the firmly accepted belief that lynchings took place in this country only because black men were wild beasts after white women; that the hardest part of my work had been to convince the British people that this was a false charge against Negro manhood and that to forsake that position now, because I was back in my own country, would be to tacitly admit that the charge was true, and I could not promise to do that." Wells felt abandoned by African Americans who were intimidated by the prospect of a racist backlash against what she considered the truth about interracial sexual relationships. She refused to compromise, and moderate black leaders remained afraid to support her.[5]

Wells also made a significant tactical error by choosing to wait in New York for support to manifest before continuing her agitation. With no meetings or additional interviews to report, the moral pressure exerted by British press coverage of Wells's campaign quickly diminished after her departure from England. Her decision to wait for the black community to rally around her squandered whatever enthusiasm for antilynching activism was left when she returned to American soil.

The ethics of Jim Crow stifled white support at home as well. Recruiting middle-class white British support was completely different from courting white American reform sentiment. Although influential American leaders such as Samuel J. Barrows, editor of the *Christian Register*, might be sensitive to the disapproval of British antilynching reformers, otherwise sympathetic Americans had no interest in allying themselves with a black woman, let alone one who had been vilified by the southern press. The only resources Wells could cultivate were in the black community, and those resources were limited.

Discouraged but not defeated, Wells decided to continue her antilynching activism on her own. Responding to invitations from individual black churches and civic organizations, she again began organizing a makeshift independent speaking tour. Wells charged fees for her appearances, stretching those funds to extend her stay in each community to lobby for local newspaper coverage and additional public speaking opportunities before white as well as black audiences. Wells had always understood that gaining a white American audience for her message, either directly or through British reformers, was essential to combat lynching. As she explained, "It was the white people of the country who had to mold the public sentiment necessary to put a stop to lynching."[6] Undeterred by the lukewarm response her efforts received, Wells celebrated the success of her transatlantic campaigns in her 1895 pamphlet, *A Red Record*, claiming that "the entire American people now feel, both North and South, that they are objects in the gaze of the civilized world and that for every lynching humanity asks that America render its account to civilization and itself."[7]

Yet the American political landscape shifted as the momentum of her British campaigns waned, making it increasingly difficult for Wells to remain an effective leader. For a time, the South refrained from committing (or at least newspapers refrained from reporting) high-profile lynchings involving torture and mass participation.[8] Without additional incidents of American atrocities to stir British moral indignation and facing fierce resistance from American lynching apologists, both the London Anti-Lynching Committee and the SRBM dissolved by 1897. Wells's style of activism fell out of favor as Booker T. Washington rose to national prominence and a wave of accommodationism swept the United States in 1895. As his social and political influence grew, Washington refrained from openly criticizing the lynching for rape narrative; instead, he encouraged blacks to move up by working through rather than against the ethics of Jim Crow segregation.[9] Wells's transatlantic efforts faltered and her antilynching campaign was soon eclipsed by other issues and other movements.

White Americans sharply criticized Wells's campaign for doing more harm than good in the effort to end lynching. In his 1905 investigation, *Lynch Law*, James E. Cutler argued that by inspiring widespread southern resistance, her activism had made no impact on American lynching practices and asserted that even "Miss Wells at length recognized the futility of further work in England and returned home."[10] On one level, Cutler's criticism of Wells's activism has merit. Wells's success in recruiting a broad coalition of white British reformers ultimately limited her ability to sustain her activism. Without an existing white middle-class American counterpart with which to coordinate their efforts, the London Anti-Lynching Committee's activism was not likely to sustain itself. Moreover, some of the committee's decisions had disastrous unintended repercussions for antilynching sentiment in the United States. Divided by the ideological diversity of its membership, the committee articulated its protests against lynching in the most general terms, favoring moral suasion and ignoring Wells's critique of lynching as a racist act of violent oppression employed to sustain white supremacy. By choosing not to engage in debate regarding the actual versus ostensible causes of lynching, British reformers made themselves an easy target for southern politicians and lynching apologists. Defenders of lynching took the opportunity to reassert the dominance of the lynching for rape narrative, forcing out more moderate arguments about the necessity of maintaining law and order. The hostile atmosphere this backlash generated pressured progressive southern governors who opposed lynching to concede ideological and rhetorical ground to lynching apologists.

While this hardening of American lynching discourse temporarily complicated southern leaders' efforts to promote law-and-order campaigns, Wells's alternative lynching narrative provided future activists with a way to attack mob violence by racializing lynching. As long as lynching remained associated with assumptions of criminal behavior, the label was powerful enough to with-stand attack. By transforming lynching into a racist act of oppression in which the mob's victims were guilty of nothing more than being black in the United States, Wells cast doubt on the idea that any lynching might be considered just.

When Cutler wrote that Wells's campaign had no direct impact on lynch-ing rates, he was also at least partially correct. It is probable that no lynch mob ever balked at the memory of Ida B. Wells, deciding to disband rather than complete its violent errand. But Wells forced the South as a whole to pause to consider the potential economic, political, and social ramifications of its brutal treatment of African Americans. She demonstrated that communities that supported mob violence faced negative consequences. The London Anti-Lynching Committee's investigation provided an avenue for lynching apolo-gists to regain control of the transatlantic debate on lynching, but Wells and her supporters' activism made lynching a matter of public debate. Wells raised the visibility of lynching and increased the perceived costs of mob violence. Lynching could no longer be considered just a natural part of the landscape of the United States—an unfortunate, inevitable natural disaster that took life much in the same way as tornadoes, train wrecks, fires, and floods. Each lynch-ing was a deliberate act of will. Every time a community chose to lynch a black man and that decision was reported by telegraph to the world, transatlantic scrutiny of those actions might result.

Wells's alternative lynching narrative was also incorporated into British public debates on American lynching. While some British commentators ac-cepted the lynching for rape narrative, many others embraced Wells's statistical evidence and assertions that a variety of social and economic motivations trig-gered lynching. More broadly, Britons generally discarded the romanticized frontier justice narrative and accepted Wells's allegation that lynching was a racist form of violent oppression.[11] The British public no longer held the illu-sion that vast territories of the United States lacked access to an institutional-ized legal system, and even those commentators who assumed that black men were lynched only for their criminal behavior understood that bigotry, fear, and anger inspired American communities to embrace mob violence rather than allow African Americans to have their day in court.

Following the end of the first wave of antilynching activism in the mid-1890s, British reformers turned their attention to other issues. Yet Wells's ideas persisted in Britain, awaiting an opportunity to reignite the transatlantic de-bate on lynching. In 1902, that opportunity came in the form of "The Negro: Another View," an *Atlantic Monthly article* by Andrew Sledd, a young Meth-

odist minister and professor of Latin from Emory College in Oxford, Georgia
(later moved to Atlanta and renamed Emory University). Written in response
to his revulsion at the 1899 lynching of Sam Hose, a black man accused of
murder and rape, in Newnan, Georgia, Sledd's polemical essay was rejected by
both the *Methodist Review* and the *Independent* and languished for more than
two years before the *Atlantic Monthly* agreed to print it. Sledd's interpretation
of lynching and race relations was unusual for a white southerner: although
he made concessions to the commonly held belief that blacks were inherently
inferior to whites, he asserted that blacks, like all Americans, had certain "inalienable rights." In his opinion, any white southerner who disregarded these
rights fed the moral degradation of the South. Sledd believed that lynchings
were primarily conducted not by grieving friends and family members but by
the lowest classes of white men, "coarse, and beastly, and drunk, mad with the
terrible blood-lust that wild beasts know" and released from the normal constraints of civilized conduct to hunt "human prey."[12]

Sledd's use of statistical evidence and assertion that race prejudice was a primary motivating factor in lynchings reflected Wells's interpretation of lynching. He asserted that lynching was "largely sectional," with up to 80 percent
of all cases occurring in the South, and "largely racial," with African Americans accounting for approximately 75 percent of all lynching victims. Sledd
believed that lynching was not reserved for vengeance against rapists but was
used in response to "murder, rape, arson, barn-burning, theft,—or suspicion of
any of these." Sledd concluded that the black man was degraded, segregated,
and lynched not because of his ignorance, viciousness, or offensiveness of manner but *"because of his blackness."*[13]

Across the Atlantic, Sledd's essay captured the attention of Edward Grubb,
one of the first members of the SRBM, a leading member of the Society of
Friends, and editor of the *British Friend*. Grubb brought Sledd's article to the
attention of the Meeting for Sufferings, the London-based central governing
body of the Society of Friends, which established a Committee on Lynching
to investigate American racial violence and produce an address on the subject
to distribute to "persons of influence" in the United States.[14]

Grubb sought Sledd's advice about how the committee could aid in the
struggle against lynching. Sledd urged caution. His outspoken assertions had
cost him dearly. Rebecca Latimer Felton, a fellow Methodist and a vocal white
supremacist who "terrorized Georgia politicians and politics" with her incendiary correspondence, launched a crusade to force Emory College to dismiss
Sledd. Not even his ties to Georgia's prominent Candler family could protect

him, and Emory president James Dickey requested Sledd's resignation. Unable to secure a position at another southern school, Sledd left the South to pursue a doctorate at Yale.[15]

Sledd consequently counseled the Quaker committee against attempts to inspire change "by any violent or sudden outside interference." Sledd had thought "that as a man of long Southern antecedents and (as I looked at it) unquestionable loyalty to my section, I might be permitted to speak where the right has so long been denied outsiders." But the backlash against his article demonstrated "the exceeding delicacy of the situation, and should make aliens think, at least what good they may be able to do by outside agitation." Sledd urged the committee to work from within existing southern organizations, encouraging its members "to take a decided stand against lynching and lawlessness in all its forms." If their work could "help to make a public sentiment [against lynching] in the South, good; but a public sentiment anywhere else" would only "aggravate the sore."[16]

In light of Sledd's advice, the committee worked in concert with American Quakers to draft a circular letter, "A Plea for Humanity," that urged all Christians to denounce lynching. Leaving "out of consideration altogether political and racial problems," the letter instead appealed to Americans "on the broad and simple grounds of Christian principle and human justice." The Society of Friends believed that the Christian "spirit of love and tenderness" had "removed the barbarous cruelties and the lawless injustices of the dark ages" and led to "the development of an ordered commonwealth, in which to the weakest members are granted the inalienable rights of life, liberty, and justice." They called on that same Christian spirit of mercy to raise a public sentiment in both Britain and America against the inhumanity of mob violence.[17]

In September 1903, the Quaker committee distributed more than thirty-five thousand copies of "A Plea for Humanity" to American newspapers, religious leaders, state governors, and attorneys general. The "Plea" was reprinted in American newspapers and provoked responses from several American clergymen, including the Reverend William McKay, who had objected to Wells's 1894 campaign in the *Spectator*.[18] According to Grubb's analysis, American responses to the "Plea" fell into three categories, with "the number in each class being nearly the same." The first expressed "warm approval and thankfulness" for the committee's efforts. The second group "includes a number of lengthy documents recognizing the good intentions and right principles of the authors . . . but protesting that they do not understand the true position of the matter and the real causes that lead to lynching." The last group contained "violent objections to the ignorant interference of Northerners and Europeans, protesting in most cases, against a misplaced sympathy which thinks everything of the person who is lynched and nothing of his innocent victims." Grubb contended that the two styles of protest shared two underlying assumptions: "the persons lynched are negroes" and "they are lynched for crimes against white women."[19]

Grubb's experience in the SRBM would have led him to doubt these assertions. Following the example of Wells's campaign a decade earlier, Grubb used statistical evidence from the *Chicago Tribune* to demonstrate that the lynching for rape narrative was cultural mythology used to defend what would otherwise be indefensible extralegal violence. He contended that "during the last twelve years not more than 72 per cent [of lynching victims] were coloured, and only 24 per cent were lynched for assaults (real or alleged) upon women." Echoing Wells's arguments, Grubb complained that white Americans could not possibly be as outraged by the crime of rape as they pretended when there was "an entire absence of expression against similar crimes when committed by white men against coloured women." Fears that excessive delays might frustrate the pursuit of justice or legal technicalities might be exploited to allow black criminals to escape punishment appeared unfounded when the entire legal system was controlled by whites. The committee concluded that further investigations needed to be made to determine how to proceed.[20]

In early 1904, Grubb conducted a joint inquiry for the Friends' Committee on Lynching and the Howard Association, a British organization dedicated to prison reform for which he served as secretary. Already scheduled to meet with the governors of Indiana, Georgia, Alabama, and Virginia as part of his prison study, Grubb used the opportunity to do informal research into lynching. He also met President Theodore Roosevelt and spent a day with Booker T. Washington.[21] Where possible, he sought information on the underlying causes of lynching, both to understand more fully the nature of American crime and to gauge southern receptivity to further British activism. Through his investigation, Grubb sought to understand cultural motivations for lynching as well as how statistical evidence contradicted popular wisdom.

His observations in the United States reinforced Grubb's sociological interpretation of lynching. Confirming Wells's analysis, Grubb noted that lynching was primarily used in retaliation for accusations of murder rather than rape. Although honorable people might firmly believe "that 90 per cent of all the lynchings . . . were for crimes committed 'by negro brutes upon white women,'" Grubb determined that the facts did not support that claim. "The place given to [assaults on white women] in speeches and articles excusing lynching," he contended, was "altogether mistaken"; murder, not rape, was "the crime of the South."[22]

The prevalence of both lynching and murder in the South, Grubb declared, resulted primarily from a combination of "race prejudice" and a "scant respect for human life, especially when" that life was "coloured." Grubb was disappointed to find that a pervasive "disbelief in the virtue of the coloured race" led even men of God to consider "terror to be the only force that would keep the negroes in their place."[23] In other words, racial bigotry ran deeper than a commitment to Christian principles in a devout section of an ostensibly Christian nation.

Despite the strong evidence that the popular southern wisdom about lynching was grossly inaccurate, Grubb determined that there was as yet no room for outside intervention. If Sledd, a native-born southerner with connections to one of the South's leading families, had been forced to resign his position and leave the region for questioning the morality of lynching, there was little chance that foreign intervention would be welcomed. Grubb reported to the committee that the issue of lynching was so tightly intertwined with racial politics that British interference during the run-up to the 1904 presidential election might do more harm than good, just as it had a decade earlier.

The Quaker committee had felt encouraged by recent statements demonstrating "signs of a better feeling in many quarters," including "instances of local authorities taking pains to anticipate and prevent such outbreaks and pronouncements against lynching by Judges of the Supreme Court & others." They were especially encouraged by Roosevelt's public statement in support of Indiana governor Winfield T. Durbin's use of the state militia to prevent a 1903 lynching. Deeply troubled by a recent lynching in Wilmington, Delaware, Roosevelt had argued that participation in a lynching or even viewing its aftermath was inherently demoralizing: "There are certain hideous sights, which when once seen, can never be wholly erased from the mental retina." Merely witnessing these events "implies degradation." But, Roosevelt warned, their impact was "a thousand fold stronger" for participants: "Whoever in any part of our country has ever taken part in lawlessly putting to death a criminal by the dreadful torture of fire must for ever after have the awful spectacle of his own handiwork seared into his brain and soul. He can never again be the same man."[24] Such powerful words from the U.S. president demonstrated that public opinion was turning against lynching and initially led the committee to believe that its voice would be welcomed. However, American beliefs about lynching and white supremacy were explosive issues that could be easily manipulated as political tools.

Roosevelt had already made a series of controversial decisions on racial issues that provoked white southerners' ire. His 1901 dinner with Washington at the White House had stirred public resentment. Political storms over black political appointments, even those made by former administrations, plagued Roosevelt. When the black postmaster of Indianola, Mississippi, Minnie Cox, received threats on her life, Roosevelt refused to accept her resignation and closed the post office. When openly racist candidates contested the seats of moderate incumbents in the Mississippi Democratic primary, racism and white supremacy became prominent national political issues. As the president struggled to maintain a balance between the lily-white and black-and-tan southern factions of the Republican Party, his reelection appeared uncertain.[25] If Roosevelt won, Washington might give African Americans some private influence over racial policies; if a Democrat took the White House, however, African American interests would have considerably less representation in national politics. But American Quakers counseled their British counterparts against sending correspondence to Roosevelt, arguing that the last thing that Roosevelt—and by extension African Americans—needed was for the issue of lynching to become part of the 1904 campaign. As long as evidence seemed to show that progress was being made, British reformers needed to wait for another invitation to intervene. In the meantime, they continued to evaluate reports of American mob violence through the lens of Wells's critique of lynching.

British beliefs that racist forces underpinned and perpetuated lynching persisted into the twentieth century, making Britain a welcome source of support for both white and African American antilynching activists who followed Wells. In 1910, John E. Milholland rallied the National Association for the Advancement of Colored People (NAACP) to protest Washington's assertions to British audiences that the problem of lynching was "greatly exaggerated" in the European press. W. E. B. Du Bois addressed a circular letter "To the People of Great Britain and Europe" in which he criticized Washington's dependency on white philanthropy, which Du Bois believed compelled Washington "to tell, not the whole truth, but that part of it which certain powerful interests in America wish to appear as the whole truth." If anyone "is giving the impression abroad that the Negro problem in America is in the process of satisfactory solution," Du Bois insisted, "he is giving an impression which is not true." African Americans still needed "the moral support of England" in the campaign against lynching and white supremacy. The NAACP continued to seek British support for its activism, even picketing outside London's Royal Albert Hall to protest lynching.[26] Time and again, American antilynching activists turned to Britain for support, and the British public answered.

While these campaigns might not have re-created the intense transatlantic debate on the causes and consequences of lynching that Wells's campaign generated, American social and political leaders were forced to respond each time British moral indignation was raised against lynching. Americans tried to stall British antilynching protests, often succeeding. Although that success might be interpreted as weakness in the British antilynching movement, it also illustrates the dynamic nature of these transatlantic debates and Britons' positive influence on American public opinion. The successive waves of international debate changed the shape of discussions of American lynching. British involvement in these debates—the exportation of British moral indignation to the United States—remained an essential element in that evolution.

Although white moderates and progressive southern governors seeking to establish a more humane system of Jim Crow segregation might have been frustrated by Wells's agitation and British moral interference, reducing the effectiveness of law-and-order campaigns might also have had benefits. By disrupting the rhetorical link between lynching and black criminality, Wells undermined romantic notions of lynching as an expression of justice. Consequently, local communities began to see an association with lynching as undesirable. The application of the term *lynching* became a social and economic liability as Wells's activism increased international scrutiny of American race relations. In response, the number of instances in which the term was used fell steadily through the first half of the twentieth century.[27] In essence, local communities became less willing to advertise their tolerance of mob violence.

Ida B. Wells played an important role in establishing the discursive space in which future debates on American lynching operated. By racializing lynching and connecting mob violence to racism, she gave future activists a way to attack lynching without having to engage in debates about black criminality; consequently, her rhetoric about the underlying causes of lynching shaped the next half century of lynching debate on both sides of the Atlantic. Her arguments were echoed by the National Association of Colored Women's Clubs, NAACP, International Labor Defense, and Association of Southern Women for the Prevention of Lynching. Her methods and rhetoric even shape how historians understand and investigate lynching today.[28] Though Wells herself was not always welcomed, her ideas remained a permanent part of subsequent debates on lynching in both the United States and Britain. Wells thus profoundly affected the development of lynching discourse and how we perceive the history of American lynching.

Notes

ABBREVIATIONS

AC	*Anti-Caste*
Axon Papers	Axon Papers, University of Manchester Library, Manchester, England
BDP	*Birmingham Daily Post*
CO&SRR v. Wells	*Chesapeake, Ohio, & Southwestern Railroad v. Ida Wells*, Circuit Court of Shelby County (Tennessee), 1885, Microfilm 1425, Tennessee State Library and Archives, Nashville
CR	*Christian Register*
Crowell Papers	John Franklin Crowell Papers, Columbia University, Rare Book and Manuscript Library, New York
CW	*Christian World*
DCL	*Daily Chronicle* (London)
DNL	*Daily News* (London)
Douglass Papers	Frederick Douglass Papers, Manuscript Division, Library of Congress, Washington, D.C.
LDP	*Liverpool Daily Post*
LP	*Liverpool Pulpit*
MFS Minutes	Meeting for Sufferings Minutes, vol. 53, Library of the Religious Society of Friends in Britain, London
Northen Papers	William J. Northen Papers, 1941-0354M, Georgia Archives, Morrow
NYT	*New York Times*
SRBM Minute Book	Minute Book of the Society for the Recognition of the Brotherhood of Man, Anti-Slavery Society Papers, MSS. Brit.

	Emp. s. 20, E/8, Bodleian Library of Commonwealth and
	African Studies, University of Oxford, Oxford, England
SRBM Scrapbook	Scrapbook of Catherine Impey, Anti-Slavery Society
	Papers, MSS. Brit. Emp. s. 20, E/7, Bodleian Library of
	Commonwealth and African Studies, University of Oxford,
	Oxford, England
TL	*The Times* (London)
Tourgée Papers	*Albion Winegar Tourgée Papers, 1801–1924.* Cleveland: Bell
	and Howell, 1967. Microfilm.

INTRODUCTION

1. Caroline Hawley, "There's Never Been an Attack as Brutal as This," *BBC News*, 31 March 2004; John Berman, "Outrage in Fallujah," *ABC News*, 31 March 2004.

2. Jeffrey Gettleman, "4 From U.S. Killed in Ambush in Iraq; Mob Drags Bodies," *NYT*, 1 April 2004; Abby Goodnough and Michael Luo, "Families of Men Slain by Mob Focus on Their Lives, Not How They Died," *NYT*, 3 April 2004; Allen et al., *Without Sanctuary*, plates 10, 11, 24–26, 37, 38, 45–52, 54, 55, 74, 75, 97.

3. This interpretation shaped early lynching scholarship (see, for example, Cutler, *Lynch Law*; Raper, *Tragedy of Lynching*; White, *Rope and Faggot*). However, it also has deeply influenced modern scholarship as historians have sought to better understand the causes and consequences of lynching through individual case studies (see Madison, *Lynching in the Heartland*; McGovern, *Anatomy of a Killing*; Smead, *Blood Justice*); state or regional studies (see Bessler, *Legacy of Violence*; Brundage, *Lynching in the New South*; Tolnay and Beck, *Festival of Violence*); investigations of antilynching activism (see Feimster, *Southern Horrors*; Hall, *Revolt against Chivalry*; Zangrando, *NAACP Crusade against Lynching*); and analysis of the cultural legacy of lynching (see Goldsby, *Spectacular Secret*; Markovitz, *Legacies of Lynching*; Wood, *Lynching and Spectacle*). Scholars have begun to examine lynching on the national (see Berg, *Popular Justice*; Pfeifer, *Rough Justice*) and international levels (see Berg and Wendt, *Globalizing Lynching History*; Carrigan and Waldrep, *Swift to Wrath*) as well as mob violence directed against other minority groups (see Carrigan and Webb, *Forgotten Dead*).

4. For examples and an exploration of the history of lynching photography, see Allen et al., *Without Sanctuary*.

5. Wells has become the focus of a significant body of scholarship, including several full-length biographies (Bay, *To Tell the Truth Freely*; Davidson, *"They Say"*; Giddings, *Ida*; McMurry, *To Keep the Waters Troubled*; Schechter, *Ida B. Wells-Barnett*; Mildred I. Thompson, *Ida B. Wells-Barnett*) and numerous essays. Scholars have paid special attention to Wells's antilynching rhetoric and transatlantic campaigns, but her activism has not been examined within the broader context of transatlantic debates on

lynching. See, for example, Bederman, *Manliness and Civilization*; Brown, *Eradicating This Evil*; Crawford, "Ida B. Wells: Her Antilynching Crusades"; Crawford, "Ida B. Wells: Some American Reactions"; Simone W. Davis, "'Weak Race'"; Giddings, *When and Where I Enter*; Karcher, "White 'Bystander'"; King, "'Colored Woman'"; Miller, *Other Reconstruction*; Royster, "To Call a Thing"; Schechter, "Unsettled Business"; Waldrep, "Ida B. Wells."

6. Although annual lynching statistics gathered by the *Chicago Daily Tribune* depicted the 1890s as the official "peak" of lynching and designated African Americans as the primary targets of lynching, scholars have begun to call into question these long-standing assumptions. William Carrigan and Clive Webb have demonstrated that in relation to their proportion of the U.S. population, Mexican Americans faced a similar risk of lynching to African Americans, while George Wright has asserted that more lynchings occurred during Reconstruction than in any other period. See Cutler, *Lynch-Law*, 170–71; Carrigan and Webb, "Lynching," 414; Wright, *Racial Violence in Kentucky*, 4, 8–9.

7. Mildred I. Thompson, *Ida B. Wells-Barnett*, 66; McMurry, *To Keep the Waters Troubled*, 219, 231, 243; Schechter, *Ida B. Wells-Barnett*, 100–101; Bederman, "'Civilization,'" 21–22.

8. Waldrep, *Many Faces of Judge Lynch*, 3. For an examination of competing definitions of lynching, see Waldrep, "Word and Deed."

9. See, for example, Schechter, *Ida B. Wells-Barnett*; Bressey, "Strange and Bitter Crop"; Karcher, "Ida B. Wells."

10. Although the antislavery and women's rights movements have frequently been studied within a transatlantic framework, scholars have recently begun to give greater attention to other transatlantic social, political, and religious reform networks. See, for example, Bender, *Nation among Nations*; Bolt, *Sisterhood Questioned*; Bolt, *Women's Movements*; Burk, *Old World, New World*; Butler, *Critical Americans*; Gilroy, *Black Atlantic*; McFadden, *Golden Cables of Sympathy*; Meer, *Uncle Tom Mania*; Quarles, *Black Abolitionists*; Rodgers, *Atlantic Crossings*; Tyrrell, *Reforming the World*; Tyrrell, *Woman's World/Woman's Empire*.

CHAPTER 1. BRITISH RESPONSES TO AMERICAN LYNCHING

1. A Genevese Traveller, "American Affairs," *TL*, 25 August 1835; "Lynch Law—Five Gamblers Hung without Trial at Vicksburg," *TL*, 25 August 1835; "Lynch Law," *Jackson's Oxford Journal*, 29 August 1835; "Foreign Miscellany," *Preston Chronicle*, 29 August 1835; editorial, *TL*, 28 August 1835; "Slavery," *Brighton Patriot and Lewes Free Press*, 1 September 1835; Weekly Epitome, *Hull Packet*, 4 September 1835; "Foreign News," *Cobbett's Weekly Political Register* (London), 5 September 1835.

2. "Express from Tamworth," *TL*, 5 September 1835; "Grand Dinner to Sir Robert

Peel," *Derby Mercury*, 9 September 1835; Waldrep, *Many Faces of Judge Lynch*, 27–29, 46.

3. "The Vicksburg Tragedy," *Vicksburg Register*, 9 July 1835, in *Lynching in America*, ed. Waldrep, 49–51; "Lynch Law—Five Gamblers Hung without Trial at Vicksburg," *TL*, 25 August 1835. For an analysis of Vicksburg attitudes toward mob violence, see Waldrep, *Roots of Disorder*.

4. Shackelford, *Proceedings*, iii–iv, 8, 11–13; Gray, *Confessions of Nat Turner*; *Historical Census Browser*, University of Virginia Library, Geospatial and Statistical Data Center, 2004, http://mapserver.lib.virginia.edu/. For an examination of the cultural impact of Nat Turner's rebellion, see French, *Rebellious Slave*.

5. Shackelford, *Proceedings*, 3, 7–8, 13; editorial, *TL*, 28 August 1835; "Lynch Law Term Reports," *TL*, 5 November 1836.

6. "Lynch Law Term Reports," *TL*, 5 November 1836.

7. Lipset, "Harriet Martineau's America," 5–6. Prominent examples include Tocqueville, *Democracy in America* (1835, 1840), and Dickens, *American Notes* (1842), but the genre remained popular throughout the nineteenth century. See also Janson, *Stranger in America* (1807); Thomson, *Tradesman's Travels* (1842); Houstoun, *Hesperos* (1850); Oldmixon, *Transatlantic Wanderings* (1855); Rae, *Westward by Rail* (1871); Stanley, *My Early Travels* (1895).

8. Grund, *Americans*, 13. For an examination of the popularity and impact of American travel narratives in Britain, see Berger, *British Traveller in America*.

9. Grimsted, *American Mobbing*, 3–4; Waldrep, *Many Faces of Judge Lynch*, 43. Leonard Richards identifies 1834–37 as the peak of "violent anti-abolitionism" (*"Gentlemen of Property and Standing*," 156).

10. Trollope, *Domestic Manners of the Americans*, 128. In 1836, Trollope wrote a satirical novel, *Life and Adventures of Jonathan Jefferson Whitlaw*, depicting the evils of slavery and lynch law in America.

11. See Temperley, "Anti-Slavery."

12. Grund, *Americans*, 179–80; Grimsted, *American Mobbing*, 17–20, 34, 38, 72; Waldrep, *Many Faces of Judge Lynch*, 38–39, 40–41; Burns and Innes, *Rethinking the Age of Reform*, 2; Innes, "'Reform' in English Public Life," 85, 92–93. For a detailed examination of the British antislavery movement, see Temperley, *British Antislavery*.

13. Martineau, *Society in America*, 1:121–22, 126–28.

14. Grimsted, *American Mobbing*, 4; Martineau, *Society in America*, 1:129; Richards, *"Gentlemen of Property and Standing*," 131–34, 155.

15. A former captain in the British Navy, Marryat penned tales of adventure on the high seas that became popular reading during the 1830s and 1840s (Warner, *Captain Marryat*, 12–13, 74, 100, 113). Martineau used her American tour to write and publish four books: *Society in America*, *Retrospect of Western Travel*, *The Martyr Age of the United States*, and *How to Observe: Morals and Manners*.

16. Frederick Marryat to Charlotte Marryat quoted in Jackman, introduction, xvi–xvii.

17. Marryat, *Diary in America*, 1:314–18, 323–24.

18. Luke Lawless, "Charge to the Grand Jury after McIntosh Burning" (1836), in *Lynching in America*, ed. Waldrep, 55.

19. Grund, *Americans*, 178–79, 180.

20. Editorial, *TL*, 1 October 1845.

21. Marryat, *Diary in America*, 1:314–16; "Lynch Law," *Penny Illustrated Paper* (London), 18 January 1862; editorial, *TL*, 1 October 1845.

22. Grund, *Americans*, 178–79; "The Americans in the Moral, Social, and Political Relations, by Francis Grund," *TL*, 25 February 1837. For a discussion of Grund's rhetorical strategy, see Berkhofer, introduction.

23. Editorial, *TL*, 28 July 1836; "Conservative Dinner at Wrexham," *TL*, 15 September 1837.

24. "America Compared with England," *TL*, 25 January 1849; editorial, *TL*, 27 November 1833.

25. Miles, "England and America" (letter to the editor), *TL*, 4 October 1843.

26. Arnstein, *Britain Yesterday and Today*, 3–18; Evans, *Parliamentary Reform*, 27–28. For an examination of the imperial context of the 1832 Reform Act, see Taylor, "Empire and Parliamentary Reform."

27. "Conservative Dinner at Wrexham," *TL*, 15 September 1837; editorial, *TL*, 5 April 1837; editorial, *TL*, 26 January 1846; McWilliam, *Popular Politics*, 17–18, 49; Adelman, *Peel and the Conservative Party*, 13; Blake, *Conservative Party*, 10–12. See also Gash, "From the Origins to Sir Robert Peel," 54–82.

28. "Great Meeting of the Liverpool Tradesmen's Conservative Association," *TL*, 22 January 1836.

29. Editorial, *TL*, 5 April 1837.

30. Ibid., 26 January 1846; Anti-Lynch, "Lynch Law" (letter to the editor), *TL*, 31 December 1850.

31. See, for example, "Public Meeting in Natchez," *TL*, 18 January 1837.

32. For an excellent example of this distinction, see Summerfield, *Illustrated Lives*, 11–13.

33. "America," *TL*, 29 September 1853; "Horrible Case of Lynching," *TL*, 5 February 1846; "A Pleasant State of Society," *TL*, 26 March 1861. For a detailed example, see R. B. Townshend, "A Trial by Lynch Law," *Nineteenth Century* 32 (August 1982): 243–53.

34. "Lynching in America," *Chambers's Journal* 7 (17 May 1890): 317; Townshend, "Trial by Lynch Law," 244; "Horrible Case of Lynching," *TL*, 5 February 1846.

35. "Horrible Case of Lynching," *TL*, 5 February 1846.

36. "Hanging by Lynch Law," *TL*, 6 May 1857.

37. "A Death Scene in Mississippi," *TL*, 20 October 1857.

38. "The United States," *TL*, 20 May 1873.

39. "Lynch Law in Arkansas," *TL*, 20 October 1860.

40. "Hanging by Lynch Law," *TL*, 6 May 1857.

41. "Lynch Law in Texas," *TL*, 4 August 1858.

42. "A Death Scene in Mississippi," *TL*, 20 October 1857.

43. "Hanging by Lynch Law," *TL*, 6 May 1857.

44. "A Pleasant State of Society," *TL*, 26 March 1861.

45. "Lynch Law—Five Gamblers Hung without Trial at Vicksburg," *TL*, 25 August 1835.

46. "American Papers," *TL*, 29 August 1836.

47. "Moral Lynching," *TL*, 22 January 1852.

48. For an excellent discussion of the evolution of American lynching definitions and the role California vigilance committees played in cultivating popular acceptance of lynching as frontier justice, see Waldrep, *Many Faces of Judge Lynch*, 49–66.

49. Summerfield, *Illustrated Lives*, 16; "Lynching in America," *Chambers's Journal*, 317.

50. "State of California," *TL*, 3 October 1849.

51. Editorial, *TL*, 7 September 1849.

52. Ibid., 27 August 1851.

53. William Kelly, "California, Ho!" (letter to the editor), *TL*, 30 November 1849; "America," *TL*, 30 July, 26 August 1851; "The United States," *TL*, 26 August 1851; "America," *TL*, 7 April 1851, 12 December 1850.

54. Editorial, *TL*, 27 August 1851.

55. The Unfortunate Owner, "The 'Government' in Australia" (letter to the editor), *TL*, 22 December 1852.

56. "The Australian Gold Diggings," *TL*, 20 August 1852.

57. "The Australian Goldfields," *TL*, 8 November 1852. For other examples, see "The Australian Gold Mines," *TL*, 6 April 1852; "The Australian Goldfields," *TL*, 16 December 1852; editorial, *TL*, 24 December 1852; "Australia," *TL*, 26 July 1855, 3 April 1858.

58. Marryat, *Diary in America*, 1:319–20; Grund, *Americans*, 166.

59. "Lynching Gamblers—From Fifty to Seventy-Five Persons Murdered," *TL*, 16 September 1841.

60. Evans, *Parliamentary Reform*, 44–45, 58.

61. Temperley, *Britain and America since Independence*, 57–58, 76; Nicholas, *United States and Britain*, 33–35, 38–46; *Case and Claims*, 6–11; Bolt, *Anti-Slavery Movement*, 25, 33, 55–56, 69–70.

62. Kasson, *Buffalo Bill's Wild West*, 65–66, 75, 77–82; Warren, *Buffalo Bill's America*, 283–90, 302. See also Gallop, *Buffalo Bill's British Wild West*.

63. Buffalo Bill's "Wild West" Show, advertisement, *Graphic* (London), 6 August 1892; "Fresh Attractions at the 'Horty,'" *Penny Illustrated Paper* (London), 30 July 1892.

64. "The United States," *TL*, 12 October 1868.

65. Ibid., 15 October 1868.

66. A. H. Paterson, "Lynch Law," *Macmillan's Magazine* 55 (March 1887): 347; Townshend, "Trial by Lynch Law," 252; "Macmillan's Magazine, 1859–1900," "The Nineteenth Century, 1877–1900," in *Wellesley Index*, ed. Houghton, 1:555, 621.

67. "Lynch Law in New Orleans," *TL*, 16 March 1891; N. J. D. Kennedy, "Lynch," *Juridical Review* 3 (July 1891): 216; "The Lynching Affair at New Orleans," *Spectator* 66 (21 March 1891): 401; Jessie White (Vedova) Mario, "Italy and the United States," *Nineteenth Century* 29 (May 1891): 703; Michael R. Haines, "Population of Cities with at Least 100,000 Population in 1990: 1790–1990," table Aa832-1033, in *Historical Statistics*, ed. Susan B. Carter et al., 1:111. For a well-articulated example of British concerns, see "Lynching in America," *Chambers's Journal*, 317–19.

68. Smith, "From the Mississippi to the Mediterranean," 61; Giose Rimanelli, "1891 New Orleans Lynching," 62–74.

69. Giose Rimanelli, "1891 New Orleans Lynching," 61, 75–77; "The Lynching at New Orleans," *TL*, 17 March 1891.

70. Giose Rimanelli, "1891 New Orleans Lynching," 77–79; Smith, "From the Mississippi to the Mediterranean," 62–63.

71. "Chief Hennessy Avenged," *NYT*, 15 March 1891; "Lynch Law in New Orleans," *TL*, 16 March 1891; Giose Rimanelli, "1891 New Orleans Lynching," 79–81. While Reuters reported a mob of two thousand people, the *New York Times* claimed ten thousand participants; Giose Rimanelli places the number at closer to eight thousand.

72. "Lynch Law in New Orleans," *TL*, 16 March 1891; Giose Rimanelli, "1891 New Orleans Lynching," 82.

73. "Lynch Law in New Orleans," *TL*, 16 March 1891.

74. "Gossip of London Town: Some English Views of the Trouble at New Orleans," *Chicago Daily Tribune*, 23 March 1891; "The United States," *TL*, 1 April 1891; "Latest Intelligence: Italy and the United States," *TL*, 2 April 1891; "Italy and the United States," *TL*, 6 April 1891; Marco Rimanelli, "1891–92 U.S.-Italian Diplomatic Crisis," 184–97, 213; Smith, "From the Mississippi to the Mediterranean," 77–81; Giose Rimanelli, "1891 New Orleans Lynching," 87–89. For an example of the exploitation of the New Orleans crisis by advocates of immigration restriction, see Henry Cabot Lodge, "Lynch Law and Unrestricted Immigration," *North American Review* 152 (May 1891): 602–13. For an exhaustive examination of the international social and political repercussions of the lynching, see Marco Rimanelli and Postman, *1891 New Orleans Lynching*.

75. "America in the Right," *Washington Post*, 4 April 1891.

76. "The Lynching at New Orleans," *TL*, 17 March 1891; Marco Rimanelli, "1891–92 U.S.-Italian Diplomatic Crisis," 199, 205–16; Giose Rimanelli, "1891 New Orleans Lynching," 86.

77. "The Lynching at New Orleans," *TL*, 8 March 1891; Mario, "Italy and the United States," 703.

78. "Lynching in America," *Chambers's Journal*, 317–19; Kennedy, "Lynch," 216; "The Lynching Affair at New Orleans," *Spectator* 66 (21 March 1891): 401; "The Lynching at New Orleans," *TL*, 17 March 1891.

79. "The Lynching at New Orleans," *TL*, 18 March 1891; "The Majesty of the Law: A Talk with Colonel John R. Fellows," *Lippincott's Magazine* 48 (July–December 1891): 764–69.

80. The rise of the frontier justice narrative corresponds to what historian Michael Pfeifer identifies as a "revolt against due process"—a period in the late nineteenth century when criticism of the adversarial system, the limitations of codified law, due-process mechanisms, and enforcement of the death penalty spread across the United States (*Rough Justice*, 94–97, 100–102, 110–12).

81. "The Lynching Affair at New Orleans," *Spectator* 66 (21 March 1891): 400–402; Mario, "Italy and the United States," 701–8; editorial, *TL*, 18 March 1891.

82. "Wild Justice at New Orleans," *Saturday Review* 71 (21 March 1891): 341; "The Lynching Affair at New Orleans," *Spectator* 66 (21 March 1891): 400–401; Coquillette, *Anglo-American Legal Heritage*, 206–8. For a similar example, see Kennedy, "Lynch," 217.

83. "The Lynching at New Orleans," *TL*, 17 March 1891; "Latest Intelligence: Italy and the United States," *TL*, 3 April 1891.

84. N. J. D. Kennedy, "Lynch II—Its International Aspect," *Juridical Review* 4 (January 1892): 46–51; Marco Rimanelli, "1891–92 U.S.-Italian Diplomatic Crisis," 217.

85. "America in the Right," *Washington Post*, 4 April 1891; editorial, *TL*, 18 March 1891; Arnstein, *Britain Yesterday and Today*, 170–71. For a fuller discussion, see Bryce, "Legal and Constitutional Aspects."

86. "Italy and the United States," *TL*, 16 April 1891.

87. "America in the Right," *Washington Post*, 4 April 1891.

88. Kennedy, "Lynch II," 46, 48.

89. Smith, "From the Mississippi to the Mediterranean," 80.

90. "The United States," *TL*, 5 January 1893.

91. Ibid., 6 January 1893.

92. "Lynching Gamblers—From Fifty to Seventy-Five Persons Murdered," *TL*, 16 September 1841; editorial, *TL*, 6 January 1893.

93. Editorial, *TL*, 6 January 1893.

94. Ibid.; "The Reported Lynching in America," *TL*, 9 January 1893. For an example of American press coverage, see "Bloody Lynching Fight: Conflict between a Sheriff's Posse and Mob," *NYT*, 5 January 1893.

95. "Calvin Snipes Smiled: He Heard the Story of His Lynching for the First Time," *NYT*, 8 January 1893.

96. Joel Wiener argues that the American emphasis on speed in journalism contributed to this cultural divide between British and American newspaper audiences ("'Get the News!'").

97. Harold Frederic, "Morocco to Eat the Leek," *NYT*, 8 January 1893.

98. See, for example, "Sensational Lynching Affray in State of Texas," *Glasgow Herald*, 2 February 1893. One British newspaper reported the mob's intentions in advance of the lynching ("The Last 24 Hours," *Bristol Mercury and Daily Post*, 2 February 1893).

99. Bishop Atticus G. Haygood quoted in Patterson, *Rituals of Blood*, 193.

100. "More Lynching Tragedies—Scenes of a Horrible Nature," *Glasgow Herald*, 2 February 1893; Buenger, *Path to a Modern South*, 19–21; Patterson, *Rituals of Blood*, 193–94; Hale, *Making Whiteness*, 206–8.

101. *Brenham (Texas) Daily Banner*, 5 February 1893.

102. "Lynch Law in the United States: Horrible Atrocities," *Reuter's Journal*, 2 February 1893; "The United States," *TL*, 8 February 1893. In the United Kingdom, reports of the Paris lynching also appeared in the *Aberdeen Weekly Journal, Belfast News-Letter, Birmingham Daily Post, Blackburn Standard and Weekly Express, Bristol Mercury and Daily Post, Derby Mercury, Glasgow Herald, Jackson's Oxford Journal, Liverpool Daily Post, Liverpool Weekly Courier, Manchester Times, North-Eastern Daily Gazette* (Middlesbrough), *Newcastle Daily Leader, Newcastle Weekly Courant, Sheffield and Rotherham Independent, Yorkshire Herald* (York), as well as several London newspapers, including the *Daily Chronicle, Daily News, News of the World, Nottinghamshire Guardian, Reynold's Newspaper, Standard*, and *Star*, and even the leading Welsh-language newspaper, *Baner ac Amserau Cymru* (Denbigh).

103. Editorial, *DCL*, 3 February 1893; "The Last 24 Hours," *Bristol Mercury and Daily Post*, 2 February 1893; "Lynch Law in Texas," *DNL*, 3 February 1893. Walter Buenger contends that racial tensions stemming from local religious conflicts over Prohibition and demographic changes sparked by economic growth inspired the unusual brutality of the Smith lynching (*Path to a Modern South*, 3–38).

104. *Brenham (Texas) Daily Banner*, 15 February 1893; "The United States," *TL*, 22 February 1892.

105. "Protection for Southern Negroes," *Chicago Daily Tribune*, 10 February 1893. A similar resolution was defeated in Oklahoma. See also "Refused to Censure Lynching," *NYT*, 9 February 1893.

106. "Excitement at the Pastors' Meeting: A Tumultuous Discussion over the Lynching of Smith at Paris, Tex.," *Chicago Daily Tribune*, 14 February 1893; "The Paris Burning," *Brenham (Texas) Daily Banner*, 24 February 1893.

107. "Lynch Law," *Fort Worth Gazette*, 8 February 1893; "Gov. Hogg Proposes Remedies," *NYT*, 8 February 1893; "The United States," *TL*, 8 February 1893; "Gov. Hogg

Aroused," *NYT*, 3 February 1893; "That Message," *Fort Worth Gazette*, 9 February 1893; Buenger, *Path to a Modern South*, 20–21; "The Paris Burning," *Brenham (Texas) Daily Banner*, 24 February 1893.

108. "Sensations: 'A Man and a Brudder,'" *Star* (London), 2 February 1893; editorial, *DCL*, 3 February 1893. For a discussion of the supplicant slave image, see Yellin, *Women and Sisters*.

109. "The Paris Burning," *Brenham (Texas) Daily Banner*, 24 February 1893.

110. See Williamson, *Crucible of Race*.

111. See Sommerville, *Rape and Race*.

112. Kennedy, "Lynch," 220; "The Lynching Affair at New Orleans," *Spectator* 66 (21 March 1891): 402.

113. Janson, *Stranger in America*, 382, 386–87; Martineau, *Society in America*, 1:373–75; "The Horrible Affair at Denton, Maryland," *TL*, 21 November 1862; "The United States," *TL*, 16 April 1884.

114. Diane Miller Sommerville convincingly argues that despite the existence of black-on-white rapes both before and after the Civil War, until the late 1880s, southern whites generally regarded black men as "complacent and innocuous." Because black rapists were seen as the exception to the rule, white southerners often sought the legal prosecution of enslaved and free black men accused of rape, who were often provided a competent legal defense and faced juries with a presumption of innocence. However, this does not account for the persistence of reports that extralegal burning was used to punish black rapists (*Rape and Race*, 21–23, 38–40, 49, 231–32, 237–40).

CHAPTER 2. THE EMERGENCE OF A TRANSATLANTIC REFORMER

1. Although Wells's brother claimed that their mother's maiden name was Warrenton, Paula Giddings suggests it may have been Arrington. See Wells, *Crusade for Justice*, 7–9; Giddings, *Ida*, 15–16, 19. The spelling of *Bolling* varied, including *Bowling* and *Boling* (see, for example, Series 1202, County Tax Rolls, Marshall County, 1858 personal, p. 18, 1862 personal, p. 7, Mississippi Department of Archives and History, Jackson).

2. Wells, *Crusade for Justice*, 8–9. The freedmen's school eventually expanded and became Rust College.

3. Mildred I. Thompson, *Ida B. Wells-Barnett*, 11–13; Wells, *Crusade for Justice*, 7–18; Crosby, *American Plague*, 87.

4. Kelley, *Right to Ride*, 41; Mack, "Law, Society, Identity," 381–82; Welke, "When All the Women Were White," 269–71, 278; Welke, *Recasting American Liberty*, 280–85. All "ladies" were expected to exemplify the core virtues of "true womanhood" such as "piety, purity, submissiveness and domesticity," but African American women were

also expected to demonstrate intelligence and to advocate for the betterment of the black community (see Welter, "Cult of True Womanhood," 152; Carlson, "Black Ideals of Womanhood," 61–62).

5. Kelley, *Right to Ride*, 15–32.

6. Ibid., 35–39.

7. *CO&SRR v. Wells*, West Tennessee 312, p. 34; Mack, "Law, Society, Identity," 389–90.

8. For example, see Terrell, *Colored Woman*, 295–98; Mack, "Law, Society, Identity," 382; Kelley, *Right to Ride*, 39; Welke, "When All the Women Were White," 280–81, 288–89.

9. Mack, "Law, Society, Identity," 393 n. 31.

10. Wells, *Memphis Diary*, 71–73, 75–76, 83–95, 147; Mack, "Law, Society, Identity," 388–90.

11. *CO&SRR v. Wells*, West Tennessee 312, pp. 19–20.

12. Ibid., 19–23, 25, 31–32; Wells, *Crusade for Justice*, 18–19.

13. Wells, *Memphis Diary*, 78, 98, 110–13, 115, 119–20, 125–27, 134.

14. Terrell, *Colored Woman*, 295–98.

15. *CO&SRR v. Wells*, West Tennessee 312, pp. 32–33, 56–69; Wells, *Crusade for Justice*, 18–19.

16. Welke, "When All the Women Were White," 273–74.

17. *CO&SRR v. Wells*, West Tennessee 312, 56–69. The 1881 Tennessee regulation requiring railroads to provide "separate but equal" facilities was passed by white legislators over the objections of black representatives as a conciliatory gesture when efforts to repeal an 1875 law permitting racial discrimination failed (Cartwright, *Triumph of Jim Crow*, 102–7).

18. Mack, "Law, Society, Identity," 388–89; Welke, "When All the Women Were White," 274.

19. *CO&SRR v. Wells*, West Tennessee 312, p. 21.

20. Ibid., 24, 58.

21. Ibid., 61, 67.

22. Ibid., 67–68.

23. Ibid., West Tennessee 319, pp. 8–15.

24. Wells, *Memphis Diary*, 76; Terrell, *Colored Woman*, 297–98.

25. "Iola," *Cleveland Gazette*, 11 December 1886; *Chesapeake, Ohio, & Southwestern Railroad Company v. Wells*, 5 April 1887, in *Reports of Cases Argued*, 1:613–15; Davidson, *"They Say,"* 72–74; Wells, *Memphis Diary*, 57, 66, 103, 137, 139, 140–41.

26. Wells, *Crusade for Justice*, 18–24; McMurry, *To Keep the Waters Troubled*, 87–88.

27. The precise origins of that pseudonym are unknown. However, it is probable that *Iola* is a derivation of *Ida* based on sloppy or flowery handwriting. Perhaps an

early criticism of her schoolwork, a personal letter, or some other incident provided her with a nickname, which she then embraced in her writing (DeCosta-Willis, "To Miss Ida Bee With Love," 91; Royster, *Southern Horrors*, 16 n. 19).

28. Mildred I. Thompson, *Ida B. Wells-Barnett*, 13–19; Wells, *Crusade for Justice*, 35–45. For a portrait of the difficulties faced by black newspaper editors, see Thornbrough, *T. Thomas Fortune*.

29. Wells, *Crusade for Justice*, 32, 86; McMurry, *To Keep the Waters Troubled*, 110–13.

30. McMurry, *To Keep the Waters Troubled*, 130–34.

31. Wells, *Crusade for Justice*, 64; McMurry, *To Keep the Waters Troubled*, 135–36; Hutton, "Rhetoric of Ida B. Wells," 29.

32. McMurry, *To Keep the Waters Troubled*, 143–46. Martha Hodes, *White Women*, argues that southerners were largely unconcerned with interracial sex during the antebellum period and that the taboo against relationships between white women and black men developed as white anxieties about black freedom increased at the end of the nineteenth century.

33. Wells, *United States Atrocities*, 1–3; McMurry, *To Keep the Waters Troubled*, 146–49; Wells, *Crusade for Justice*, 61–67.

34. Wells, *Crusade for Justice*, 83–85.

35. For examples of African American activists courting British support, see McFeely, *Frederick Douglass*; Blackett, *Building an Antislavery Wall*; Marsh, *Story*; Andrew Ward, *Dark Midnight*; Adi and Sherwood, *1945 Manchester Pan-African Congress*; Branch, *Parting the Waters*.

36. *Case and Claims*, 4–6; Bolt, *Anti-Slavery Movement*, 54, 59.

37. Bolt, *Anti-Slavery Movement*, 105; Friends Central Committee, *Report*; Nicholas, *United States and Britain*, 38–39. British travelers to the United States after the Civil War expressed concern regarding black idleness and lack of thrift (Wynes, "Race Question," 223–32).

38. Nicholas, *United States and Britain*, 33–35, 38–46; *Case and Claims*, 6–11; Bolt, *Anti-Slavery Movement*, 25, 33, 55–56, 59–61, 69–70.

39. Nicholas, *United States and Britain*, 43–44, 47.

40. For a discussion of the end of Reconstruction, see Richardson, *Death of Reconstruction*.

41. Temperley, *Britain and America since Independence*, 82–88; Nicholas, *United States and Britain*, 45–50; Dobson, *Anglo-American Relations*, 11.

42. Bolt, *Anti-Slavery Movement*, 38–39; Holt, *Problem of Freedom*, 263–67, 290–307.

43. Bolt, *Anti-Slavery Movement*, 38, 41–45, 52; Holt, *Problem of Freedom*, 278–85, 307–9.

44. Dilke, *Greater Britain*, 318; Reynolds, *Minstrel Memories*, 9; Bolt, *Anti-Slavery Movement*, 142–43, 146, 150–51; Meer, "Competing Representations."

45. Marsh, *Story*, 52–58, 64–65, 70–71, 73, 76–78, 81–87; Gilroy, *Black Atlantic*,

88–90. For a detailed depiction of the history of the Jubilee Singers and their tours in Europe and North America, see Andrew Ward, *Dark Midnight*.

46. Marsh, *Story*, 80; Gilroy, *Black Atlantic*, 237 n. 37.

47. See, for example, Rice and Crawford, "Triumphant Exile"; Blackett, "Cracks in the Antislavery Wall"; McFeely, "Visible Man"; Hamilton, "Frederick Douglass." For a discussion of the rise of reform movements within U.S. black and white communities, see Carle, *Defining the Struggle*; Foster, *Moral Reconstruction*; Gilmore, *Gender and Jim Crow*; Greenwood, *Bittersweet Legacy*; Luker, *Social Gospel*; Tyrrell, *Reforming the World*.

48. Catherine Impey to the Grand Lodge of England, 26 April 1889, SRBM Scrapbook; Catherine Impey to William E. A. Axon, 4 June 1889, Axon Papers, 2972; Catherine Impey, "An Appeal Concerning the Treatment of Coloured Races," January 1888, SRBM Minute Book; "Negro Mission Fund," *Good Templars' Watchword* 11 (3 March 1884): 139; Fahey, *Temperance and Racism*, 114, 139, 141–42, 144.

49. Frederick Douglass to Catherine Impey, 9 July 1888, SRBM Scrapbook; Catherine Impey to Emma Kilborn and Albion Winegar Tourgée, 3 January–2 March 1893, 6700, *Tourgée Papers*; Gen. Samuel Chapman Armstrong to Catherine Impey, 6 July 1890, SRBM Scrapbook.

50. Frederick Douglass to Catherine Impey, 9 July 1888, SRBM Scrapbook.

51. Catherine Impey to Emma K. Tourgée, 12 April 1893, 6854, *Tourgée Papers*.

52. Ibid.

53. Wells, *Crusade for Justice*, 89.

54. Catherine Impey, "Private," 17 August 1893, SRBM Scrapbook.

55. Catherine Impey to Emma K. and Albion W. Tourgée, 3 January–2 March 1893, 6700, *Tourgée Papers*.

56. Catherine Impey, "Private," 17 August 1893, SRBM Scrapbook; "Lynch Law in the United States: Horrible Atrocities," *Reuter's Journal*, 2 February 1893; Catherine Impey to Emma K. and Albion W. Tourgée, 3 January–2 March 1893, 6700, *Tourgée Papers*.

57. Catherine Impey, "Private," 17 August 1893, SRBM Scrapbook.

58. Ibid.; Wells, *Crusade for Justice*, 83–85, 89. The SRBM's initial efforts to end American lynching fit into a broader anti-imperialist agenda, and the SRBM carved a discursive space for future anti-imperial movements, including the Pan-African Conference of 1900 (Ware, *Beyond the Pale*; Schneer, "Pan-African Conference").

59. Schechter, *Ida B. Wells-Barnett*, 92.

60. Ida B. Wells, "Lynch Law in All Its Phases" *Our Day* 11 (May 1893): 333–47.

61. Wells, *Crusade for Justice*, 85–86. For analysis of black protests against the Chicago World's Fair, see Rydell, *All the World's a Fair*; Rydell, introduction to *Reason Why*; Rudwick and Meier, "Black Man."

62. Catherine Impey, "Private," 17 August 1893, SRBM Scrapbook.

63. Wells, *Crusade for Justice*, 3–5; "Lynch Law in the United States," *LP* 3 (April

1894): 49–51. For an examination of Fortune's career and connections to Washington, see Thornbrough, *T. Thomas Fortune*. For Washington's account of the public reaction to his Atlanta Exposition address, see *Up from Slavery*, 217–37. For an examination of the racial politics surrounding the Cotton States Exposition, see Perdue, *Race*.

64. Catherine Impey, "An Appeal Concerning the Treatment of Coloured Races," January 1888, SRBM Minute Book.

65. Catherine Impey, "Private," 17 August 1893, SRBM Scrapbook.

66. Midgley, *Women against Slavery*, 143. See also Tamarkin, "Black Anglophilia."

67. Catherine Impey, "Private," 17 August 1893, SRBM Scrapbook.

68. McMurry, *To Keep the Waters Troubled*, 167.

69. "Declaration Form as Used April till August 1893," SRBM Minute Book.

70. "Early Record of 'Brotherhood' Society," SRBM Scrapbook.

71. Catherine Impey, "An Appeal Concerning the Treatment of Coloured Races," January 1888, SRBM Minute Book.

72. Catherine Impey, "Who Shall Make America Listen?" *AC* 6 (February 1893): 3.

73. "A Lynching Scene in Alabama," *AC* 6 (January 1893): 1.

74. Wells, "Lynch Law in All Its Phases."

75. See, for example, "Lynch Law in the United States," *Birmingham Daily Gazette*, 18 May 1893; "Lynch Law in America," *BDP*, 18 May 1893.

76. Wells, "Lynch Law in All its Phases," 344.

77. "Lynch Law in America," *BDP*, 18 May 1893.

78. "Lynch-Law in the United States," *Aberdeen Daily Free Press*, 24 April 1893.

79. "Lynch Law in the United States," *LDP*, 18 May 1893.

80. "Lynch Law in the Southern States of America," *Huntly Express*, 29 April 1893. Charles Wynes notes that few British travelers to the United States remarked on racial segregation ("Race Question," 231–32).

81. Woodward, *Strange Career of Jim Crow*, 31–44; Woodward, "Capitulation to Racism," 9–13.

82. "Lynch Law in America," *BDP*, 18 May 1893.

83. "Lynch Law in the United States," *Birmingham Daily Gazette*, 18 May 1893.

84. Wells, *United States Atrocities*, 2.

85. S. J. Celestine Edwards, introduction, v–vi.

86. See, for example, N. J. D. Kennedy, "Lynch," *Juridical Review* 3 (July 1891): 213–22. Alison Piepmeier argues that Wells emphasized black female bodies in her rhetoric to claim both a right to black womanhood and American citizenship (*Out in Public*, 129–71).

87. Wells, *United States Atrocities*, 8–9, 19–21.

88. Ibid., 2, 3, 4–6, 10–13, 20.

89. Ibid., 19.

90. Ibid., 9, 19–21.

91. S. J. Celestine Edwards, introduction, vi.

92. Wells, *United States Atrocities*, 9, 15–18, 27–28; S. J. Celestine Edwards, introduction, vii.

CHAPTER 3. THE STRUGGLE FOR LEGITIMACY

1. Peterson, *"Doers of the Word,"* 137–38.

2. Meer, *Uncle Tom Mania*, 164, 189.

3. Mattingly, *Well-Tempered Women*, 97.

4. Christine Bolt argues that the small number of African American women abolitionists in Britain inhibited interracial tensions, making them "interesting and useful" to white reformers (*Sisterhood Questioned*, 8–11). For an examination of British attitudes toward race in Britain, see Lorimer, *Colour, Class, and the Victorians*; Gerzina, *Black Victorians/Black Victoriana*. For British attitudes toward race in the colonial and postcolonial context, see Bolt, *Victorian Attitudes to Race*.

5. McCaskill, "'Yours Very Truly.'" For a broader discussion of African American abolitionist activism in Britain, see Blackett, "Cracks in the Antislavery Wall"; Meer, "Competing Representations"; Quarles, *Black Abolitionists*, 116–42; Rice and Crawford, "Triumphant Exile."

6. Meer, *Uncle Tom Mania*, 184–85, 186, 189; Gardner, "Stowe Takes the Stage," 80–81; Clark, "Solo Black Performance," 346, 347–48.

7. Meer, *Uncle Tom Mania*, 189; Fisch, *American Slaves*, 83–87.

8. Midgley, *Women against Slavery*, 143, 170–71; Brownlee, "Out of the Abundance," 127–29, 132, 134; Peterson, *"Doers of the Word,"* 137–38; Coleman, "'Like Hot Lead,'" 177–82.

9. Mattingly, *Well-Tempered Women*, 96–120.

10. Ibid., 17, 65, 97, 111, 115. For a broader discussion of efforts to establish an acceptable role for women in policymaking, see Muncy, *Creating a Female Dominion*.

11. "Lynch-Law in the United States," *Aberdeen Daily Free Press*, 24 April 1893.

12. Sommerville, *Rape and Race*, 25.

13. "Lynch Law in America," *DCL*, 28 April 1894.

14. "Lynch Law in the Southern States," *Scottish Pulpit*, 10 May 1893; *Lady's Pictorial* 25 (20 May 1893): 809.

15. Mattingly, *Well-Tempered Women*, 96–120.

16. "Lynch Law in the Southern States of America," *Newcastle Daily Leader*, 10 May 1893.

17. "Lynch Law in the Southern States," *Scottish Pulpit*, 10 May 1893.

18. Schechter, *Ida B. Wells-Barnett*, 20; Wells, *Crusade for Justice*, 22–23.

19. "Lynch Law in the Southern States of America," *Huntly Express*, 29 April 1893.

20. "Aberdeen—Lynch Law in America," *Aberdeen Daily Free Press*, 25 April 1893.

21. "Lynch Law in the Southern States," *Scottish Pulpit*, 10 May 1893.
22. Ibid.
23. McCaskill, "'Yours Very Truly,'" 524.
24. Still, *Underground Railroad*, 374–76.
25. McCaskill, "'Yours Very Truly,'" 521; Wells, *Crusade for Justice*, 109–10, 113.
26. "Aberdeen—Lynch Law in America," *Aberdeen Daily Free Press*, 25 April 1893.
27. Remond's career was quickly eclipsed by traditional male antislavery lecturers, including Frederick Douglass. See Gardner, "Stowe Takes the Stage," 80; Meer, *Uncle Tom Mania*, 188; Brownlee, "Out of the Abundance," 127, 134–35, 138.
28. "Lynch Law in the Southern States of America," *Newcastle Daily Leader*, 10 May 1893.
29. "Lynch Law in the Southern States of America," *Huntly Express*, 29 April 1893.
30. "Lynch Law in the Southern States," *Scottish Pulpit*, 10 May 1893; "Lynch Law in the Southern States of America," *Aberdeen Journal*, 25 April 1893; "Aberdeen—Lynch Law in America," *Aberdeen Daily Free Press*, 25 April 1893. For an analysis of Wells's womanly "performance" on the British platform, see King, "'Colored Woman.'"
31. "Lynch Law in America," *BDP*, 18 May 1893.
32. "Lynch Law in the Southern States of America," *Newcastle Daily Leader*, 10 May 1893; "Lynch Law in the Southern States of America," *Huntly Express*, 29 April 1893; "The Negro Question in South America," *Glasgow Herald*, 3 May 1893.
33. "Lynch Law in the Southern States," *Scottish Pulpit*, 10 May 1893.
34. "The Negro Question in South America," *Glasgow Herald*, 3 May 1893.
35. "Lynch Law in America," *BDP*, 18 May 1893; "Lynch Law in the United States," *Birmingham Daily Gazette*, 18 May 1893.
36. "Lynch Law in the Southern States of America," *Aberdeen Journal*, 25 April 1893; "Lynch Law in the Southern States of America," *Huntly Express*, 29 April 1893; "Lynch Law in America," *BDP*, 18 May 1893; "Lynch Law in the United States," *Birmingham Daily Gazette*, 18 May 1893.
37. *Lady's Pictorial* 25 (20 May 1893): 809; editorial, *BDP*, 18 May 1893; "Lynch Law in the United States," *LDP*, 18 May 1893.
38. "Negro Mission Fund," *Good Templars' Watchword* 11 (3 March 1884): 139; David M. Fahey, "Impey, Catherine (1847–1923)," in *Oxford Dictionary*, ed. Matthew and Harrison, 29:213–14.
39. Frederick Douglass to Catherine Impey, 9 July 1888, SRBM Scrapbook; Catherine Impey to William E. A. Axon, 25 February 1889, Axon Papers, 2939; Fahey, *Temperance and Racism*, 114.
40. Catherine Impey, "An Appeal Concerning the Treatment of Coloured Races," January 1888, SRBM Minute Book; "Appeal on Behalf of the Coloured People of America," n.d., LSF box L267, Library of the Religious Society of Friends in Britain, London; Fahey, *Temperance and Racism*, 114, 139; Fahey, "Impey, Catherine."

41. Catherine Impey, "An Appeal Concerning the Treatment of Coloured Races," January 1888, SRBM Minute Book.

42. Gen. Samuel Chapman Armstrong to Catherine Impey, 6 July 1890, SRBM Scrapbook.

43. Catherine Impey, "Extracts from the Editor's Diary of a Visit to 'Cedar Hill,'" *AC* 7 (April–May 1895): 14.

44. Catherine Impey to Emma K. Tourgée, 12 April 1893, 6854, *Tourgée Papers*.

45. Catherine Impey to William E. A. Axon, 9 November 1894, Axon Papers, 3329.

46. Wells, *Crusade for Justice*, 103.

47. Catherine Impey to William E. A. Axon, 9 November 1894, Axon Papers, 3329. As the secretary of the Edinburgh Ladies' Emancipation Society and a key figure in early transatlantic reform movements, Wigham helped raise funds to support fugitive slaves, including William and Ellen Craft (Midgley, *Women against Slavery*, 132–33, 135–37, 139).

48. Catherine Impey to William E. A. Axon, 9 November 1894, Axon Papers, 3329. Charges of monomania, a disorder in which an individual becomes convinced of "a single false notion" but whose thoughts remain "otherwise unclouded," could be applied to anyone who displayed a behavior or asserted a belief that deviated from social norms. Accusations of monomania would have been damaging and extremely difficult to refute, since a person's reasonable behavior in all other areas of life would not constitute evidence of sanity (Prichard, *On the Different Forms of Insanity*, 67).

49. Wells, *Crusade for Justice*, 104–5.

50. Wells, *Memphis Diary*, 82.

51. Wells, *Crusade for Justice*, 239–41.

52. Ibid., 105, 109–10; Catherine Impey, "Private," 17 August 1893, SRBM Scrapbook.

53. Wells, *Crusade for Justice*, 104.

54. Gen. Samuel Chapman Armstrong to Catherine Impey, 6 July 1890, SRBM Scrapbook; McMurry, *To Keep the Waters Troubled*, 185.

55. Rice and Crawford, "Triumphant Exile," 7–8. See also Fisch, *American Slaves*, 69–90. Lindy Moore argues that Mayo supported both interracial marriage and a woman's right to propose marriage but viewed Impey's behavior as impulsive and reckless ("Reputation," 76–79).

56. Catherine Impey to William E. A. Axon, 9 November 1894, Axon Papers, 3329.

57. Isabella Fyvie Mayo to Isabella Spring Brown, 30 September 1905, 22 August 1906, 2 November, Christmastide 1907, 29 March, 29 April 1908, 11 January, Easter Day 1910, n.d., NLS: MS. 1890, 97–102, 104–11, 113–15, 168–74, National Library of Scotland, Edinburgh.

58. Ibid., 2 November 1907, 105–8.

59. Emma Plaskitt, "Mayo, Isabella (1843–1914)," in *Oxford Dictionary*, ed. Mat-

thew and Harrison, 37:619–20; Catherine Impey to Emma K. Tourgée, 23 June 1893, 7064, *Tourgée Papers*.

60. Catherine Impey to Emma K. Tourgée, 23 June 1893, 7064, Catherine Impey to Albion W. Tourgée, 24 June 1893, 7069, T. Thomas Fortune to Albion W. Tourgée, 9, 15 July 1893, 7112, 7129, Albion W. Tourgée to T. Thomas Fortune, n.d., 7179, *Tourgée Papers*.

61. Showalter, *Female Malady*, 29, 74–75, 131; Catherine Impey to Emma K. Tourgée, 23 June 1893, 7064, *Tourgée Papers*.

62. Albion W. Tourgée to T. Thomas Fortune, n.d., 7179, *Tourgée Papers*; Showalter, *Female Malady*, 55, 59, 121–25.

63. Catherine Impey to William E. A. Axon, 9 November 1894, Axon Papers, 3329.

64. Isichei, *Victorian Quakers*, 118–19, 139–41.

65. Catherine Impey to Albion W. and Emma K. Tourgée, 23 September 1894, 8044, *Tourgée Papers*.

66. Catherine Impey to William E. A. Axon, 9 November 1894, Axon Papers, 3329.

67. Wells, *Crusade for Justice*, 109. An exact date for Wells's departure from England has not been determined, although Mildred I. Thompson claims that Wells returned in June 1893. See Schechter, *Ida B. Wells-Barnett*, 94; McMurry, *To Keep the Waters Troubled*, 197–98; Mildred I. Thompson, *Ida B. Wells-Barnett*, 39.

68. "Lynch Law in the Southern States of America," *Newcastle Daily Leader*, 10 May 1893; handwritten notation, *AC* 6 (May–June 1893), SRBM Scrapbook; Wells, *United States Atrocities*; Catherine Impey, "Private," 17 August 1893, SRBM Scrapbook.

69. "Early Record of 'Brotherhood' Society," SRBM Scrapbook.

70. Jonathan Schneer, "Edwards, (Samuel Jules) Celestine (1857?–1894)," in *Oxford Dictionary*, ed. Matthew and Harrison, 17:912–13; Fryer, *Staying Power*, 277–79; "Early Record of 'Brotherhood' Society," SRBM Scrapbook.

71. Schneer, "Edwards, (Samuel Jules) Celestine."

72. Isabella Fyvie Mayo to Ida B. Wells, 12 September 1893, Douglass Papers.

73. Ida B. Wells to Frederick Douglass, 6 April 1894, in ibid.

74. Ibid., 13 March, 6 April 1894.

75. Ibid., 6 April 1894.

76. "What We Think," *Fraternity* 1 (April 1894): 1; "Ex-Senator Green in Scotland," *Fraternity* 1 (June 1894): 16; *Cleveland Gazette*, 28 April 1894.

77. Ida B. Wells to Frederick Douglass, 6 April 1894, Douglass Papers.

78. S. J. Celestine Edwards, (open letter), *Lux* 2 (20 January 1894): 393; "Sparks," *Lux* 2 (10 March 1894): 90; Schneer, "Edwards, (Samuel Jules) Celestine."

79. E. J. Norris, (open letter), *Lux* 2 (31 March 1894): 137.

80. Ida B. Wells to Frederick Douglass, 6 April 1894, Douglass Papers.

81. Ibid., 13 March, 6 April, 10 May 1894.

82. Ibid., 6 April 1894.

83. Frederick Douglass to Ida B. Wells, 27 March 1894, in ibid.

84. Ida B. Wells to Frederick Douglass, 6 April, 6, 10 May 1894, in ibid.

85. Catherine Impey to Albion W. and Emma K. Tourgée, 23 September 1894, 8044, *Tourgée Papers*; Schneer, "Edwards, (Samuel Jules) Celestine."

86. "The Female Accusation," *Fraternity* 1 (August 1894): 4; Mattingly, *Well-Tempered Women*, 104.

87. "The Female Accusation," *Fraternity* 1 (August 1894): 4–5.

88. Ibid., 5.

89. "The Present Position of Our Society," *Fraternity* 1 (September 1894): 5–6.

90. The name change was first discussed in *Fraternity* 2 (November 1894): 2.

91. "An Anti-Lynching Committee," *Fraternity* 1 (October 1894): 7.

92. "The Late Frederick Douglass," *Great Thoughts of Master Minds* 4 (16 March 1895): 387; Frederick Douglass to Catherine Impey, 9 July 1888, SRBM Scrapbook. For a more thorough examination of Impey's struggles for control of the SRBM and ultimate decision to leave the organization, see Silkey, "'More Sinned against Than Sinning.'"

CHAPTER 4. BUILDING A TRANSATLANTIC
DEBATE ON LYNCHING

1. Ida B. Wells to Frederick Douglass, 13 March, 6 April 1894, Douglass Papers.

2. Ibid., 6 April 1894.

3. Ibid.; Wells, *Crusade for Justice*, 141–42.

4. Ida B. Wells to Frederick Douglass, 6 April 1894, Douglass Papers.

5. "Interviews with Local Celebrities: Rev. C. F. Aked, the New Evangel," *Porcupine*, 16 September 1893, in Aked Clipping File, Liverpool Record Office, Liverpool Libraries, Liverpool, England.

6. Ibid.; Charles F. Aked, "Five Years in Liverpool, a Personal Retrospect," *LP* 4 (October 1895), 112–15.

7. Charles F. Aked, "Five Years in Liverpool, a Personal Retrospect," *LP* 4 (October 1895), 112; Hundley, *George Kennan*; Marsden, *On Sledge and Horseback*; Schechter, *Ida B. Wells-Barnett*, 98.

8. Ida B. Wells to Frederick Douglass, 6 April 1894, Douglass Papers.

9. Claiming that "Wells was poorly positioned to dictate terms," Patricia Schechter characterizes Wells's relationship with Aked as prescribed by his personal and political ambitions. She concludes that Wells banked too heavily on "Aked's rising star" to make her campaign a success (*Ida B. Wells-Barnett*, 98–99, 101). Linda McMurry mentions Aked only briefly (*To Keep the Waters Troubled*, 208, 209, 215, 217).

10. Ida B. Wells to Frederick Douglass, 13 March 1894, Douglass Papers.

11. "'American Atrocities': Demonstration in Liverpool," *LDP*, 23 March 1894; "Lynching in the United States," *LDP*, 6 April 1894; "A Sermon on Ibsen: A Coloured Woman in the Pulpit," *CW* 38 (15 March 1894): 187; A. J. A. Morris, "Russell, Edward

Richard, First Baron Russell of Liverpool (1834–1920)," in *Oxford Dictionary*, ed. Matthew and Harrison, 48:232–33.

12. *Christian News* (Glasgow), 10 June 1893; "Interviews with Local Celebrities: Rev. C. F. Aked, the New Evangel," *Porcupine*, 16 September 1893, Aked Clipping File.

13. Charles F. Aked, "Lynch Law Rampant," *CW* 38 (12 April 1894): 259; Charles F. Aked, "One Woman's Work," *CW* 38 (19 July 1894): 545; "Lynch Law in the United States," *LP* 3 (April 1894): 49–51; "More Lynch Law," *LP* 3 (May 1894): 65–66; "American Christians and Lynch Law," *LP* 3 (July 1894): 97–98; "Appeal to the Ministers of Religion and Members of the Churches of the United States," *LP* 3 (August 1894): 113–14.

14. *LP* 3 (April 1894): 49.

15. "A Sermon on Ibsen: A Coloured Woman in the Pulpit," *CW* 38 (15 March 1894): 187; Charles F. Aked, "Lynch Law Rampant," *CW* 38 (12 April 1894): 259; "Lynch Law in America," *CW* 38 (19 April 1894): 287; "Negro Lynching in America: A Talk with Miss Ida B. Wells," *CW* 38 (3 May 1894): 334; Charles F. Aked, "One Woman's Work," *CW* 38 (19 July 1894): 545.

16. "Lynch Law in the United States," *LP* 3 (April 1894): 49; Charles F. Aked, "Lynch Law Rampant," *CW* 38 (12 April 1894): 259; Frederick Douglass to Ida B. Wells, 27 March 1894, Ida B. Wells to Frederick Douglass, 6 April 1894, Douglass Papers.

17. Charles F. Aked to Frederick Douglass, 12 April 1894, Douglass Papers.

18. Richard Acland Armstrong, "Lynch Law in America: An English Protest" (letter to the editor), *CR* 73 (12 April 1894): 227; "Lynching in the United States," *Inquirer* 53 (31 March 1894): 203; "Lynching in the United States," *LDP*, 6 April 1894.

19. "Triennial Conference of Unitarians . . . Lynch Law in America," *LDP*, 14 April 1894; Ida B. Wells, "Miss Wells Maintains Her Accusations of 'Pulpit and Press'" (letter to the editor), *Inquirer* 53 (5 May 1894): 274.

20. "Triennial Conference of Unitarians . . . Lynch Law in America," *LDP*, 14 April 1894; Philippa Levine, "Chant, Laura Ormiston (1848–1923)," in *Oxford Dictionary*, ed. Matthew and Harrison, 11:19.

21. Charles Roper to William E. A. Axon, 10 May 1894, Axon Papers, 3299; "National Conference: Fifth Triennial Meeting," *Inquirer* 53 (14 April 1894): 232; "Triennial Conference of Unitarians . . . Lynch Law in America," *LDP*, 14 April 1894.

22. Ida B. Wells to Frederick Douglass, 6 May 1894, Ambrose N. Blatchford to Ida B. Wells, 30 April 1894, Douglass Papers.

23. "Lynch Law in the South," *CR* 73 (12 April 1894): 225; Richard Acland Armstrong, "Lynch Law in America: An English Protest" (letter to the editor), *CR* 73 (12 April 1894): 227; "Triennial Conference of Unitarians . . . Lynch Law in America," *LDP*, 14 April 1894.

24. "Lynch Law in the South," *CR* 73 (12 April 1894): 225.

25. Ida B. Wells, "Miss Wells Maintains Her Accusations of 'Pulpit and Press'" (letter to the editor), *Inquirer* 53 (5 May 1894): 274–75.

26. "Topics and Events," *Inquirer* 53 (28 April 1894): 257.

27. Brooke Herford to William E. A. Axon, 8 May 1894, Axon Papers, 3298; Charles Roper to William E. A. Axon, 10 May 1894, Axon Papers, 3299; Ida B. Wells to William E. A. Axon, [May 1894], Axon Papers, 3583.

28. Ida B. Wells to William E. A. Axon, [May 1894], Axon Papers, 3583; Ambrose N. Blatchford to Ida B. Wells, 30 April 1894, Douglass Papers.

29. "Lynch Law in America," *CW* 38 (19 April 1894): 287.

30. David M. Thompson, "Clifford, John (1836–1923)," in *Oxford Dictionary*, ed. Matthew and Harrison, 12:100–101.

31. Charles F. Aked to Frederick Douglass, 12 April 1894, Douglass Papers.

32. Frederick Douglass to Charles F. Aked, 27 March 1894, Ida B. Wells to Frederick Douglass, 13 March 1894, Douglass Papers; "Lynch Law in America," *CW* 38 (19 April 1894): 287.

33. Editorials, *DCL*, 25, 28 April 1894.

34. "The Baptist Union," *CW* 38 (26 April 1894): 303.

35. (Lady Henry) Isabel Somerset to Frederick Douglass, 22 May 1894, Douglass Papers; "B.W.T.A. Council Meetings," *Woman's Signal* 1 (17 May 1894): 340; *DCL*, 14 May 1894. For an excellent examination of the controversy surrounding Wells's criticism of Willard, see Mattingly, *Well-Tempered Women*, 75–95. Vron Ware argues that the conflict over Wells's critique of Willard's assumptions reveals the important interconnections between race and gender oppression (*Beyond the Pale*, 212–21).

36. "Women's Yearly Meeting," *British Friend* 3 (July 1894): 204.

37. "London Yearly Meeting," *British Friend* 3 (9 June 1894): 174; "The May Meetings: The Friends' Yearly Meeting," *CW* 38 (31 May 1894): 422.

38. *DCL*, 14 May 1894.

39. "May Meetings: The Congregational Union," *DCL*, 12 May 1894; Elaine Kaye, "Horton, Robert Forman (1855–1934)," in *Oxford Dictionary*, ed. Matthew and Harrison, 28:214–16.

40. *DCL*, 14 May 1894; "Lynching in the South: The Awful Stories Told to the English," *Columbus (Georgia) Enquirer-Sun*, 13 May 1894, clipping, Northen Papers, box 5, vol. 4, p. 15.

41. "Topics and Events," *Inquirer* 53 (5 May 1894): 273; "British and Foreign Unitarian Association: Annual Meeting," *Inquirer* 53 (19 May 1894): 306–7; "Unitarian Association," *DCL*, 16 May 1894; "The Unitarian Meetings," *CW* 38 (17 May 1894): 381; W. Copeland Bowie to the editor, 30 May 1894, Douglass Papers; A Refreshed Unit., "Impressions of the Meetings" (letter to the editor), *Inquirer* 53 (26 May 1894): 334.

42. Frederick Douglass to Charles F. Aked, 22 May 1894, Frederick Douglass to Richard A. Armstrong, 22 May 1894, Ida B. Wells to Frederick Douglass, 3 June 1894, Douglass Papers; Charles F. Aked, "One Woman's Work," *CW* 38 (19 July 1894): 545; Wells, *Crusade for Justice*, 176.

43. Charles F. Aked, "Race Problem in America," *Contemporary Review* 65 (June

1894): 823–25, 827; "Lynch Law in America," *DCL*, 28 April 1894. Although journalists used the phrase *criminal assaults* to refer to offenses ranging from inappropriate sexual advances to rape, audiences most commonly interpreted it as the latter.

44. Wells's arguments appear in Wells, *Southern Horrors*, 11–12; Rydell, *Reason Why*, 30–33.

45. "Lynch-Law in America," *Spectator* 72 (2 June 1894): 743–44; "The Lynching of Negroes in America," *Economist* 52 (2 June 1894): 664.

46. William McKay, "Lynching in Georgia: A Correction" (letter to the editor), *Spectator* 73 (28 July 1894): 111.

47. "Lynching in America and English Interference," *Spectator* 73 (11 August 1894): 169.

48. For examples of renewed coverage, see "Black versus White," *Labour Leader*, 12 May 1894; "Lynch Law in America," *DCL*, 28 April 1894; "Miss Ida B. Wells," *Sun* (London), 31 May 1894.

49. "Lynch Law in America," *DCL*, 28 April 1894; "Lynching in the United States," *Newcastle Daily Leader*, 20 April 1894; "Miss Ida B. Wells," *Sun* (London), 31 May 1894.

50. "Lynch Law in America," *DCL*, 28 April 1894.

51. Editorial, *Bradford Observer*, 11 May 1894; "Lynching in the United States," *Newcastle Daily Leader*, 20 April 1894; editorial, *DCL*, 28 April 1894.

52. Editorial, *DCL*, 3 February 1893; "Lynch Law in Texas," *DNL*, 3 February 1893.

53. Editorial, *DCL*, 28 April 1894; "Lynch Law in America," *DCL*, 28 April 1894.

54. Editorial, *DCL*, 29 May 1894.

55. Ibid.

56. Wells, *Crusade for Justice*, 213–14; "May Meetings: The Baptist Union," *DNL*, 26 April 1894; "The Congregational Union," *DNL*, 12 May 1894; G. S. Woods, "Clayden, Peter William (1827–1902)," rev. H. C. G. Matthew, in *Oxford Dictionary*, ed. Matthew and Harrison, 11:971–72.

57. Wells, *Crusade for Justice*, 175–76.

58. "Lynching in America: A Parliamentary Protest," *DCL*, 7 June 1894; Charlotte Fell-Smith, "Pease, Sir Joseph Whitwell, First Baronet (1828–1903)," rev. M. W. Kirby, in *Oxford Dictionary*, ed. Matthew and Harrison, 43:356–57.

59. Florence Balgarnie, "The Story of Miss Ida B. Wells," *Great Thoughts of Master Minds* 4 (16 March 1895): 386; "An Anti-Lynching Committee," *Fraternity* 2 (October 1894): 7; Wells, *Crusade for Justice*, 216.

60. Society for the Recognition, *Annual Report 1894*, 6; editorial, *TL*, 6 October 1894; William M. Fishback to Anti-Lynching Committee of England, 8 November 1894, Crowell Papers.

61. J. Hiles Hitchens, "Lynch Law in the United States" (letter to the editor), *DCL*, 6 June 1894; Lloyd C. Griscom to J. Hiles Hitchens, 29 May 1894, reprinted in Hitchens, letter to the editor, *DCL*, 6 June 1894.

62. "Miss Wells's Second English Trip," *Fraternity* 2 (August 1894): 4; Minutes, 3 May, 8 June 1894, SRBM Minute Book; Society for the Recognition, *Annual Report 1894*, 9–10.

63. Editorial, *DCL*, 29 May 1894; *Anglo-American Times*, 16 June 1894; J. Moffat Logan, "Bristol," *Freeman* 40 (15 June 1894): 396.

64. "The Lynching of Negroes in America," *Economist* 52 (2 June 1894): 664.

65. "Negro Lynching in America: A Talk with Miss Ida B. Wells," *CW* 38 (3 May 1894): 334; Charles F. Aked, "Race Problem in America," *Contemporary Review* 65 (June 1894): 826–27; Florence Balgarnie, "The Story of Miss Ida B. Wells," *Great Thoughts of Master Minds* 4 (16 March 1895): 385.

CHAPTER 5. AMERICAN RESPONSES
TO BRITISH PROTEST

1. The ultimate resolution of post-Reconstruction tensions through disfranchisement, segregation, and other "reform" measures designed to rationalize southern society through the lens of white supremacy became known as southern progressivism. See Woodward, *Origins of the New South*; Kirby, *Darkness at the Dawning*; Kantrowitz, *Ben Tillman*.

2. Doyle, *New Men*, 313–18; Cobb, *Away Down South*, 67–73, 76–78.

3. Godshalk, "William J. Northen's Public and Personal Struggles," 141–42; Northen, *To the General Assembly*. Proponents of the New South creed struggled to overcome the image of the South as a backwards region that required missionary and regulatory intervention similar to colonial possessions. See Ring, *Problem South*.

4. Steeples, *Democracy in Desperation*, 27–28.

5. Godshalk, "William J. Northen's Public and Personal Struggles," 141–42; Northen, *To the General Assembly*.

6. "Lynch Law and Capital," *Elbert County (Georgia) Star*, [ca. June 1893], clipping, Northen Papers, box 5, vol. 3, p. 70.

7. "Capital Chat" and "Dunham Commended by the Governor," clippings, Northen Papers, box 5, vol. 3, p. 71; George W. Dunham to William J. Northen, 21 August 1893, William J. Northen to George W. Dunham, 24 August 1893, Northen Papers, box 1, folder 7.

8. Waldrep, *Many Faces of Judge Lynch*, 152, 163.

9. "An Act to Prevent Mob Violence," 19 December 1893, Northen Papers, box 3, folder 6.

10. Thomas Goode Jones, "Mob Violence," *Montgomery Daily Advertiser*, 7 February 1893.

11. Jones, *Inaugural Address*, 15.

12. Thomas Goode Jones, "Mob Violence," *Montgomery Daily Advertiser*, 7 February 1893; "Executive Messages," *Montgomery Daily Advertiser*, 7 February 1893;

Thomas Goode Jones, "Report to the Governor (1883)," in *Lynching in America*, ed. Waldrep, 136–37.

13. W. M. Waltrip to Thomas G. Jones, 3 April 1891, W. R. Carter to Thomas G. Jones, 3 April 1891, J. K. Jackson to J. T. Hamiter, 20 September 1893, J. T. Hamiter to Thomas G. Jones, 22 September 1893, W. A. Pinkerton to Thomas G. Jones, 24, 27, 29 November 1893, Alabama Governor (1890–1894: Jones), Administrative Files, SG8, 415 Reels 5–13, Alabama Department of Archives and History, Montgomery. See also Aucoin, "Thomas Goode Jones," 48–64.

14. Brundage, *Lynching in the New South*, 166–68, 173; George A. Mushbach to Charles T. O'Ferrall, 8 February 1894, Executive Papers of Charles T. O'Ferrall, 1894–97, Accession 43210, State Government Records Collection, Library of Virginia, Richmond; N. C. Watts to Captain of the Monticello Guards, 29 April 1894, O'Ferrall Papers; "Staunton's Brutal Tragedy," *Roanoke Times*, 2 May 1894; "Spiller Quickly Convicted," *Richmond Times*, 3 May 1894; editorial, *Richmond Planet*, 5 May 1894; Waldrep, *Many Faces of Judge Lynch*, 163.

15. Steeples, *Democracy in Desperation*, 91–92; Cobb, *Away Down South*, 71.

16. Southern states include Delaware, Maryland, West Virginia, Virginia, North Carolina, South Carolina, Georgia, Florida, Kentucky, Tennessee, Alabama, Mississippi, Louisiana, Oklahoma, and Texas. The District of Columbia is also considered part of the South. See Michael R. Haines, "Population, by Sex, Nativity, and Citizenship Status: 1890–1990," table Ad280-318, and Susan B. Carter, "Geographic Concentration of the Foreign-Born Population—Top Three States and the South: 1850–1990," table Ad696, in *Historical Statistics*, ed. Susan B. Carter et al., 1:598, 613.

17. Susan B. Carter and Richard Sutch, "U.S. Immigrants and Emigrants: 1820–1998," table Ad1-2, and Robert Barde, Susan B. Carter, and Richard Sutch, "Immigrants, by Country of Last Residence—Europe: 1820–1997," table Ad106-120, in ibid., 541, 561.

18. William J. Northen, "Lynching in the South," *CR* 73 (10 May 1894): 291; Northen, *Negro at the South*.

19. "Lynch Law in the South," *CR* 73 (12 April 1894): 225.

20. Wells, *United States Atrocities*, 16; Charles F. Aked, "One Woman's Work," *CW* 38 (19 July 1894): 545.

21. Wells, *United States Atrocities*, 15.

22. "'Tis Miss Ida," *Atlanta Constitution*, 28 July 1894, clipping, Northen Papers, box 5, vol. 4, p. 20.

23. "Governor Northen Expresses His Views of Attacks on the South," *Atlanta Constitution*, 27 June 1894, clipping, Northen Papers, box 5, vol. 4, p. 15.

24. "Voice of the Press," *Topeka Call*, 24 July 1892; "Organized Last Week: North-Western Emigration Association," *Springfield (Illinois) State Capitol*, 10 September 1892; "An Emigration Association," *Indianapolis Freeman*, 17 September 1892.

25. Examples include William E. A. Axon (*Manchester Guardian*), Percy Bunting

(*Contemporary Review*), Sir Edward Russell (*Liverpool Daily Post*), A. E. Fletcher (*Daily Chronicle*), and P. W. Clayden (*Daily News*). See Wells, *Crusade for Justice*, 216.

26. "Negro Lynching in America," *CW* 38 (3 May 1894): 334; J. J. Hall, "The South and the Negro: An Answer to the Charges Made against the White People of the South," *Norfolk Landmark*, 15 September 1894.

27. J. J. Hall to John Franklin Crowell, 24 October 1894, Crowell Papers.

28. J. J. Hall, "The South and the Negro: An Answer to the Charges Made against the White People of the South," *Norfolk Landmark*, 15 September 1894.

29. J. J. Hall to John Franklin Crowell, 24 October 1894, Crowell Papers.

30. J. J. Hall, "South and the Negro: An Answer to the Charges Made against the White People of the South," *Norfolk Landmark*, 15 September 1894.

31. William J. Northen to Col. C. B. Howard, 18 May 1894, Northen Papers, box 2, folder 19.

32. William J. Northen, "Lynching in the South," *CR* 73 (10 May 1894): 291; Samuel J. Barrows to William J. Northen, 16 April 1894, Northen Papers, box 5, vol. 4, p. 13; Richard Acland Armstrong, "Lynch Law in America: An English Protest" (letter to the editor), *CR* 73 (12 April 1894): 227.

33. "Masterly Defense," *Athens (Georgia) Weekly Banner*, clipping, Northen Papers, box 5, vol. 4, p. 15; W. P. Turner to William J. Northen, 6 June 1894, Northen Papers, box 2, folder 19.

34. Northen, *Negro at the South*; W. P. Turner to William J. Northen, 6 June 1894, Northen Papers, box 2, folder 19.

35. William J. Northen to William E. Hatcher, 24 May 1894, Northen Papers, box 2, folder 19. Christopher Waldrep, "Ida B. Wells," argues that Wells's activism received significant resistance from white southerners because her rhetoric challenged deeply entrenched beliefs in legal localism.

36. Editorial, *DCL*, 28 April 1894; William J. Northen, "Lynch Law in the Southern States" (letter to the editor), *DCL*, 5 June 1894.

37. William J. Northen, "Lynch Law in the Southern States" (letter to the editor), *DCL*, 5 June 1894; A. E. Fletcher, "Lynch Law in the Southern States" (editor's note), *DCL*, 5 June 1894.

38. "The Wells Woman," 26 May 1894, clipping, Northen Papers, box 5, vol. 4, p. 15.

39. Schechter, *Ida B. Wells-Barnett*, 91, 275 n. 49.

40. Editorial, *DCL*, 6 June 1894.

41. Ida B. Wells, "Lynching in America" (letter to the editor), *DCL*, 9 June 1894.

42. For an examination of Felton's pro-lynching rhetoric and activism, see Feimster, *Southern Horrors*.

43. Collins Denny, Questionnaire 7, Crowell Papers.

44. J. J. Hall, Questionnaire 12, E. E. Hoss, Questionnaire 14, William J. Northen, Questionnaire 34, Crowell Papers.

45. Collins Denny, Questionnaire 7, Crowell Papers; Wells, *United States Atrocities*, 3, 5–7, 9.

46. H.E.S., "Lynch-Law in America" (letter to the editor), *Spectator* 73 (7 July 1894): 16. Meredith White Townsend and Richard Holt Hutton were coeditors of the *Spectator*, but Townsend was in charge of political issues. John St. Loe Strachey also worked as assistant editor at this time (A. J. A. Morris, "Townsend, Meredith White [1831–1911]," in *Oxford Dictionary*, ed. Matthew and Harrison, 55:129–31).

47. "Lynch-Law in America" (editor's note), *Spectator* 73 (7 July 1894): 16.

48. "Lynch-Law in America," *Spectator* 72 (2 June 1894): 744.

49. H.E.S., "Lynch-Law in America" (letter to the editor), *Spectator* 73 (7 July 1894): 16; William McKay, "Lynching in Georgia: A Correction" (letter to the editor), *Spectator* 73 (28 July 1894): 111.

50. Edward Grubb, "Journal of American Tour" (1904), MSS 16A/7/7, Archives of the Howard League for Penal Reform (MSS.16), Modern Records Centre, University of Warwick, Coventry, England.

51. "Governor Northen Expresses His Views of Attacks on the South," *Atlanta Constitution*, 27 June 1894, clipping, Northen Papers, box 5, vol. 4, p. 15; *Spectator* 72 (16 June 1894): 810; William McKay, "Lynching in Georgia: A Correction" (letter to the editor), *Spectator* 73 (28 July 1894): 111.

52. William McKay, "Lynching in Georgia: A Correction" (letter to the editor), *Spectator* 73 (28 July 1894): 111; "Glad to Get Truth … Gov. Northen's Words Welcomed," *Atlanta Constitution*, 29 July 1894.

53. S. Alfred Steinthal, "Lynching in America" (letter to the editor), *Spectator* 73 (4 August 1894): 142.

54. Bapbapoσ, "Lynch-Law in the United States" (letter to the editor), *Spectator* 73 (8 September 1894): 303.

55. Elizabeth L. Banks, "The Negro Problem," *Sun* (London), 6 July 1894; Philip C. Ivens, "Colour Prejudice" (letter to the editor), *Sun* (London), 9 July 1894.

56. George Shute, "The Negro Problem: Miss E. L. Banks Criticised" (letter to the editor), *Sun* (London), 9 July 1894.

57. "Lynching in America," *TL*, 6 October 1894; Florence Balgarnie, "Anti-Lynching Committee" (letter to the editor), *Manchester Guardian*, 4 August 1894.

58. Editorial, *TL*, 6 October 1894; Florence Balgarnie to Thomas G. Jones, 10 October 1894, Alabama Governor (1890–1894: Jones), Administrative Files, SG8, 415 Reels 5–13, Alabama Department of Archives and History, Montgomery.

59. "Lynching in America and English Interference," *Spectator* 73 (11 August 1894): 169.

60. Florence Balgarnie, "Anti-Lynching Committee" (letter to the editor), *Manchester Guardian*, 4 August 1894; "Sir John Gorst's Report," *NYT*, 10 September 1894; "Governors Speak Out," *New York World*, 14 September 1894; "Get Out Englishmen!" 10 September 1894, clipping, Northen Papers, box 5, vol. 4, p. 23.

61. "Get Out Englishmen!" 10 September 1894, clipping, Northen Papers, box 5, vol. 4, p. 23.

62. Ibid.; "Our English Invaders," [September 1894], clipping, Northen Papers, box 5, vol. 4, p. 23.

63. Tillman, *Inaugural Address*, 6; Kantrowitz, *Ben Tillman*, 156–57, 162–70, 174–81. For Wells's criticisms of Tillman's record on lynching, see "Black versus White," *Labour Leader*, 12 May 1894.

64. "Our English Invaders," [September 1894], clipping, Northen Papers, box 5, vol. 4, p. 23.

65. "Get Out Englishmen!" 10 September 1894, clipping, Northen Papers, box 5, vol. 4, p. 23; "Governors Speak Out," *New York World*, 14 September 1894.

66. "Lynching in America," *TL*, 6 October 1894.

67. Editorial, *TL*, 6 October 1894.

68. Editorial, *Daily Telegraph* (London), 8 October 1894; editorial, *TL*, 6 October 1894.

69. "London Week of Excitement," *NYT*, 7 October 1894; "Lessons for Busybodies," *NYT*, 15 October 1894; "Impertinence That Amazes Labouchere," *NYT*, 20 October 1894; "Anti-Lynching Committee's Snubbing," *NYT*, 25 October 1894.

70. "It Cut to the Quick," *Montgomery Daily Advertiser*, 25 October 1894.

71. Florence Balgarnie, "The Governor of Alabama and the English Anti-Lynching Committee" (letter to the editor), *TL*, 8 October 1894.

72. William Lloyd Garrison Jr., "The Anti-Lynching Committee" (letter to the editor), *TL*, 9 November 1894.

73. "Anti-Lynching Committee," *TL*, 20 December 1895.

CHAPTER 6. A TRANSATLANTIC LEGACY

1. Wells, *Crusade for Justice*, 218–19.

2. Ibid., 39–42.

3. Ibid., 39–42, 78–80.

4. John W. Jacks to Florence Balgarnie, 19 March 1895, reprinted in "A Timely Call," *Indianapolis Freeman*, 22 June 1895; National Association of Colored Women's Clubs, *History*, 3–5; Elizabeth Lindsay Davis, *Lifting as They Climb*. See also Lerner, "Early Community Work"; Rief, "Thinking Locally, Acting Globally"; Stetson, "Black Feminism"; Terborg-Penn, "African American Women's Networks." Black women employed "racial uplift" and the "politics of respectability" in their struggle for equality beyond the NACW. See, for example, Gaines, *Uplifting the Race*; Higginbotham, *Righteous Discontent*.

5. Wells, *Crusade for Justice*, 220–23; Wells, *Red Record*, 80–89.

6. Wells, *Crusade for Justice*, 219.

7. Wells, *Red Record*, 81. David Tucker, "Miss Ida B. Wells," supports Wells's assess-

ment, arguing that the international scrutiny generated by her activism forced Memphis officials to suppress lynching.

8. Statistics regarding mob violence are problematic as a consequence of the political nature of the label *lynching*. Therefore, whether white southerners truly paused in their exercise of lynch law or merely became less willing to advertise their lawlessness by labeling incidents of mob violence *lynchings* remains unclear. It is indisputable, however, that the transatlantic press printed fewer reports of mob violence in the immediate aftermath of Wells's campaign. For discussions of the sources for lynching statistics and the challenges associated with compiling useful data for comparisons, see Tolnay and Beck, *Festival of Violence*, 259–63; Waldrep, *Many Faces of Judge Lynch*, 112–16. For representative lynching statistics, see Cutler, *Lynch-Law*, 170–72; Tolnay and Beck, *Festival of Violence*, 29–32, 271–72; National Association for the Advancement of Colored People, *Thirty Years of Lynching*.

9. While Washington has been widely criticized for dismissing African American political agitation, recent scholarship has revealed Washington's private efforts to undermine segregation and disfranchisement measures through personal appeals and court challenges. See, for example, Riser, *Defying Disfranchisement*.

10. Cutler, *Lynch-Law*, 229–30.

11. See, for example, D. E. Tobias, "A Negro on the Position of the Negro in America," *Nineteenth Century* 46 (December 1899): 957–73; Ray Stannard Baker, "What Is a Lynching?: A Study of Mob Justice, South and North," *McClure's* 24 (January 1905): 299–314.

12. Andrew Sledd, "The Negro: Another View," *Atlantic Monthly* 90 (July 1902): 65–67, 70–71.

13. Ibid., 68.

14. Society for the Recognition of the Brotherhood of Man, "To the Friends of Justice and Humanity Everywhere," August 1893, SRBM Scrapbook; *Extracts from the Minutes and Proceedings* (1903), 191.

15. Warnock, "Andrew Sledd," 251–61, 269; Terry L. Matthews, "Voice of a Prophet," 1, 8–13. See also Terry L. Matthews, "Emergence of a Prophet." Although his career fell victim to Felton's personal feuds with Emory College; the Methodist Episcopal Church, South; and his father-in-law, Bishop Warren A. Candler, Sledd eventually became the president of the University of Florida.

16. Andrew Sledd to Warren Candler, 8 November 1902, box 11, folder 2, Warren A. Candler Papers, Manuscript, Archives, and Rare Book Library, Emory University, Atlanta.

17. Society of Friends in Great Britain, "A Plea for Humanity," MFS Minutes, vol. 53, insert 341–42.

18. MFS Minutes, 4 September 1903, 451–57; Edward Grubb, "Journal of American Tour" (1904), MSS 16A/7/7, Archives of the Howard League for Penal Reform (MSS.16), Modern Records Centre, University of Warwick, Coventry, England; Wil-

liam McKay, "Lynching in Georgia: A Correction" (letter to the editor), *Spectator* 73 (28 July 1894): 111.

19. MFS Minutes, 4 September 1903, 452–53.

20. Ibid., 453–55; Religious Society of Friends Central Committee on Lynching, Minute Book, 5 December 1902, Library of the Religious Society of Friends in Britain, London.

21. Dudley, *Life of Edward Grubb*, 83–85; *Extracts from the Minutes and Proceedings* (1904), 198; Grubb, *Methods*, 56.

22. Grubb, *Methods*, 56–58.

23. Ibid., 56–57.

24. MFS Minutes, 4 September 1903, 454–56; Edmund Morris, *Theodore Rex*, 246–49, 250, 261–62.

25. Booker T. Washington to James Sullivan Clarkson, 18 January 1904, Theodore Roosevelt to Booker T. Washington, 9 May 1904, in *Booker T. Washington Papers*, ed. Harlan and Smock, 7:394–95, 497–98; Edmund Morris, *Theodore Rex*, 52–58, 198–200, 258–62.

26. Sledd, "Negro"; *Extracts from the Minutes and Proceedings* (1903), 191; "Negro's Position Shows Progress," *New York Herald*, 7 October 1910; "An Open Letter to the People of Great Britain and Europe by William Edward Burghardt Du Bois and Others," in *Booker T. Washington Papers*, ed. Harlan and Smock, 10:422; "British NAACP Pickets"; Roy Wilkins to Martin Luther King Jr., 17 April 1960, in *Papers of the National Association for the Advancement of Colored People*, ed. Meier.

27. Cutler, *Lynch-Law*, 170–72; Tolnay and Beck, *Festival of Violence*, 29–32, 271–72.

28. Waldrep, *Many Faces of Judge Lynch*, 4–5; Waldrep, *Lynching in America*, 3.

Bibliography

ARCHIVAL MATERIAL AND MANUSCRIPTS

Alabama Department of Archives and History, Montgomery

Alabama Governor (1890–1894: Jones), Administrative Files of Thomas Goode Jones,
  SG8, 415 Reels 5–13

Columbia University, Rare Book and Manuscript Library, New York

John Franklin Crowell Papers

Emory University, Manuscript, Archives, and Rare Book Library, Atlanta

Warren A. Candler Papers

Georgia Archives, Morrow

William J. Northen Papers, 1941-0354M

Library of Congress, Manuscript Division, Washington, D.C.

Frederick Douglass Papers

Library of the Religious Society of Friends in Britain, London

LSF Box L267
Records of the Central Committee on Lynching
Records of the Meeting for Sufferings

Library of Virginia, Richmond

Executive Papers of Governor Charles T. O'Ferrall, 1894–1897, Accession 43210

Liverpool Record Office, Liverpool Libraries, Liverpool, England
Aked Clipping File

Mississippi Department of Archives and History, Jackson
Series 1202, County Tax Rolls, 1818–1902

National Library of Scotland, Manuscripts and Archive Collections, Edinburgh
NLS: MS. 1890

Tennessee State Library and Archives, Nashville
Chesapeake, Ohio, & Southwestern Railroad v. Ida Wells, Circuit Court of Shelby
County (Tennessee), 1885, West Tennessee 312, 319, Microfilm 1425

University of Chicago, Special Collections Research Center,
Joseph Regenstein Library, Chicago
Ida B. Wells Papers

University of Manchester Library, Manchester, England
Axon Papers

University of Oxford, Bodleian Library of Commonwealth
and African Studies, Oxford, England
Anti-Slavery Society Papers (MSS Brit. Emp. s. 20, E/7–8)

University of Warwick, Modern Records Centre, Coventry, England
Archives of the Howard League for Penal Reform (MSS.16)

PUBLISHED MANUSCRIPT SOURCES

Albion Winegar Tourgée Papers, 1801–1924. Cleveland: Bell and Howell, 1967. Microfilm.
Blassingame, John W., and John R. McKivigan, eds. *The Frederick Douglass Papers.*
Series 1, *Speeches, Debates, and Interviews.* 5 vols. New Haven: Yale University
Press, 1991–92.
Harlan, Louis R., and Raymond W. Smock, eds. *The Booker T. Washington Papers.* 14
vols. Urbana: University of Illinois Press, 1972–89.
Meier, August, ed. *Papers of the National Association for the Advancement of Colored
People.* Frederick, Md.: University Publications of America, 1982. Microfilm.
Williams, Lillian Serece, and Randolph Boehm, eds. *Records of the National Associa-
tion of Colored Women's Clubs, 1895–1992.* Bethesda, Md.: University Publications
of America, 1993–94. Microfilm.

NEWSPAPERS AND PERIODICALS

Aberdeen Daily Free Press
Aberdeen Journal
Aberdeen Weekly Journal
Anglo-American Times
Anti-Caste
Atlanta Constitution
Baner ac Amserau Cymru
  (Denbigh, Wales)
Belfast News-Letter
Birmingham Daily
  Gazette
Birmingham Daily Post
Blackburn Standard and
  Weekly Express
Bond of Brotherhood
Bradford Observer
Brenham (Texas) Daily
  Banner
Brighton Patriot and
  Lewes Free Press
Bristol Mercury and
  Daily Post
British Friend
Chicago Daily Tribune
Christian News
Christian Register
Christian World
Cleveland Gazette
Cobbett's Weekly Political
  Register (London)
Daily Chronicle
  (London)
Daily News (London)

Daily Telegraph
  (London)
Derby Mercury
Economist
Evening Gazette
  (Edinburgh)
Fort Worth Gazette
Fraternity
Freeman
Glasgow Herald
Graphic (London)
Hull Packet
Huntly Express
Indianapolis Freeman
Inquirer
Jackson's Oxford Journal
Labour Leader
Lady's Pictorial
Liverpool Daily Post
Liverpool Echo
Liverpool Mercury
Liverpool Pulpit
Liverpool Weekly Courier
Lux
Manchester Guardian
Manchester Times
Montgomery Daily
  Advertiser
Newcastle Daily Leader
Newcastle Weekly
  Courant
New York Herald
New York Times

New York World
News of the World
  (London)
Norfolk Landmark
North-Eastern
  Daily Gazette
  (Middlesbrough)
Nottinghamshire
  Guardian (London)
Penny Illustrated Paper
  (London)
Preston Chronicle
Reuter's Journal
Reynold's Newspaper
  (London)
Richmond Planet
Richmond Times
Roanoke Times
Scottish Leader
Scottish Pulpit
Sheffield and Rotherham
  Independent
Spectator
Springfield (Illinois) State
  Capitol
Standard (London)
Star (London)
Sun (London)
The Times (London)
Topeka Call
Washington Post
Westminster Gazette
Yorkshire Herald (York)

PRIMARY SOURCES

Aked, Charles F. "Five Years in Liverpool, a Personal Retrospect." *Liverpool Pulpit* 4 (October 1895): 112–15.
———. "Lynch Law Rampant." *Christian World* 38 (12 April 1894): 259.

———. "One Woman's Work." *Christian World* 38 (19 July 1894): 542.

———. "The Race Problem in America." *Contemporary Review* 65 (June 1894): 818–27.

"America and Italy." *Spectator* 66 (4 April 1891): 466–67.

"American Christians and Lynch Law." *Liverpool Pulpit* 3 (July 1894): 97–98.

"An Anti-Lynching Committee." *Christian World* 38 (2 August 1894): 573.

"An Anti-Lynching Committee." *Fraternity* 2 (October 1894): 7.

"Appeal to the Ministers of Religion and Members of the Churches of the United States." *Liverpool Pulpit* 3 (August 1894): 113–14.

Armstrong, Richard Acland. "Lynch Law in America: An English Protest" (letter to the editor). *Christian Register* 73 (12 April 1894): 227.

Baker, Ray Stannard. "What Is a Lynching?: A Study of Mob Justice, South and North." *McClure's Magazine* 24 (January 1905): 299–314.

Balgarnie, Florence. "The Story of Miss Ida B. Wells." *Great Thoughts of Master Minds* 4 (16 March 1895): 384–86.

Bapbapoσ. "Lynch-Law in the United States" (letter to the editor). *Spectator* 73 (8 September 1894): 303.

"Baptist." *Christian World* 38 (3 May 1894): 335.

"The Baptist Union." *Christian World* 38 (26 April 1894): 302–3.

Benjamin, Robert C. O. *Southern Outrages: A Statistical Record of Lawless Doings.* [Los Angeles?]: n.p., 1894.

Bishop, Joseph B. "The Negro and Public Office." *International Quarterly* 8 (March–June 1903): 231–40.

Bliss, William D. P., ed. *Encyclopedia of Social Reform.* New York: Funk and Wagnalls, 1897.

Bradford, Amory H. "Race Prejudice: The Other Side." *Christian World* 38 (12 July 1894): 529.

"British and Foreign Unitarian Association: Annual Meeting." *Inquirer* 53 (19 May 1894): 306–7.

"British NAACP Pickets with Anti-Lynching Placards." Photograph [ca. 1910–40]. Prints and Photographs Division, Library of Congress, Washington, D.C.

Brooks, John Graham. *As Others See Us: A Study of Progress in the United States.* New York: Macmillan, 1909.

Bryce, James. "Legal and Constitutional Aspects of the Lynching at New Orleans." *New Review* 4 (May 1891): 385–97.

———. *Social Institutions of the United States.* New York: Chautauqua, 1891.

Butler, Chas. S. "The Lynching of Negroes in America" (letter to the editor). *Spectator* 73 (25 August 1894): 240.

"B.W.T.A. Council Meetings." *Woman's Signal* 1 (17 May 1894): 340.

Case and Claims of the Emancipated Slaves of the United States: Being the Address of the Central Committee of the Society of Friends in Great Britain and Ireland, to their

Fellow-Members and the British Public. London: [Religious Society of Friends in Britain], March 1865.

Dennis, Alfred Pearce. "The Political and Ethical Aspects of Lynching." *Ethics (International Journal of Ethics)* 15 (January 1905): 149–61.

Dickens, Charles. *American Notes for General Circulation*. 2 vols. London: Chapman and Hall, 1842.

Dilke, Charles. *Greater Britain: A Record of Travel in English-Speaking Countries during 1866 and 1867*. London: Macmillan, 1868.

Edwards, S. J. Celestine. Introduction to *United States Atrocities: Lynch Law*, by Ida B. Wells, v–vii. London: Lux, 1893.

E.W. "Lynch-Law" (letter to the editor). *Spectator* 62 (13 April 1889): 511.

Extracts from the Minutes and Proceedings of the Yearly Meeting of Friends Held in London. London: Office of the Society of Friends, 1903, 1904.

An Ex-Vigilante. "An Apology for the Short Shrift" (letter to the editor). *Saturday Review* 85 (28 May 1898): 717–18.

"The Foreign Relations of the United States." *Saturday Review* 71 (11 April 1891): 430–31.

"Friendly Interference into the Domestic Affairs of Other Countries." *American Law Review* 28 (November–December 1894): 904–6.

Friends Central Committee of the Emancipated Negro. *Report of the Emancipated Negroes Relief Committee*. 3 vols. London: [Religious Society of Friends in Britain], 1865–66.

"Friends' Yearly Meeting." *Christian World* 38 (24 May 1894): 392.

Gray, Thomas R. *The Confessions of Nat Turner, The Leader of the Late Insurrection in Southampton, VA*. Baltimore: Thomas R. Gray, 1831.

Grubb, Edward. *Methods of Penal Administration in the United States: Notes of a Personal Enquiry, February and March, 1904*. London: Wertheimer, Lea, 1904.

Grund, Francis J. *The Americans in Their Moral, Social, and Political Relations*. 1837. Intro. Robert Berkhofer Jr. Rpt. New York: Johnson Reprint, 1968.

H.E.S. "Lynch-Law in America" (letter to the editor). *Spectator* 73 (7 July 1894): 16.

Hobson, J. A. "'Lynching' in the Southern States." *Speaker* 8 (29 August 1903): 498–99.

Houstoun, Matilda Charlotte. *Hesperos; or, Travels in the West*. 2 vols. London: Parker, 1850.

Impey, Catherine. "Who Shall Make America Listen?" *Anti-Caste* 6 (February 1893): 3.

"The Italian Countercheck Quarrelsome." *Saturday Review* 71 (4 April 1891): 406.

Janson, Charles William. *The Stranger in America, 1793–1806*. 1807. Rpt. New York: Press of the Pioneers, 1935.

Jones, Thomas G. *Inaugural Address of Thomas G. Jones, Governor of Alabama, Delivered before the General Assembly, December 1st, 1890*. Montgomery, Ala.: Brown, 1890.

Kennedy, N. J. D. "Lynch." *Juridical Review* 3 (July 1891): 213–22.

———. "Lynch II—Its International Aspect." *Juridical Review* 4 (January 1892): 44–57.

"The Late Frederick Douglass." *Great Thoughts of Master Minds* 4 (16 March 1895): 387.

Lodge, Henry Cabot. "Lynch Law and Unrestricted Immigration." *North American Review* 152 (May 1891): 602–13.

Logan, J. Moffat. "Bristol." *Freeman* 40 (15 June 1894): 396.

"London Yearly Meeting." *British Friend* 3 (9 June 1894): 174.

Love, Emanuel K. *A Sermon on Lynch Law and Raping: Preached by Rev. E. K. Love, D.D., at 1st. African Baptist Church, Savannah, Ga., of Which He is Pastor, November 5th, 1893.* Augusta, Ga.: Georgia Baptist, 1894.

"Lynch Law." *Saturday Review* 71 (30 May 1891): 643.

"Lynch-Law in America." *Christian World* 38 (19 April 1894): 287.

"Lynch-Law in America." *Spectator* 72 (2 June 1894): 743–44.

"Lynch Law in the South." *Christian Register* 73 (12 April 1894): 225.

"Lynch Law in the United States." *Liverpool Pulpit* 3 (April 1894): 49–51.

"The Lynching Affair at New Orleans." *Spectator* 66 (21 March 1891): 400–402.

"Lynching in America." *Chambers's Journal* 7 (17 May 1890): 317–19.

"Lynching in America and English Interference." *Spectator* 73 (11 August 1894): 169–70.

"Lynching in the United States." *Inquirer* 53 (31 March 1894): 203.

"The Lynching of Negroes in America." *Economist* 52 (2 June 1894): 664.

Macrae, David. "The Lynching of Negroes in America" (letter to the editor). *Speaker* 14 (4 August 1906): 408–9.

"The Majesty of the Law: A Talk with Colonel John R. Fellows." *Lippincott's Magazine* 48 (July–December 1891): 764–69.

Mario, Jessie White (Vedova). "Italy and the United States." *Nineteenth Century* 29 (May 1891): 701–8.

Marryat, Frederick. *A Diary in America, with Remarks on Its Institutions.* 2 vols. Paris: Baudy's European Library, 1839.

Marsden, Kate. *On Sledge and Horseback to the Outcast Siberian Lepers.* New York: Cassell, 1892.

Marsh, J. B. T. *The Story of the Fisk Jubilee Singers with Their Songs.* London: Hodder and Staughton, 1875.

Martineau, Harriet. *How to Observe: Morals and Manners.* London: Knight, 1838.

———. *The Martyr Age of the United States.* Boston: Weeks, Jordan/Otis, Broaders, 1839.

———. *Retrospect of Western Travel.* 3 vols. London: Saunders and Otley, 1838.

———. *Society in America.* 3 vols. New York: Saunders and Otley, 1837.

"The May Meetings: The Friends' Yearly Meeting." *Christian World* 38 (31 May 1894): 422.

McKay, William. "Lynching in Georgia: A Correction" (letter to the editor). *Spectator* 73 (28 July 1894): 111.

"Miss Wells's Second English Trip." *Fraternity* 2 (August 1894): 4.

"More Lynch Law." *Liverpool Pulpit* 3 (May 1894): 65–66.

Mossell, N. F. *The Work of the Afro-American Woman*. Philadelphia: Ferguson, 1908.

National Association of Colored Women's Clubs. *A History of the Club Movement Among the Colored Women of the United States of America*. n.p., 1902.

"Negro Lynching in America: A Talk with Miss Ida B. Wells." *Christian World* 38 (3 May 1894): 334.

"Negro Mission Fund." *Good Templars' Watchword* 11 (3 March 1884): 139.

Northen, William J. "Lynching in the South." *Christian Register* 73 (10 May 1894): 291.

———. *The Negro at the South: Letters by Gov. W. J. Northen*. Atlanta: Franklin, 1894.

———. *To the General Assembly of Georgia: Inaugural Address of Gov. Wm. J. Northen*. Atlanta: Southern Cultivator and Dixie Farmer, 1890.

Oldmixon, John W. *Transatlantic Wanderings; or, A Last Look at the United States*. 1855. Rpt. New York: Johnson Reprint, 1970.

Paterson, A. H. "Lynch Law." *Macmillan's Magazine* 55 (March 1887): 342–50.

Prichard, James Cowels. *On the Different Forms of Insanity, in Relation to Jurisprudence, Designed for the Use of Persons Concerned in Legal Questions Regarding Unsoundness of Mind*. London: Bailliére, 1842.

"Protest against Lynching." *Christian World* 38 (17 May 1894): 381.

Rae, W. F. *Westward by Rail: The New Route to the East*. New York: Appleton, 1871.

A Refreshed Unit. "Impressions of the Meetings" (letter to the editor). *Inquirer* 53 (26 May 1894): 334.

Reports of Cases Argued and Determined in the Supreme Court of Tennessee for the Eastern Division, September Term, 1886; for the Middle Division, December Term 1886, and for the Western Division, April Term, 1887. Nashville: Marshall and Bruce, 1887.

Roberts, William. "The Administration of Justice in America." *Fortnightly Review* 57 (1 January 1892): 91–108.

Royster, Jacqueline Jones, ed. *Southern Horrors and Other Writings: The Anti-Lynching Campaign of Ida B. Wells, 1892–1900*. Boston: Bedford, 1997.

Rydell, Robert W., ed. *The Reason Why the Colored American Is Not in the World's Columbian Exposition, by Ida B. Wells, Frederick Douglass, Irvine Garland Penn, and Ferdinand L. Barnett*. 1893. Rpt. Urbana: University of Illinois Press, 1999.

"A Sermon on Ibsen." *Christian World* 38 (15 March 1894): 187.

Shackelford, Thomas. *Proceedings of the Citizens of Madison County, Mississippi, at Livingston, in July, 1835, in Relation to the Trial and Punishment of Several Individuals Implicated in a Contemplated Insurrection in this State*. Jackson, Miss.: Mayson and Smoot, 1836.

Sledd, Andrew. "The Negro: Another View." *Atlantic Monthly* 90 (July 1902): 65–73.

Society for the Recognition of the Brotherhood of Man. *Annual Report 1894, includ-ing Ida B. Wells's Summary of Her Anti-Lynching Campaign in England.* London: Society for the Recognition of the Brotherhood of Man, 1894.

Stanley, Henry M. *My Early Travels and Adventures in America.* 1895. Foreword by Dee Brown. Rpt. Lincoln: University of Nebraska Press, 1982.

Steinthal, S. Alfred. "Lynching in America" (letter to the editor). *Spectator* 73 (4 August 1894): 142.

Still, William. *The Underground Railroad: A Record of Facts, Authentic Narratives, Letters, &c.* 1872. Rpt. New York: Arno, 1968.

Summerfield, Charles. *Illustrated Lives and Adventures of the Desperadoes of the New World: Containing an Account of the Different Modes of Lynching . . . Together with the Lives of the Most Notorious Regulators and Moderators in the Known World.* Philadelphia: Peterson, 1849.

Terrell, Mary Church. *A Colored Woman in a White World.* 1940. Rpt. New York: Hall, 1996.

Thompson, Maurice. "The Court of Judge Lynch." *Lippincott's Magazine* 64 (August 1899): 254–62.

Thomson, William. *A Tradesman's Travels in the United Sates in the Years 1840, 41, and 42.* Edinburgh: Oliver and Boyd, 1842.

Tillman, Benjamin R. *Inaugural Address of B. R. Tillman, Governor of South Caro-lina, Delivered at Columbia, S.C., December 4, 1890.* Columbia, S.C.: Woodrow, 1890.

Tobias, D. E. "A Negro on the Position of the Negro in America." *Nineteenth Century* 46 (December 1899): 957–73.

Tocqueville, Alexis de. *Democracy in America.* 2 vols. London: Saunders and Otley, 1835, 1840.

Townshend, R. B. "A Trial by Lynch Law." *Nineteenth Century* 32 (August 1892): 243–55.

Trollope, Frances. *Domestic Manners of the Americans.* 5th ed. London: Bentley, 1839.

———. *The Life and Adventures of Jonathan Jefferson Whitlaw; or, Scenes on the Mis-sissippi.* London: Bentley, 1836.

"The Unitarian Meetings." *Christian World* 38 (17 May 1894): 381.

Washington, Booker T. *Up from Slavery.* Garden City, N.Y.: Doubleday, 1901.

Wells, Ida B. *Crusade for Justice: The Autobiography of Ida B. Wells.* Ed. Alfreda M. Duster. Chicago: University of Chicago Press, 1970.

———. "Lynch Law in All Its Phases." *Our Day* 11 (May 1893): 333–47.

———. *The Memphis Diary of Ida B. Wells.* Ed. Miriam DeCosta-Willis. Boston: Beacon, 1995.

———. "Miss Wells Maintains Her Accusations of 'Pulpit and Press'" (letter to the editor). *Inquirer* 53 (5 May 1894): 274–75.

———. "The Negro's Case in Equity." *Humanitarian* 16 (June 1900): 421–23.

———. *A Red Record: Tabulated Statistics and Alleged Causes of Lynching in the United States*. Chicago: Donohue and Henneberry, 1895.

———. *Southern Horrors: Lynch Law in All its Phases*. [New York]: New York Age Print, 1892.

———. *United States Atrocities: Lynch Law*. London: Lux, 1893.

Wells-Barnett, Ida B. *Lynch Law in Georgia*. Chicago: Chicago Colored Citizens, 1899.

"Wild Justice at New Orleans." *Saturday Review* 71 (21 March 1891): 341–42.

Winskill, Peter T. *The Temperance Movement and Its Workers: A Record of Social, Moral, Religious, and Political Progress*. 4 vols. London: Blackie, 1891–92.

"Women's Yearly Meeting." *British Friend* 3 (July 1894): 204.

SECONDARY SOURCES

Adelman, Paul. *Peel and the Conservative Party, 1830–1850*. Harlow, Eng.: Pearson Longman, 1990.

Adi, Hakim, and Marika Sherwood. *The 1945 Manchester Pan-African Congress Revisited*. London: New Beacon, 1995.

Allen, James, Hilton Als, John Lewis, and Leon F. Litwack. *Without Sanctuary: Lynching Photography in America*. Sante Fe: Twin Palm, 2000.

Arnstein, Walter L. *Britain Yesterday and Today: 1830 to the Present*. 8th ed. Boston: Houghton Mifflin, 2001.

Aucoin, Brent J. "Thomas Goode Jones, Redeemer and Reformer: The Racial Policies of a Conservative Democrat in Pursuit of a 'New South,' 1874–1914." Master's thesis, Miami University, 1993.

Bay, Mia. *To Tell the Truth Freely: The Life of Ida B. Wells*. New York: Hill and Wang, 2009.

Bederman, Gail. "'Civilization,' the Decline of Middle-Class Manliness, and Ida B. Wells's Antilynching Campaign (1892–94)." *Radical History Review* 52 (Winter 1992): 5–30.

———. *Manliness and Civilization: A Cultural History of Gender and Race in the United States, 1880–1917*. Chicago: University of Chicago Press, 1995.

Bender, Thomas. *A Nation among Nations: America's Place in World History*. New York: Hill and Wang, 2006.

Berg, Manfred. *Popular Justice: A History of Lynching in America*. Chicago: Ivan R. Dee, 2011.

Berg, Manfred, and Simon Wendt, eds. *Globalizing Lynching History: Vigilantism and Extralegal Punishment from an International Perspective*. New York: Palgrave Macmillan, 2011.

Berger, Max. *The British Traveller in America, 1836–1860*. New York: Columbia University Press, 1943.

Berkhofer, Robert F. Introduction to *The Americans in Their Moral, Social, and Politi-*

cal Relations, by Francis J. Grund, v–xxii. 1837. Rpt. New York: Johnson Reprint, 1968.

Bessler, John D. *Legacy of Violence: Lynch Mobs and Executions in Minnesota*. Minneapolis: University of Minnesota Press, 2003.

Blackett, R. J. M. *Building an Antislavery Wall: Black Americans in the Atlantic Abolitionist Movement, 1830–1860*. Baton Rouge: Louisiana State University Press, 1983.

———. "Cracks in the Antislavery Wall: Frederick Douglass's Second Visit to England (1859–1860) and the Coming of the Civil War." In *Liberating Sojourn: Frederick Douglass and Transatlantic Reform*, ed. Alan J. Rice and Martin Crawford, 187–206. Athens: University of Georgia Press, 1999.

Blake, Robert. *The Conservative Party from Peel to Major*. London: Heinemann, 1997.

Bolt, Christine. *The Anti-Slavery Movement and Reconstruction: A Study in Anglo-American Co-Operation, 1833–77*. London: Oxford University Press, 1969.

———. *Sisterhood Questioned? Race, Class, and Internationalism in the American and British Women's Movements, c. 1880s–1970s*. London: Routledge, 2004.

———. *Victorian Attitudes to Race*. Toronto: University of Toronto Press, 1971.

———. *The Women's Movements in the United States and Britain from the 1790s to the 1920s*. New York: Harvester Wheatsheaf, 1993.

Branch, Taylor. *Parting the Waters: America in the King Years, 1954–63*. New York: Touchstone, 1988.

Bressey, Caroline. "A Strange and Bitter Crop: Ida B. Wells' Anti-Lynching Tours, Britain 1893 and 1894." *Centre for Capital Punishment Studies Occasional Paper* 1 (December 2003): 8–28.

Brown, Mary Jane. *Eradicating This Evil: Women in the American Anti-Lynching Movement, 1892–1940*. New York: Garland, 2000.

Brownlee, Sibyl Ventress. "Out of the Abundance of the Heart: Sarah Ann Parker Remond's Quest for Freedom." PhD diss., University of Massachusetts–Amherst, 1997.

Brundage, W. Fitzhugh. *Lynching in the New South: Georgia and Virginia, 1880–1930*. Urbana: University of Illinois Press, 1993.

Buenger, Walter L. *The Path to a Modern South: Northeast Texas between Reconstruction and the Great Depression*. Austin: University of Texas Press, 2001.

Burk, Kathleen. *Old World, New World: Great Britain and America from the Beginning*. New York: Atlantic Monthly Press, 2008.

Burns, Arthur, and Joanna Innes, eds. *Rethinking the Age of Reform: Britain, 1780–1850*. Cambridge: Cambridge University Press, 2003.

Butler, Leslie. *Critical Americans: Victorian Intellectuals and Transatlantic Liberal Reform*. Chapel Hill: University of North Carolina Press, 2007.

Carle, Susan D. *Defining the Struggle: National Organizing for Racial Justice, 1880–1915*. New York: Oxford University Press, 2013.

Carlson, Shirley J. "Black Ideals of Womanhood in the Late Victorian Era." *Journal of Negro History* 77 (Spring 1992): 61–73.

Carrigan, William D., and Christopher Waldrep, eds. *Swift to Wrath: Lynching in Global Historical Perspective*. Charlottesville: University of Virginia Press, 2013.

Carrigan, William D., and Clive Webb. *Forgotten Dead: Mob Violence against Mexicans in the United States, 1848–1928*. New York: Oxford University Press, 2013.

———. "The Lynching of Persons of Mexican Origin or Descent in the United States, 1848–1928." *Journal of Social History* 37 (Winter 2003): 411–38.

Carter, Susan B., Scott Sigmund Gartner, Michael R. Haines, Alan L. Olmstead, Richard Sutch, and Gavin Wright, eds. *Historical Statistics of the United States, Earliest Times to the Present: Millennial Edition*. New York: Cambridge University Press, 2006.

Cartwright, Joseph H. *The Triumph of Jim Crow: Tennessee Race Relations in the 1880s*. Knoxville: University of Tennessee Press, 1976.

Clark, Susan F. "Solo Black Performance before the Civil War: Mrs. Stowe, Mrs. Webb, and *The Christian Slave*." *New Theatre Quarterly* 13 (November 1997): 339–48.

Cobb, James C. *Away Down South: A History of Southern Identity*. New York: Oxford University Press, 2005.

Coleman, Willi. "'Like Hot Lead to Pour on the Americans . . .': Sarah Parker Remond—From Salem, Mass., to the British Isles." In *Women's Rights and Transatlantic Antislavery in the Era of Emancipation*, ed. Kathryn Kish Sklar and James Brewer Stewart, 173–88. New Haven: Yale University Press, 2007.

Coquillette, Daniel R. *The Anglo-American Legal Heritage: Introductory Materials*. 2nd ed. Durham: Carolina Academic, 2004.

Crawford, Floyd W. "Ida B. Wells: Her Anti-Lynching Crusades in Britain and Repercussions from Them in the United States." 1958. Unpublished. Ida B. Wells Papers, Box 9, Folder 2, University of Chicago Library, Chicago.

———. "Ida B. Wells: Some American Reactions to Her Anti-Lynching Crusades in Britain," 1963. Unpublished. Ida B. Wells Papers, Box 9, Folder 2, University of Chicago Library, Chicago.

Crosby, Molly Caldwell. *The American Plague: The Untold Story of Yellow Fever, the Epidemic That Shaped Our History*. New York: Berkley, 2007.

Cutler, James Elbert. *Lynch-Law: An Investigation into the History of Lynching in the United States*. 1905. Rpt. Montclair, N.J.: Patterson Smith, 1969.

Davidson, James West. *"They Say": Ida B. Wells and the Reconstruction of Race*. New York: Oxford University Press, 2009.

Davis, Elizabeth Lindsay. *Lifting as They Climb*. Washington, D.C.: National Association of Colored Women, 1933.

Davis, Simone W. "The 'Weak Race' and the Winchester: Political Voices in the Pamphlets of Ida B. Wells-Barnett." *Legacy* 12.2 (1995): 77–97.

DeCosta-Willis, Miriam. "To Miss Ida Bee with Love." In *Flat-Footed Truths: Telling Black Women's Lives*, ed. Patricia Bell-Scott and Juanita Johnson-Bailey, 72–96. New York: Holt, 1998.

Dobson, Alan P. *Anglo-American Relations in the Twentieth Century: Of Friendship, Conflict, and the Rise and Decline of Superpowers.* New York: Routledge, 1995.

Doyle, Don H. *New Men, New Cities, New South: Atlanta, Nashville, Charleston, Mobile, 1860–1910.* Chapel Hill: University of North Carolina Press, 1990.

Dudley, James. *The Life of Edward Grubb, 1854–1939: A Spiritual Pilgrimage.* London: Camelot, 1946.

Evans, Eric J. *Parliamentary Reform, c. 1770–1918.* Harlow, Eng.: Pearson Education, 2000.

Fahey, David M. *Temperance and Racism: John Bull, Johnny Reb, and the Good Templars.* Lexington: University Press of Kentucky, 1996.

Feimster, Crystal Nicole. *Southern Horrors: Women and the Politics of Rape and Lynching.* Cambridge: Harvard University Press, 2009.

Fisch, Audrey A. *American Slaves in Victorian England: Abolitionist Politics in Popular Literature and Culture.* Cambridge: Cambridge University Press, 2000.

Foster, Gaines M. *Moral Reconstruction: Christian Lobbyists and the Federal Legislation of Morality, 1865–1920.* Chapel Hill: University of North Carolina Press, 2002.

French, Scot. *The Rebellious Slave: Nat Turner in American Memory.* Boston: Houghton Mifflin, 2004.

Fryer, Peter. *Staying Power: The History of Black People in Britain.* London: Pluto, 1984.

Gaines, Kevin K. *Uplifting the Race: Black Leadership, Politics, and Culture in the Twentieth Century.* Chapel Hill: University of North Carolina Press, 1996.

Gallop, Alan. *Buffalo Bill's British Wild West.* Stroud, Eng.: Sutton, 2001.

Gardner, Eric. "Stowe Takes the Stage: Harriet Beecher Stowe's *The Christian Slave.*" *Legacy: A Journal of American Women Writers* 15.1 (1998): 78–84.

Gash, Norman. "From the Origins to Sir Robert Peel." In *The Conservatives: A History from Their Origins to 1965,* ed. Lord Butler, 19–108. London: Allen and Unwin, 1977.

Gerzina, Gretchen Holbrook, ed. *Black Victorians/Black Victoriana.* New Brunswick, N.J.: Rutgers University Press, 2003.

Giddings, Paula. *Ida: A Sword among Lions.* New York: Amistad, 2008.

———. *When and Where I Enter: The Impact of Black Women on Race and Sex in America.* New York: Bantam, 1984.

Gilmore, Glenda Elizabeth. *Gender and Jim Crow: Women and the Politics of White Supremacy in North Carolina, 1896–1920.* Chapel Hill: University of North Carolina Press, 1996.

Gilroy, Paul. *The Black Atlantic: Modernity and Double Consciousness.* London: Verso, 1993.

Godshalk, David F. "William J. Northen's Public and Personal Struggles against Lynching." In *Jumpin' Jim Crow: Southern Politics from Civil War to Civil Rights,* ed. Jane Dailey, Glenda Elizabeth Gilmore, and Bryant Simon, 140–61. Princeton: Princeton University Press, 2000.

Goldsby, Jacqueline. *A Spectacular Secret: Lynching in American Life and Literature.* Chicago: University of Chicago Press, 2006.

Greenwood, Janette Thomas. *Bittersweet Legacy: The Black and White "Better Classes" in Charlotte, 1850–1910.* Chapel Hill: University of North Carolina Press, 1994.

Grimsted, David. *American Mobbing, 1828–1861: Toward Civil War.* New York: Oxford University Press, 1998.

Hale, Grace Elizabeth. *Making Whiteness: The Culture of Segregation in the South, 1890–1940.* New York: Pantheon, 1998.

Hall, Jacquelyn Dowd. *Revolt against Chivalry: Jesse Daniel Ames and the Women's Campaign against Lynching.* New York: Columbia University Press, 1993.

Hamilton, Cynthia S. "Frederick Douglass and the Gender Politics of Reform." In *Liberating Sojourn: Frederick Douglass and Transatlantic Reform*, ed. Alan J. Rice and Martin Crawford, 73–92. Athens: University of Georgia Press, 1999.

Higginbotham, Evelyn Brooks. "African-American Women's History and the Meta-language of Race." *Signs* 17 (Winter 1992): 251–74.

———. *Righteous Discontent: The Women's Movement in the Black Baptist Church, 1880–1920.* Cambridge: Harvard University Press, 1993.

Hodes, Martha. *White Women, Black Men: Illicit Sex in the Nineteenth-Century South.* New Haven: Yale University Press, 1997.

Holt, Thomas C. *The Problem of Freedom: Race, Labor, and Politics in Jamaica and Britain, 1832–1938.* Baltimore: Johns Hopkins University Press, 1992.

Houghton, Walter Edwards, ed. *The Wellesley Index to Victorian Periodicals, 1824–1900.* 5 vols. Toronto: University of Toronto Press, 1966.

Hundley, Helen Sharon. *George Kennan and the Russian Empire: How America's Conscience became an Enemy of Tsarism.* Washington, D.C.: Kennan Institute for Advanced Russian Studies, Woodrow Wilson International Center for Scholars, 2000.

Hutton, Mary Magdelene Boone. "The Rhetoric of Ida B. Wells: The Genesis of the Anti-Lynch Movement." PhD diss., Indiana University, 1975.

Innes, Joanna. "'Reform' in English Public Life." In *Rethinking the Age of Reform: Britain, 1780–1850*, ed. Arthur Burns and Joanna Innes, 71–97. Cambridge: Cambridge University Press, 2003.

Isichei, Elizabeth. *Victorian Quakers.* London: Oxford University Press, 1970.

Jackman, Sydney. Introduction to *A Diary in America with Remarks on Its Institutions*, by Frederick Marryat, ix–xxvi. Ed. Sydney Jackman. Westport, Conn.: Greenwood, 1973.

Kantrowitz, Stephen. *Ben Tillman and the Reconstruction of White Supremacy.* Chapel Hill: University of North Carolina Press, 2000.

Karcher, Carolyn L. "Ida B. Wells and Her Allies against Lynching: A Transnational Perspective." *Comparative American Studies* 3 (June 2005): 131–51.

———. "The White 'Bystander' and the Black Journalist 'Abroad': Albion W. Tourgée and Ida B. Wells as Allies against Lynching." *Prospects* 29 (October 2005):
85–119.

Kasson, Joy S. *Buffalo Bill's Wild West: Celebrity, Memory, and Popular History*. New
York: Hill and Wang, 2000.

Kelley, Blair L. *Right to Ride: Streetcar Boycotts and African American Citizenship
in the Era of Plessy v. Ferguson*. Chapel Hill: University of North Carolina Press,
2010.

Kirby, Jack Temple. *Darkness at the Dawning: Race and Reform in the Progressive
South*. Philadelphia: Lippincott, 1972.

King, Nicole. "'A Colored Woman in Another Country Pleading for Justice in Her
Own': Ida B. Wells in Great Britain." In *Black Victorians/Black Victoriana*, ed.
Gretchen Holbrook Gerzina, 88–109. New Brunswick, N.J.: Rutgers University
Press, 2003.

Lerner, Gerda. "Early Community Work of Black Club Women." *Journal of Negro
History* 59 (April 1974): 158–67.

Lipset, Seymour Martin. "Harriet Martineau's America." In Harriet Martineau, *Society in America*, ed. Seymour Martin Lipset, 5–41. New Brunswick, N.J.: Transac-
tion, 1981.

Lorimer, Douglas A. *Colour, Class, and the Victorians: English Attitudes to the Negro
in the Mid-Nineteenth Century*. New York: Holmes and Meier, 1978.

Luker, Ralph E. *The Social Gospel in Black and White: American Reform, 1885–1912*.
Chapel Hill: University of North Carolina Press, 1991.

Mack, Kenneth W. "Law, Society, Identity, and the Making of the Jim Crow South:
Travel and Segregation on Tennessee Railroads, 1875–1905." *Law and Social
Inquiry* 24 (Spring 1999): 377–409.

Madison, James H. *A Lynching in the Heartland: Race and Memory in America*. New
York: St. Martin's, 2000.

Markovitz, Jonathan. *Legacies of Lynching: Racial Violence and Memory*. Minneapolis: University of Minnesota Press, 2004.

Matthew, H. C. G., and Brian Harrison, eds. *Oxford Dictionary of National Biography*. Oxford: Oxford University Press, 2004.

Matthews, Terry L. "The Emergence of a Prophet: Andrew Sledd and the 'Sledd
Affair' of 1902." PhD diss., Duke University, 1990.

———. "The Voice of a Prophet: Andrew Sledd Revisited." *Journal of Southern Religion* 6 (December 2003): 1–13.

Mattingly, Carol. *Well-Tempered Women: Nineteenth-Century Temperance Rhetoric*.
Carbondale: Southern Illinois University Press, 1998.

McCaskill, Barbara. "'Yours Very Truly': Ellen Craft—The Fugitive as Text and Arti-
fact." *African American Review* 28 (Winter 1994): 509–29.

McFadden, Margaret H. *Golden Cables of Sympathy: The Transatlantic Sources of Nineteenth-Century Feminism*. Lexington: University Press of Kentucky, 1999.

McFeely, William S. *Frederick Douglass*. New York: Norton, 1991.

———. "Visible Man: Frederick Douglass for the 1990s." In *Liberating Sojourn: Frederick Douglass and Transatlantic Reform*, ed. Alan J. Rice and Martin Crawford, 15–27. Athens: University of Georgia Press, 1999.

McGovern, James R. *Anatomy of a Lynching: The Killing of Claude Neal*. Baton Rouge: Louisiana State University Press, 1982.

McMurry, Linda O. *To Keep the Waters Troubled: The Life of Ida B. Wells*. New York: Oxford University Press, 1998.

McWilliam, Rohan. *Popular Politics in Nineteenth Century England*. London: Routledge, 1998.

Meer, Sarah. "Competing Representations: Douglass, the Ethiopian Serenaders, and Ethnic Exhibition in London." In *Liberating Sojourn: Frederick Douglass and Transatlantic Reform*, ed. Alan J. Rice and Martin Crawford, 141–65. Athens: University of Georgia Press, 1999.

———. *Uncle Tom Mania: Slavery, Minstrelsy, and Transatlantic Culture in the 1850s*. Athens: University of Georgia Press, 2005.

Midgley, Clare. *Women against Slavery: The British Campaigns, 1780–1870*. London: Routledge, 1992.

Miller, Ericka M. *The Other Reconstruction: Where Violence and Womanhood Meet in the Writings of Wells-Barnett, Grimké, and Larsen*. New York: Garland, 2000.

Moore, Lindy. "The Reputation of Isabella Fyvie Mayo: Interpretations of a Life." *Women's History Review* 19 (January 2010): 71–88.

Morris, Edmund. *Theodore Rex*. New York: Random House, 2001.

Muncy, Robyn. *Creating a Female Dominion in American Reform, 1890–1935*. New York: Oxford University Press, 1994.

National Association for the Advancement of Colored People. *Thirty Years of Lynching in the United States, 1889–1918*. 1919. Rpt. New York: Arno, 1969.

Nicholas, H. G. *The United States and Britain*. Chicago: University of Chicago Press, 1975.

Patterson, Orlando. *Rituals of Blood: Consequences of Slavery in Two American Centuries*. Washington, D.C.: Civitas/Counterpoint, 1998.

Perdue, Theda. *Race and the Atlanta Cotton States Exposition of 1895*. Athens: University of Georgia Press, 2010.

Peterson. Carla L. *"Doers of the Word": African-American Women Speakers and Writers in the North (1830–1880)*. New York: Oxford University Press, 1995.

Pfeifer, Michael J. *Rough Justice: Lynching and American Society, 1874–1947*. Urbana: University of Illinois Press, 2004.

Piepmeier, Alison. *Out in Public: Configurations of Women's Bodies in Nineteenth-Century America*. Chapel Hill: University of North Carolina Press, 2004.

Quarles, Benjamin. *Black Abolitionists*. 1969. Rpt. New York: Da Capo, 1991.

Raper, Arthur F. *The Tragedy of Lynching*. Chapel Hill: University of North Carolina Press, 1933.

Reynolds, Harry. *Minstrel Memories: The Story of Burnt Cork Minstrelsy in Great Britain from 1836 to 1927*. London: Alston Rivers, 1928.

Rice, Alan J., and Martin Crawford. "Triumphant Exile: Frederick Douglass in Britain, 1845–1847." In *Liberating Sojourn: Frederick Douglass and Transatlantic Reform*, ed. Alan J. Rice and Martin Crawford, 1–12. Athens: University of Georgia Press, 1999.

Richards, Leonard L. *"Gentlemen of Property and Standing": Anti-Abolition Mobs in Jacksonian America*. London: Oxford University Press, 1970.

Richardson, Heather Cox. *The Death of Reconstruction: Race, Labor, and Politics in the Post–Civil War North, 1865–1901*. Cambridge: Harvard University Press, 2001.

Rief, Michelle. "Thinking Locally, Acting Globally: The International Agenda of African American Clubwomen, 1880–1940." *Journal of African American History* 89 (Summer 2004): 203–22.

Rimanelli, Giose. "The 1891 New Orleans Lynching: Southern Politics, Mafia, Immigration, and the American Press." In *The 1891 New Orleans Lynching and U.S.-Italian Relations: A Look Back*, ed. Marco Rimanelli and Sheryl L. Postman, 53–105. New York: Lang, 1992.

Rimanelli, Marco. "The 1891–92 U.S.-Italian Diplomatic Crisis and War-Scare: Foreign and Domestic Policies of the Harrison and di Rudini Governments." In *The 1891 New Orleans Lynching and U.S.-Italian Relations: A Look Back*, ed. Marco Rimanelli and Sheryl L. Postman, 183–285. New York: Lang, 1992.

Rimanelli, Marco, and Sheryl L. Postman, eds. *The 1891 New Orleans Lynching and U.S.-Italian Relations: A Look Back*. New York: Lang, 1992.

Ring, Natalie J. *The Problem South: Region, Empire, and the New Liberal State, 1880–1930*. Athens: University of Georgia Press, 2012.

Riser, R. Volney. *Defying Disfranchisement: Black Voting Rights Activism in the Jim Crow South, 1890–1908*. Baton Rouge: Louisiana State University Press, 2010.

Rodgers, Daniel T. *Atlantic Crossings: Social Politics in a Progressive Age*. Cambridge: Belknap Press of Harvard University Press, 1998.

Royster, Jacqueline Jones, ed. Introduction to *Southern Horrors and Other Writings: The Anti-Lynching Campaign of Ida B. Wells, 1892–1900*, 1–41. Boston: Bedford, 1997.

———. "To Call a Thing by Its True Name: The Rhetoric of Ida B. Wells." In *Reclaiming Rhetorica: Women in the Rhetorical Tradition*, ed. Andrea A. Lunsford, 167–184. Pittsburgh: University of Pittsburgh Press, 1995.

Rudwick, Elliott M., and August Meier. "Black Man in the 'White City': Negroes and the Columbian Exposition, 1893." *Phylon* 26 (Winter 1965): 354–61.

Rydell, Robert W. *All the World's a Fair: Visions of Empire at American International Expositions, 1876–1916*. Chicago: University of Chicago Press, 1984.

———, ed. Introduction to *The Reason Why the Colored American Is Not in the World's Columbian Exposition, by Ida B. Wells, Frederick Douglass, Irvine Garland Penn, and Ferdinand L. Barnett*, xi–xlviii. 1893. Rpt. Urbana: University of Illinois Press, 1999.

Schechter, Patricia A. *Ida B. Wells-Barnett and American Reform, 1880–1930*. Chapel Hill: University of North Carolina Press, 2001.

———. "Unsettled Business: Ida B. Wells against Lynching; or, How Antilynching Got Its Gender." In *Under Sentence of Death: Lynching in the South*, ed. W. Fitzhugh Brundage, 292–317. Chapel Hill: University of North Carolina Press, 1997.

Schneer, Jonathan. "Anti-Imperial London: The Pan-African Conference of 1900." In *Black Victorians/Black Victoriana*, ed. Gretchen Holbrook Gerzina, 175–86. New Brunswick, N.J.: Rutgers University Press, 2003.

Showalter, Elaine. *The Female Malady: Women, Madness, and English Culture, 1830–1980*. New York: Pantheon, 1985.

Silkey, Sarah L. "British Public Debates and the 'Americanization' of Lynching." In *Swift to Wrath: Lynching in Global Historical Perspective*, ed. William D. Carrigan and Christopher Waldrep, 160–80. Charlottesville: University of Virginia Press, 2013.

———. "'More Sinned against Than Sinning': Ida B. Wells and the Challenges of a Transatlantic Anti-Lynching Reform Movement." Master's thesis, University of East Anglia, 2001.

———. "Redirecting the Tide of White Imperialism: The Impact of Ida B. Wells's Transatlantic Antilynching Campaign on British Conceptions of American Race Relations." In *Women Shaping the South: Creating and Confronting Change*, ed. Angela Boswell and Judith N. McArthur, 97–119. Columbia: University of Missouri Press, 2006.

———. "Southern Politicians, British Reformers, and Ida B. Wells's 1893–1894 Transatlantic Antilynching Campaign." In *The U.S. South and Europe: Transatlantic Relations in the Nineteenth and Twentieth Centuries*, ed. Cornelis A. van Minnen and Manfred Berg, 145–64. Lexington: University Press of Kentucky, 2013.

Smead, Howard. *Blood Justice: The Lynching of Mack Charles Parker*. New York: Oxford University Press, 1986.

Smith, David A. "From the Mississippi to the Mediterranean: The 1891 New Orleans Lynching and Its Effects on United States Diplomacy and the American Navy." *Southern Historian* 19 (1998): 60–85.

Sommerville, Diane Miller. *Rape and Race in the Nineteenth-Century South*. Chapel Hill: University of North Carolina Press, 2004.

Steeples, Douglas O. *Democracy in Desperation: The Depression of 1893*. Westport, Conn.: Greenwood, 1998.

Stetson, Erlene. "Black Feminism in Indiana, 1893–1933." *Phylon* 46 (Winter 1983): 292–98.

Tamarkin, Elisa. "Black Anglophilia; or, The Sociability of Antislavery." *American Literary History* 14 (Autumn 2002): 444–78.

Taylor, Miles. "Empire and Parliamentary Reform: The 1832 Reform Act Revisited." In *Rethinking the Age of Reform: Britain, 1780–1850*, ed. Arthur Burns and Joanna Innes, 295–311. Cambridge: Cambridge University Press, 2003.

Temperley, Howard. "Anti-Slavery." In *Pressure from Without in Early Victorian England*, ed. Patricia Hollis, 27–51. London: Arnold, 1974.

———. *Britain and America since Independence*. New York: Palgrave, 2002.

———. *British Antislavery, 1833–1870*. London: Longman, 1972.

Terborg-Penn, Rosalyn. "African American Women's Networks in the Anti-Lynching Crusade." In *Gender, Class, Race, and Reform in the Progressive Era*, ed. Noralee Frankel and Nancy S. Dye, 148–61. Lexington: University Press of Kentucky, 1991.

Thompson, Mildred I. *Ida B. Wells-Barnett: An Exploratory Study of an American Black Woman, 1893–1930*. Brooklyn, N.Y.: Carlson, 1990.

Thornbrough, Emma Lou. *T. Thomas Fortune: Militant Journalist*. Chicago: University of Chicago Press, 1972.

Tolnay, Stewart E., and E. M. Beck. *A Festival of Violence: An Analysis of Southern Lynchings, 1882–1930*. Urbana: University of Illinois Press, 1995.

Tucker, David M. "Miss Ida B. Wells and Memphis Lynching." *Phylon* 32 (Summer 1971): 112–22.

Tyrrell, Ian. *Reforming the World: The Creation of America's Moral Empire*. Princeton: Princeton University Press, 2010.

———. *Woman's World/Woman's Empire: The Woman's Christian Temperance Union in International Perspective, 1800–1930*. Chapel Hill: University of North Carolina Press, 1991.

Waldrep, Christopher. "Ida B. Wells, Higher Law, and Community Justice." In *The Human Tradition in the Gilded Age and Progressive Era*, ed. Ballard C. Campbell, 37–52. Wilmington, Del.: Scholarly Resources, 2000.

———. ed. *Lynching in America: A History in Documents*. New York: New York University Press, 2006.

———. *The Many Faces of Judge Lynch: Extralegal Violence and Punishment in America*. New York: Palgrave Macmillan, 2002.

———. *Roots of Disorder: Race and Criminal Justice in the American South, 1817–80*. Urbana: University of Illinois Press, 1998.

———. "War of Words: The Controversy over the Definition of Lynching, 1899–1940." *Journal of Southern History* 66 (February 2000): 75–100.

Ward, Andrew. *Dark Midnight When I Rise: The Story of the Jubilee Singers, Who Introduced the World to the Music of Black America.* New York: Farrar, Straus, and Giroux, 2000.

Ware, Vron. *Beyond the Pale: White Women, Racism, and History.* London: Verso, 1992.

Warner, Oliver. *Captain Marryat: A Rediscovery.* London: Constable, 1953.

Warnock, Henry Y. "Andrew Sledd, Southern Methodists, and the Negro: A Case History." *Journal of Southern History* 31 (August 1965): 251–71.

Warren, Louis S. *Buffalo Bill's America: William Cody and the Wild West Show.* New York: Knopf, 2005.

Welke, Barbara Y. "When All the Women Were White, and All the Blacks Were Men: Gender, Class, Race, and the Road to *Plessy,* 1855–1914." *Law and History Review* 13 (Autumn 1995): 261–316.

———. *Recasting American Liberty: Gender, Race, Law, and the Railroad Revolution, 1865–1920.* New York: Cambridge University Press, 2001.

Welter, Barbara. "The Cult of True Womanhood: 1820–1860." *American Quarterly* 18 (Summer 1966): 151–74.

White, Walter Francis. *Rope and Faggot: A Biography of Judge Lynch.* New York: Knopf, 1929.

Wiener, Joel H. "'Get the News! Get the News!': Speed in Transatlantic Journalism, 1830–1914." In *Anglo-American Media Interactions, 1850–2000,* ed. Joel H. Wiener and Mark Hampton, 48–66. New York: Palgrave Macmillan, 2007.

Williamson, Joel. *The Crucible of Race: Black-White Relations in the American South since Emancipation.* New York: Oxford University Press, 1984.

Wood, Amy Louise. *Lynching and Spectacle: Witnessing Racial Violence in America, 1890–1940.* Chapel Hill: University of North Carolina Press, 2009.

Woodward, C. Vann. "Capitulation to Racism." In *The Black Man in America since Reconstruction,* ed. David M. Reimers, 9–13. New York: Crowell, 1970.

———. *Origins of the New South, 1877–1913.* Baton Rouge: Louisiana State University Press, 1951.

———. *The Strange Career of Jim Crow.* 3rd rev. ed. New York: Oxford University Press, 1974.

Wright, George C. *Racial Violence in Kentucky, 1865–1940: Lynchings, Mob Rule, and "Legal Lynchings."* Baton Rouge: Louisiana State University Press, 1990.

Wynes, Charles E. "The Race Question in the South as Viewed by British Travelers, 1865–1914." *Louisiana Studies* 13 (Fall 1974): 223–40.

Yellin, Jean Fagan. *Women and Sisters: The Antislavery Feminists in American Culture.* New Haven: Yale University Press, 1989.

Zangrando, Robert L. *The NAACP Crusade against Lynching, 1909–1950.* Philadelphia: Temple University Press, 1980.

Index

Rankin, John G., 41
reactions in America to British antilynching
movement, 116, 122–27, 145–46, 148, 149;
attempts to discredit Wells, 124, 125–26,
126–27; blame criminality of African
Americans, 129–30; deny lynching reports,
130–32; outrage over London Anti-
Lynching Committee delegation, 135, 136–
37; point to violence in North, 124–25. *See
also* New South
Reform Act (1832), 16
Reform Act (1867), 26
Remond, Sarah Parker, 74–75, 78
Reynolds, Robert J., 135
Reynolds, W., 99
Robinson, W. D., 126
Roosevelt, Theodore, 146, 147–48
Roper, Charles, 99, 100, 102
Russell, Edward, 96
Rust College, 160n2
Ryder, Dudley (Lord Sandon), 17

Sandon, Lord (Viscount Sandon; Dudley
Ryder, 2nd Earl of Harrowby), 17
San Francisco Vigilance Committee, 25
Saxton, Rufus, 56
segregation, 46–52, 53, 60, 64, 65–66, 79–80,
81, 164n80 , 173n1
sexuality, 83–84, 86, 91. *See also* interracial
relationships; women
Shackelford, Thomas, 8–9
Shaftesbury, 7th Earl of (Anthony Ashley
Cooper), 59
Shakespeare, Joseph, 32
Sheldon, Charles H., 134
Sherman, William T., 56
Shortridge, Eli C. D., 135
Shute, George, 132
Sledd, Andrew, 143–45, 147
Smith, Henry, 38, 40, 42, 110. *See also* Paris,
Texas, lynching (1893)
Society for the Recognition of the

Brotherhood of Man (SRBM), 72,
93; Christian support, 66–67; and
colonialism, 163n58 ; creation of, 61, 63–
64; dissolution of, 142; under Edwards's
leadership, 87–89; International Society
for the Recognition of the Brotherhood
of Man, 91; local chapters, 112–13; loss of
Edwards's leadership, 89, 90; Northern
Federation of Branches, 88; relationship
with London Anti-Lynching Committee,
112; relationship with Wells, 80–81, 138;
schisms in leadership, 84–85, 88, 91–92,
93–94. *See also* Edwards, S. J. Celestine;
Impey, Catherine; Mayo, Isabella Fyvie
Society of Friends: antilynching resolutions,
104–5, 145–46; Committee on Lynching,
144–48; hearing on Impey's sanity, 86–87;
refusal to hear Wells, 104–5
Somerset, Lady Henry, 104
southern progressivism, 173n1
Steinthal, S. Alfred, 98–100, 102, 103, 131
Stewart, Henry, 53. *See also* Memphis,
Tennessee, lynching (1892)
Stone, John Marshall, 124
Stone, William J., 134
Stowe, Harriet Beecher, 73, 74
Strachey, John St. Loe, 175n46
Stubbs, Charles William, 97

Tarrant, William George, 101–2
Tennessee Rifles, 53
Terrell, Mary Church, 49, 51
Texarkana, Arkansas, lynching (1892), 40,
68–69
Thoumaian, Madame (Lucy), 95
Tillman, Benjamin R., 134–35
Tourgée, Albion W., 61, 85–86
Townsend, Meredith White, 129–30
Townshend, R. B., 28
travel narratives, 9, 10, 43. *See also* Marryat,
Frederick; Martineau, Harriet
Trollope, Frances, 10

10|13|15 3x 10|14|15